*In memory of Lizzie Rummel
and Ken Jones
with great respect
and affection*

Disclaimer

Cross country skiing, whether on a groomed and trackset trail or far back in the wilderness, is potentially dangerous. Cold weather and exposure, falls, river crossings, avalanches and the possibility of losing one's way are only some of the very real dangers that must be accepted and dealt with if one is to venture onto these mountain trails. For many of us the existence of the dangers forms an integral part of the attraction of this activity.

Hopefully, this guidebook will provide information to help make your time in the mountains a safe and enjoyable experience. However, it is only a book—another tool to help you along the way. You must still learn all the techniques and skills required to venture safely into the backcountry, and you must still learn to show good judgement in applying all of these techniques. Furthermore, due to continually changing conditions and weather, the information presented in this book provides only a limited part of the overall picture. It is up to you to collect all the information necessary to make intelligent and safe decisions. This guidebook is not a substitute for experience and good judgement.

Ski Trails
the Canadian Rockies
Chic Scott

Rocky Mountain Books
#108 – 17665 66A Avenue
Surrey, BC V3S 2A7
www.rmbooks.com

Rocky Mountain Books
PO Box 468
Custer, WA
98240-0468

Library and Archives Canada Cataloguing in Publication

Scott, Chic, 1945-

 Ski trails in the Canadian Rockies / Chic Scott. — 4th ed.

Includes index.

ISBN 978-1-894765-59-6

 1. Cross-country skiing—Rocky Mountains, Canadian (B.C. and Alta.)—Guidebooks. 2. Trails—Rocky Mountains, Canadian (B.C. and Alta.)—Guidebooks. 3. Rocky Mountains, Canadian (B.C. and Alta.)—Guidebooks. I. Title.

GV854.8.C3S37 2005   796.93'2'09711   C2005-901166-1

Front cover: Ski touring on the south side of Dolomite Pass with a view toward the pass. Photo Pat Morrow. First Page: Ken Jones from Ken Jones Collection and Lizzie Rummel, Whyte Museum of the Canadian Rockies. Title Page: Above a sea of clouds at Burstall Pass. Mount Sir Douglas in the background. Photo Clive Cordery. All photos by the author unless otherwise credited.

Printed in Canada

Rocky Mountain Books acknowledges the financial support for its publishing program from the Government of Canada through the Book Publishing Industry Development Program (BPIDP), Canada Council for the Arts, and the province of British Columbia through the British Columbia Arts Council and the Book Publishing Tax Credit.

Disclaimer

The actions described in this book may be considered inherently dangerous activities. Individuals undertake these activities at their own risk. The information put forth in this guide has been collected from a variety of sources and is not guaranteed to be completely accurate or reliable. Many conditions and some information may change owing to weather and numerous other factors beyond the control of the authors and publishers. Individual climbers and/or hikers must determine the risks, use their own judgment, and take full responsibility for their actions. Do not depend on any information found in this book for your own personal safety. Your safety depends on your own good judgment based on your skills, education, and experience.

 It is up to the users of this guidebook to acquire the necessary skills for safe experiences and to exercise caution in potentially hazardous areas. The authors and publishers of this guide accept no responsibility for your actions or the results that occur from another's actions, choices, or judgments. If you have any doubt as to your safety or your ability to attempt anything described in this guidebook, do not attempt it.

CONTENTS

RMB

Victoria Vancouver Calgary

Preface to the First Edition

As far back as 1970, my good friend Lloyd MacKay was urging me to write this book. However I was too busy travelling the globe, climbing and skiing, to get my act together and sit down at the typewriter. By 1974 I had begun to think it was a good idea and I started to organize myself and collect information. I even took the winter off to work on the project. But fate decreed that things should be otherwise and my life swept me along other channels. Someone else wrote the book.

Time and fate however have an uncanny way of bringing things back to you that you thought lost forever. Several years ago, when Tony and Gill asked me to write this book I knew the time was right. I had continued over the years, to ski and explore the trails of the Rockies. I had personally covered most of the ground in this book and had honed my writing and research skills. I jumped at the prospect and now after a year of intense work it is done.

I hope that you find the peace and happiness, gliding along these trails, that I have. Many years ago I realized something was wrong with the society that we live in. Somehow out on the trails, with the winter snows around and the mountains gleaming above, I found what was missing. If this book can get more of us out there, safely exploring our Canadian winter wilderness, then my goal will have been achieved.

I wish you happy and safe skiing and a crackling fire and good company at the end of the day.

Chic Scott

Preface to the Second Edition

It has been almost ten years since I realized a dream and wrote my own version of *Ski Trails in the Canadian Rockies*. The book has now taken thousands of skiers out onto the backcountry trails, as I hoped it would. I have gone on to make a living as a writer with new guide books to high alpine skiing and even a history book.

Over the years I have continued to explore the backcountry, so you will find in this edition some new trail descriptions and better versions of others. Gillean Daffern has very generously allowed me to use information from her ski guidebook and so I have included descriptions of some of the most popular Kananaskis trails. I have included, as well, expanded information on the huts and lodges which are so popular with backcountry ski tourers.

Enjoy this new edition of *Ski Trails* and may you all continue to discover the magic of winter in the Canadian Rockies.

Chic Scott

Publishing History of Ski Trails in the Canadian Rockies

First edition, 1977, by Rick Kunelius, published by Summerthought

Revised edition, 1981, by Rick Kunelius and Dave Biederman, published by Summerthought

Second edition, 1992. Third edition, 2002. Revised edition, 2005 by Chic Scott, published by Rocky Mountain Books.

Skiing in the Canadian Rockies

Skiing in the Canadian Rockies is a wonderful and varied experience. You can enjoy a safe and easy trackset trail or explore the high and wild backcountry. You can camp in the solitude of a remote valley or stay in the luxury and comfort of one of our historic lodges.

Skiing in these mountains offers you the opportunity to escape from the noise and rush of our culture. In the winter you need venture only a few hundred metres from the road to enter a world of silence and poetry. In the winter all is clean, new and fresh. The beauty of the snow formations, the wind and the clouds can put new life in your soul. The fresh air and hard exercise can put roses in your cheeks.

The Canadian Rockies have been home to ski adventure since the late 1920s. Long before the development of ski resorts and mechanical lifts, skiers from around the world journeyed to the Rockies to experience the winter wilderness. Much of that history is still around us. Thankfully, most of the areas covered in this book are protected as National or Provincial Parks and little has changed over the years. You can still experience the same adventure and beauty that the pioneers enjoyed.

There are, however, serious hazards for ski tourers in the Canadian Rockies. You must be well prepared and use good judgement to venture safely into these mountains. The penalty for mistakes can be harsh indeed. Judgement comes with experience and it is advised that you begin slowly with modest trips, then gradually work your way into the more demanding ski tours.

The area covered by this book is very large and there are endless possibilities for ski adventures. We have collected only the most popular and obvious trails. You could spend a lifetime exploring the remote backcountry and you would rarely encounter a soul.

Good ski touring skills and techniques are required to go far in these mountains. In addition, the Canadian Rockies have some distinctive characteristics with which you should become familiar.

Snow Conditions

The snow which falls in the Canadian Rockies is usually very dry and some years can be minimal for long periods of time. Because temperatures are often low, the snow does not consolidate or settle fast. As a result of long spells of cold weather combined with a shallow snow pack, a loose and unstable type of snow, called depth hoar, often develops. Early season trail breaking can be extremely frustrating and it is not uncommon to find yourself sinking deep into unconsolidated snow. The best time to undertake serious ski touring is from mid February on, when the snowpack is deeper and more consolidated.

You should give serious consideration to the condition of the snowpack before you head out on long distance tours. A telephone call to the appropriate agency (see the numbers at the back of the book) will give you all the information you need to make a decision.

Avalanches

The snowpack in the Canadian Rockies is often unstable and unpredictable. Snow stability is difficult to evaluate, even for knowledgeable and experienced tourers. Avalanche accidents are a regular occurrence, usually during periods when forecasters are predicting high or extreme hazard. Consequently you are advised to check the avalanche hazard forecast by phoning the appropriate numbers found at the end of this book.

You are also advised to take an avalanche awareness course where you will learn to travel safely in avalanche terrain and to recognize signs of snowpack instability.

Ski tourers should all wear an avalanche beacon and carry a snow shovel and probe when skiing in avalanche terrain. Your beacon should be switched on at the beginning of the tour and worn until you are safely back at your car. Batteries should be fresh and your group should do a beacon check at the beginning of each day. Everyone should know how to conduct a beacon search in the event of an avalanche incident. Avalanche beacons should not be an excuse to push the limits of safe judgement—remember that despite these electronic devices many avalanches still prove fatal.

You should ski with a high degree of awareness. Most of the tours in this book can be done without exposing yourself or your group to the possibility of being avalanched. If you find yourself anywhere which seems to be steep and dangerous, you are likely off route. If you are skiing terrain which makes you nervous, look for a more comfortable route. Keen observation, good routefinding and extreme caution are the keys to safe travel in the Canadian Rockies.

Parks Canada Avalanche Terrain Exposure Scale

This exposure scale developed by Grant Statham and Bruce McMahon, and the associated avalanche terrain ratings, attempts to assess how serious the terrain is from the perspective of avalanche hazards. Used in conjunction with the daily avalanche bulletins, it will enable you to evaluate the hazard and manage personal risk when skiing the trails described in this guidebook. For more information on the rating system go to any of the mountain parks web sites such as www.pc.gc.ca/banff. The scale recognizes three levels of terrain:

1 Simple

Exposure to low angle or primarily forested terrain. Some forest openings may involve the runout zones of infrequent avalanches. Many options to reduce or eliminate exposure. No glacier travel.

2 Challenging

Exposure to well defined avalanche paths, starting zones or terrain traps; options exist to reduce or eliminate exposure with careful routefinding. Glacier travel is straightforward but crevasse hazards may exist.

3 Complex

Exposure to multiple overlapping avalanche paths or large expanses of steep, open terrain; multiple avalanche starting zones and terrain traps below; minimal options to reduce exposure. Complicated glacier travel with extensive crevasse bands or icefalls.

In this guidebook, a number 1, 2 or 3 after the type of skiing shown alongside the trail name corresponds to the ratings above.

Read *Avalanche Safety for Skiers, Climbers and Snowboarders* by Tony Daffern for advice on travelling safely in the backcountry.

Weather

Weather in the Canadian Rockies can be extreme. There can be long periods when the thermometer drops to -30° or -40° Celsius. Chinook winds can change this in a matter of hours and raise the temperature well above freezing. Carrying the proper protection against the wind and cold is essential and if your tour takes you above treeline you should be particularly well prepared. A night out in the Rockies is a serious matter so carry survival equipment on longer tours.

The mean temperature in the Rockies is reasonable however, and the area receives a large amount of sunshine. A typical Rockies day is perhaps -15°C and sunny. Springtime ski touring can be a real treat—often a sweater or windbreaker is all that is needed. An effective sun cream and quality sunglasses are required, particularly later in the season when the sun rises higher in the sky.

Weather reports can be obtained in Banff by phoning 403-762-2088 and in Jasper by phoning 780-852-3185.

Remoteness

Many of the tours in this book take you through wilderness areas. There are no man made facilities on many of these trails and often there will be no other skiers in the area. You will be on your own and you must deal with any eventuality with your own resources. Self reliance is the byword in the Canadian Rockies. This remoteness is indeed one of the great attractions of these mountains.

Environment

Most of these trails are in National or Provincial Parks where the environment is protected. Cutting of trees and branches and feeding of animals is prohibited. All garbage must be packed out.

Emergency Procedures

Before venturing far into the backcountry you should obtain the knowledge and skills necessary to carry out a few emergency procedures. You should know how to build an emergency shelter, how to start a fire and how to stay warm and dry. You should also be familiar with avalanche rescue procedures because it unlikely that outside help will do more than recover bodies. If you venture onto glaciers you should be able to perform a crevasse rescue.

If you are embarking on any of the more serious ski tours, you should consider registering out with the Park Wardens or Rangers for some added security. In an emergency you can raise the alarm by phoning the appropriate number listed on the final page of the book.

Throughout most of Alberta the number to call in the event of emergency is 911.

Equipment and Clothing

Here are a few tips on the type of equipment and clothing commonly used in winter in the Canadian Rockies

Skis Metal edged 'Telemark' style skis are popular for backcountry touring. Three pin bindings still work well and nowadays many people are using the NNNBC binding, but breakage is proving a real problem with these. If you use a cable binding be sure to carry a spare cable. Waxes are still used on

the flats but when the going gets steep most folks use skins. Fish scale waxless skis are not recommended. Look for quality in your ski equipment—it is no fun to have to walk several kilometres back to the trail head with a broken ski or binding.

Ski Poles Poles that adapt to form an avalanche probe are very popular. However, it is recommended that several people in the group carry regular sectional probes.

Headgear A warm toque or insulated hat is essential. A Balaclava which can be pulled down to cover the face and neck is highly recommended.

Handgear Warm mitts, rather than gloves, are the most effective.

Boots Well made, leather touring boots still work well for backcountry use and should provide room to accommodates extra socks. Many skiers are now using the plastic Scarpa T3 touring boots and report that they are very warm and comfortable. Heat moulded Intuition liners make for a perfect fit.

Insulating Materials Down is still the insulating material of choice in the Rockies. The climate is dry and can be very cold, necessitating a high quality four season sleeping bag. Synthetic pile fabrics are popular for clothing and work very well. Synthetic underclothes are now used almost exclusively.

Shell Material Most folks use Gore-Tex shell material but it does ice up badly from body moisture in cold weather. Breathable nylon fabrics work well if you can find them.

Avalanche Beacons Single-frequency 457 kHz beacons are now the standard in north America.

Stoves White gas stoves such as the MSR models are the norm in the Canadian Rockies. Butane has difficulty vaporizing in the cold weather so if you use this type of stove you must use cartridges with a propane/butane mix.

Food, Gear and Other Supplies

The mountain communities of Banff, Canmore, Lake Louise and Jasper have a wide variety of stores and shops to serve you. White gas for stoves is readily available as is gasoline for your vehicle. Ski equipment and backcountry gear can be purchased at:

Monod Sports (Banff) 403-762-4571
Mountain Magic Sports (Banff)
403-762-2591
Altitude Sports (Canmore)
403-678-1636
Valhalla Pure Outfitters (Canmore)
403-678-5610
Wilson's Sports (Lake Louise)
403-522-3636
Totem Ski Shop (Jasper) 780-852-3078
Gravity Gear (Jasper) 1-888-852-3155

If necessary you can drive to Calgary to get what you need. Here you can check:

Mountain Equipment Co-op
403-269-2420

Opposite: One of the cabins at Mount Assiniboine Lodge. Photo Alf Skrastins.

Grading and Other Trail Info

All trails have been designated as either Nordic skiing, ski touring or ski mountaineering. In addition, a simple grading system of easy, intermediate and advanced has been used. To apply this system to 150 trails, where the conditions are constantly changing, means that there will be times when you must use your own discretion.

The grading takes in to account that Nordic skiing requires less knowledge and experience than ski touring, which in turn requires less than ski mountaineering. Consequently an easy ski along a trackset trail would be less challenging than an easy ski tour. An easy ski mountaineering tour may be much more demanding than appropriate for a novice skier.

The following definitions apply to the descriptions and grades used in the book.

Nordic Skiing Takes place on well maintained trails which are usually packed and often trackset. The trails are normally near to the town or road and you will most likely encounter other skiers along the way.

Ski Touring Takes you into the backcountry, usually below treeline but sometimes up into the subalpine. Trail breaking is often required and you may go long distances without encountering any man made facilities or other skiers. Route finding and wilderness survival skills are essential as is proper equipment.

Ski Mountaineering Takes you into the alpine zone, high above treeline. Glacier travel is usually involved and a more advanced level of skills is required. One should have solid skiing abilities and at least one individual in the group should be completely familiar with all the requisite skills—route finding, avalanche avoidance and emergency procedures such as first aid, crevasse rescue and improvised survival techniques.

A number 1, 2 or 3 after the type of skiing indicates the Avalanche Terrain Rating (see page 8).

Each trail has also been given a grading which should be interpreted as follows:

Easy These trails are normally suitable for a novice or inexperienced skier (within the parameters of the above trail designations). Route finding is not difficult and there are few hills. The length of the trip should always be taken into consideration for beginner skiers.

Intermediate These trails are more challenging and will often have steep hills which require more advanced skiing abilities. For ski tours and ski mountaineering a more advanced level of route finding skills will be required.

Advanced These trails may have extensive sections requiring advanced skiing skills and may also present serious route finding challenges. Often these tours will be into isolated and remote areas and you must rely solely on your own resources and ability.

Directions are almost always given in the direction of travel (i.e., ski along the right bank of the creek; turn left at the trail junction). Often a compass direction will be given in brackets (south) to add clarity. In a few instances the true left or right bank of a glacier or stream are referred to. In these cases the direction is derived from the direction of flow of the glacier or stream and may be different from the direction of travel of the skier. For example, if you are skiing upstream along the right bank of a creek, you are actually skiing on the true left bank.

Times Times given are for an average party under average conditions. Skiing times can vary greatly depending on the strength and ability of the party, the weight of their packs, and the depth of the trail breaking. What might take several days under one set of circumstances could be skied in several hours on another day. You must always integrate all the factors and arrive at your own estimate of the time your trip will require. The times given are only guidelines.

Distances are given in kilometres and are noted as being one way, return or loop. The distances given in the text are approximate—I did not ski these trails with a tape measure. They are accurate enough that with a little judgement you will be able to make the right decisions.

Elevations are given in metres and were determined from the contour lines on the map. They are intended to give you an idea of how much climbing will be required on a given trail and what will be the maximum elevation reached. Elevation gains given within the text are referred to as vertical metres to differentiate them from horizontal distances. These elevation gains are approximate and one should use a little discretion in interpreting them.

Grid References Many specific objects such as huts are given a grid reference to help you accurately locate the object (i.e., Bow Hut GR 355203). On the right hand border of each map you will find instructions on how to use the Univer-

sal Transverse Mercator Grid System to locate the object on the map.

If you are using a GPS receiver, be sure to check the map datum. In this book all grid references are derived from the older NAD 27 datum. Some of the newer maps have now switched to NAD 83 and it may be necessary to make a small adjustment.

Maps
Map references given are all to the 1:50,000 National Topographic Series. These can be obtained from private sources such as Mountain Equipment Co-op (403-269-2420) or Map Town (403-266-2241) in Calgary or at The Alpine Club of Canada in Canmore (403-678-3200). If you live far away you can obtain maps from the federal government in Ottawa:

Canada Map Office
130 Bentley Avenue
Nepean, Ontario
Canada, K1A 0E9
US and Canada 1-800-465-6277
613-952-7000

Take care when using some of the newer maps where the contour interval is 20 m below 2000 m and 40 m above. These maps are truly hard to read.

Some trails marked on topographic maps are incorrect. It is best to cross check with other references whenever possible.

A new series of topographic maps to the province of British Columbia, at a scale of 1:20,000 and a contour interval of 20 meters based on the B.C. government TRIM data, are now available from Clover Point Cartographics Ltd. The company can be reached through their website at www.cloverpoint.com.

Trip Planning

You should always have at least an informal plan in the back of your mind, even for the most casual day of skiing. The more serious the trip, the better planned it should be. If you do one of the multi-day trips virtually nothing should be left to chance. The following are some items that you should consider when planning your tour:

Register Out Let someone know where you are going and when you will be back.

Route Study the map and any other information so as to be completely familiar with the route. Be aware of options and alternatives along the way.

Team Know the people you are skiing with and their skill and experience level. Don't get them in over their heads.

Times Establish a start time and a finish time. Leave plenty of room in your schedule to deal with the unforeseen. Check your time along the way to gauge your progress. You should decide on a turn back time and stick to it.

Equipment Run through an equipment check before departing. Check the rest of the group for proper skis, boots and clothing. Always do a beacon check before heading out.

Weather Obtain the latest weather forecast before starting out.

Snow Stability Check the avalanche hazard and snow stability forecast before making a final decision on your route.

Equipment Checklist—to refresh your memory

Skis
Poles
Boots
Skins
Wax kit
Avalanche beacon
Avalanche probe
Shovel
Snow saw
Compass
Altimeter
GPS receiver
Map
Repair kit
First aid kit
Emergency toboggan
Snow study kit
Headlamp
Bivouac sack
Water bottle
Thermos
Sun glasses

Ski goggles
Pocket knife
Toilet paper
Camera and film
Lighter or matches
Lip balm
Sun cream
Notebook and pencil
Pack sack

Clothing
Underwear
Socks
Pants
Overpants
Jacket
Shirt
Pile jacket or sweater
Down jacket
Toque
Mitts or gloves
Polypro gloves

Gaiters
Spare mitts, socks
Spare underwear

If you are going overnight
Tent
Sleeping bag
Insulated sleeping pad
Insulated booties
Stove and fuel
Pots & pot scrubber
Cup, bowl and spoon
Toilet kit

For glacier travel
Harness
Rope
Several prussik slings
Several locking carabiners
Several regular carabiners
Ice axe
Ice screw

Regulations

Most of the ski tours in this book are in areas where backcountry use is controlled to some degree. The majority of the tours lie within the boundaries of five national parks: Waterton, Banff, Yoho, Kootenay and Jasper, or are located within a provincial park: Assiniboine or Robson or in Kananaskis Country. Each of these areas have similar backcountry regulations and a summary is presented here.

National Park Entrance Fees
The drivers of all motor vehicles stopping in national parks are required to pay an entrance fee. The Great Western Pass, which is valid for all national parks covered in this book, is $67.70/year for a single adult and $136.40/year for an adult group (2-7 persons). The Great Western Pass is valid for one year from date of issue. A National Park Day Pass is $9.80 for a single adult and $19.60 for an adult group (2-7 persons). Passes are available at the park entrance or park information centres.

Wilderness Pass
In the national parks it is necessary to get a Wilderness Pass if you stay overnight in the backcountry. The Wilderness Pass is $9.80/night. Annual Wilderness Passes are available at a cost of $68.70/person. The annual pass is valid for one year from date of issue. Wilderness Passes can be obtained at park information centres or, if you are staying at an ACC hut, from the Alpine Club of Canada. If you are just going out for a day trip, a wilderness pass is not required.

Registration
A voluntary registration system is provided by the Parks Service for hazardous activities within the National Parks. It is a very good idea to use the service if you are skiing in a remote area.

It is necessary to register in person at either park information centres or at a warden office. Note that all overdue registrations are checked out. There are two important considerations to bear in mind when you register out:

1. Because all overdue registrations are checked out you must provide a reasonable estimate of the time your trip will take.
2. You must notify the Parks Service upon completion of your trip. This is done by either dropping the registration slip off at one of the warden offices or information centres, or by telephoning the offices or centres. If you are late, phone at your earliest convenience.

Note Failure to notify the Park Service of your return is very serious and is grounds for prosecution.

Rescue personnel will exercise some discretion about when to commence a search. This depends on many factors like weather, amount of time overdue, estimate of the individuals ability, number in party, etc. For this reason you must be prepared to spend at least one night out before expecting help to arrive.

Travel Information

Public transportation in the Rockies is poor, particularly in winter. It is almost imperative that you have a vehicle if you want to reach most of the trailheads. The Canadian Rockies however, can be reached easily by air, car or bus. But once you are there it is best to drive.

By Air

There are international airports in both Edmonton and Calgary. It is possible to fly direct to these cities from within North America and from Europe and Asia. The areas described in this book are only a few hours drive, along excellent highways, from the airports. In other words, it is possible to fly from Europe and be skiing in the Canadian wilderness the following day.

By Bus

There are regular scheduled buses along the Trans Canada Highway (Highway 1). These buses stop at all the major centres between Calgary and Vancouver such as Canmore, Banff and Lake Louise. There are also regular scheduled buses which travel Highway 16 between Edmonton and Jasper. Phone Greyhound Bus Lines for further Information. Check with Brewster Transport (403-762-6767) for Icefields Parkway buses.

By Car

Cars can be rented from the major international chains (Hertz, Avis, Budget etc.) in Calgary, Edmonton, Jasper and Banff. The highways described in this book are all in excellent condition and are well maintained in the winter. Driving in the Canadian Rockies in winter is normally a reasonable proposition,

however, the cold can make extreme demands on both car and driver. Be sure that your car has antifreeze adequate for -40°C, and that it is equipped with snow tires, a block heater and a strong battery. You should carry jumper cables in your trunk in the event of a dead battery. If the thermometer plunges it is advisable to plug your car in, if at all possible. Propane and diesel powered vehicles can be hard to start on cold winter mornings. It is best not to park along the roadside as high speed snowplows regularly maintain the highways.

Telephone Numbers

The telephone exchange for southern Alberta is 403 and northern Alberta (including Red Deer) is 780. The telephone exchange for British Columbia is 250, except in the lower mainland area, near Vancouver, where it is 604.

Guides

Ski Guides and instruction can be obtained through:

White Mountain Adventures
www.canadiannatureguides.com
phone: 1-800-408-0005 or
403-678-4099

Yamnuska Inc.
www.yamnuska.com
phone: 403-678-4164

The Association of Canadian Mountain Guides
www.acmg.ca

Where To Stay

When you get off the plane in Calgary or Edmonton you are in a major city, each having populations in excess of 800,000. There is an endless variety of accommodation, from five star hotels to hostels. The four major mountain towns are Canmore, Banff, Lake Louise and Jasper. All of these communities have a variety of hotels, bed and breakfast establishments and hostels. More information can be obtained from:

Travel Alberta
phone: 1-800-254-3782
website: www.travelalberta.com

Tourism British Columbia
phone: 1-800-663-6000
website: www.hellobc.com

The Alpine Club of Canada

The ACC operates a clubhouse and many backcountry huts. They are reasonably priced (particularly if you choose to become a member). Bookings can be made through the ACC office.

The Alpine Club of Canada
Box 8040, Canmore,
Alberta, T1W 2T8
phone: 403-678-3200
website: www.alpineclubofcanada.ca
email: info@alpineclubofcanada.ca

The Club House Located on the outskirts of Canmore, this lovely facility has beds for 43. There is a comfortable reading room, sauna and complete kitchen facilities.

Huts The ACC operates many backcountry huts which tend to be rustic and lean toward a philosophy of self reliance. Many of these huts are locked with a combination lock. Making a booking is a simple matter of exchanging your visa or Mastercard number for the combination lock number. The ACC huts described in this book are classified as follows:

Class A+ Huts equipped with foamies, cooking and eating utensils, propane cooking stoves and lanterns and a wood heating stove.
Bow Hut (Wapta Icefields)
Elizabeth Parker Hut (Lake O'Hara)
Stanley Mitchell Hut (Little Yoho)

Class A Huts equipped as above but with Coleman cooking stoves and lanterns.
Wates-Gibson Hut (Tonquin)
Sydney Vallence Hut (Fryatt Creek)
Fay Hut (Prospectors Valley)

Class B+ Huts equipped with foamies, cooking and eating utensils, propane cooking stoves and lanterns. There is no heating stove.
Peyto Hut (Wapta Icefields)

Class B Huts equipped as above but with Coleman cooking stoves and lanterns.
Balfour Hut (Wapta Icefields)
Scott Duncan Hut (Wapta Icefields)

Hostels

The Southern Alberta Hostelling Association (SAHA) operates two luxurious hostels as well as a number of more rustic hostels throughout the Rocky Mountains. They are moderately priced and are used extensively by backcountry skiers.

SAHA

#203, 1414 Kensington Road N.W.
Calgary, Alberta, T2N 3P9
phone: 403-283-5551

Ribbon Creek Hostel Located near Kananaskis Village, this comfortable hostel has dormitory accommodation for 30 and five 4 person private rooms. Bookings can be made through the Banff Hostel.

The Banff Hostel is a large modern structure with beds for 250. There is a restaurant, lounge and self serve kitchen. Phone 403-762-4122.

The Lake Louise Alpine Centre is owned and operated in conjunction with The Alpine Club of Canada. This fully modern facility offers 155 beds, restaurant, sauna, library, lounge and a self serve kitchen. Phone 403-522-2200.

Castle Mountain Hostel, located along the Bow Valley Parkway at Castle Junction, has beds for 36. Bookings can be made through the Banff Hostel.

The Icefields Parkway Hostels there are several hostels which are more rustic and are almost like backcountry cabins. These are located along the Icefields Parkway at Mosquito Creek, Ramparts Creek and Hilda Creek. They are inexpensive but very comfortable. Bookings can be made through the Banff Hostel.

The **Alberta Hostelling Association** (AHA) operates several hostels near Jasper. For information contact:
10926 - 88 Ave.
Edmonton, Alberta, T6G 0Z1
phone: 780-432-7798
phone 1-877-852-0781 for reservations at Jasper Hostels

AHA Hostels include
Jasper Hostel (7 km from Jasper)
Maligne Canyon Hostel (11 km from Jasper)
Athabasca Falls Hostel (30 km south of Jasper)
Edith Cavell Hostel (ski access only, 13 km from the trailhead)
Beauty Creek Hostel (82 km south of Jasper)

Commercial Lodges
The Canadian Rockies are blessed with a rich skiing history and some very beautiful backcountry lodges. These are described in the book along with a contact number for reservations and information. They can provide a truly memorable experience and are highly recommended.

Miscellaneous Huts
There are several other huts that are referred to in this book. These are the Egypt Lake and Bryant Creek Shelters which are operated by Parks Canada, the Naiset Huts which are operated by B.C. Provincial Parks and the Shangri La Cabin which is operated by the Maligne Lake Ski Club. Reservations are required and can be obtained by phoning 403-762-1550 (for the Egypt Lake and Bryant Creek shelters), 403-678-2883 (for the Naiset Huts) and 780-852-3665 (for the Shangri La Cabin).

Campgrounds
The Canadian Parks Service plows several campgrounds and keeps them open all winter for folks with RV vehicles. These are Tunnel Mountain (near Banff), Lake Louise, Mosquito Creek (Icefields Parkway) and Wapiti (near Jasper). Contact the park information centre for more current information.

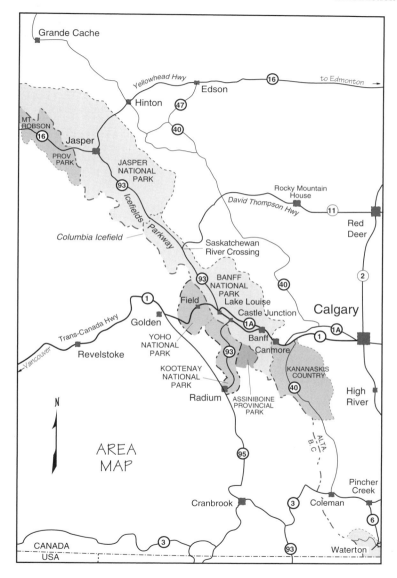

Grande Cache

Yellowhead Hwy

Edson

16 to Edmonton

Hinton

47

MT ROBSON PROV PARK

40

16 Jasper

JASPER NATIONAL PARK

93

Icefields Parkway

Rocky Mountain House

David Thompson Hwy

11

Red Deer

Columbia Icefield

Saskatchewan River Crossing

2

93 BANFF NATIONAL PARK

40

1 Field

Lake Louise

Calgary

Golden

Castle Junction

1A

Trans-Canada Hwy

YOHO NATIONAL PARK

93 Banff

1A

Vancouver

Canmore

1

Revelstoke

KANANASKIS COUNTRY

KOOTENAY NATIONAL PARK

Radium

ASSINIBOINE PROVINCIAL PARK

40

High River

N

ALTA B.C.

AREA MAP

95

Pincher Creek

Cranbrook

3 Coleman

6

CANADA
USA

3

93 Waterton

19

WATERTON LAKES NATIONAL PARK

1 Dipper	intermediate	p. 21
2 Cameron Lake	easy	p. 22
3 Summit Lake	intermediate	p. 23
4 Akamina Pass to Wall Lake & Forum Lake	easy/intermediate	p. 24

Waterton Lakes National Park, the most southerly area covered in this book, is the Canadian section of the International Peace Park. Glacier National Park on the U.S. side of the border forms the southern portion. Situated in the extreme southwest corner of Alberta, this small (518 sq. km) park is popular in summer for its backpacking and hiking trails. However, in winter Waterton is a very quiet park indeed and there are few amenities available.

In good snow periods the skiing, especially in the Akamina Pass area, can be excellent. However, the area is affected by Chinooks—warm westerly winds prevalent from December to April—that, when combined with a somewhat lower snowfall than other mountain regions, may result in only marginal skiing.

Access to Waterton Park is via Highway 6 from Pincher Creek, located 48 km north, or by Highway 5 connecting to Cardston, 45 km east. The townsite is located 8 km along a spur road off Highway 6. Chief Mountain Highway, which provides access from the United States, is closed in winter. Within the Park, the Akamina Highway is the only road open, being plowed to a parking area 2.5 km short of Cameron Lake.

Facilities Little is available in winter.

Accommodation Crandell Mountain Lodge (403-859-2288) and Kilmorey Lodge (403-859-2334) are open in winter.

Information Phone the Visitor Centre 403-859-5133 weekdays from 8:00 am to 4:00 pm. Phone or visit the Warden Office (403-859-5140) located on the right-hand side as you approach the townsite.

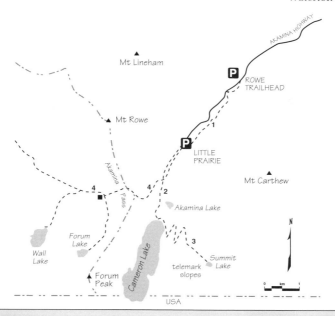

1 DIPPER

Nordic skiing 1

Grade Intermediate
Distance 6.5 km return
Time 2 hours
Height gain 50 m
Max elevation 1680 m
Map Sage Creek 82 G/1

This is a rolling and challenging trail which requires decent snow conditions to be enjoyable. It runs between the Little Prairie parking lot and the Rowe Creek trailhead and is downhill in that direction. You can use two cars and ski the trail one way if you choose. Not recommended when icy or in crusty snow conditions.

Facilities At the Little Prairie parking lot there are picnic tables, a camp shelter and toilets.

Access Park at Little Prairie parking lot, at the end of the plowed section of the Akamina Highway, 13.5 km west of the town of Waterton.

From the picnic shelter head south for about 50 m (the opposite direction that you would anticipate) to a small meadow.

Turn left and cross Cameron Creek on a narrow bridge then continue north along the right bank of the creek. The trail crosses the creek another three times on small bridges and ascends and descends numerous short, steep hills. It is very narrow until the final kilometre where it follows the old bridle road again.

21

2 CAMERON LAKE

Grade Easy
Distance 5 km return
Time 1.5 hours
Height gain Minimal
Max elevation 1680 m
Map Sage Creek 82 G/1

This trail follows the unplowed section of the Akamina Highway to the north shore of Cameron Lake. It is a good trail for beginners and children but is exposed to the wind resulting frequently in filled-in tracks.

Access Park at the Little Prairie parking lot at the end of the plowed section of the Akamina Highway, 13.5 km west of the town of Waterton.

Facilities Picnic tables, a camp shelter and toilets at the Little Prairie parking lot.

Options On the return back to the Little Prairie parking lot you can follow a variation on the east side of the road. This is an old road which gives you a nice downhill glide much of the way if skied in a south to north direction. It begins about half way along the road, opposite the Akamina Pass Trail.

Ski around the gate and continue down the unplowed roadway. The trail climbs very gently to begin with then descends to the lake. Cameron lake is a beautiful spot to eat your lunch and admire the scenery.

Skiing the snow-covered Akamina Highway to Cameron Lake. Photo Gillean Daffern.

Looking down on Cameron Lake from above Summit Lake. Photo Brent Kozachenko.

3 SUMMIT LAKE

Ski touring 2

Grade Intermediate
Distance 13 km return from Little Prairie
Time 4 hours return from Little Prairie
Height gain 310 m
Max elevation 1,960 m
Map Sage Creek 82 G/1

A scenic trail for Telemark skiers who want to make a few turns on the hill west of Summit Lake.

Hazards Not recommended in icy conditions. Telemarking slopes above Summit Lake have the potential to avalanche.

Access Park at the trailhead for Cameron Lake Trail.

Follow the Cameron Lake trail to Cameron Lake and continue along the north shore of the lake to Cameron Creek which is crossed on a bridge. The trail then climbs the steepening hillside in 5 long switchbacks. The trail itself is not too steep but the angle of the slope is. Consequently if there is deep snow you can be traversing under difficult conditions. Half way along the fifth zag the angle eases and from here it is a pleasant ski along a bench then a gentle descent to the lake. You are just below treeline so there are wonderful views across the border to the peaks of Glacier National Park. This is a good place to spend a few hours practising your Telemark turns. In good conditions it can be a fun descent back to Cameron Lake.

23

4 AKAMINA PASS TO WALL LAKE & FORUM LAKE   Ski touring 2, 1

Grade Easy/intermediate
Distance 1.6 km from Akamina Hwy to
Akamina Pass, 4.7 km to Forum Lake,
5.6 km to Wall Lake one way
Time You can visit both lakes in a 5 hour
day
Height gain 220 m to Wall Lake, 360 m
to Forum Lake
Max elevation 1800 m at Akamina
Pass, 1780 m at Wall Lake, 2000 m at
Forum Lake
Map Sage Creek 82 G/1

This is a popular trail with skiers who want
something a little more challenging. It has
the best snow in the area. When you cross
Akamina Pass into British Columbia you are
in the Akamina/Kishinena Recreation Area.
Snowmobiles are allowed here so you may
share the trail with these machines. Forum
Lake is perhaps a more exciting destination
than Wall Lake, particularly if you are looking
for Telemark slopes.

Facilities There are picnic tables, a camp
shelter and toilets at the Little Prairie
parking lot.

Hazards Snowmobiles

Options Some people reach Forum Lake
from Akamina Pass by skiing south up
the boundary cut line then descending
through open timber to the lake.

Access Park at the Little Prairie parking
lot at the end of the plowed section of
the Akamina Highway, 13.5 km west of
the town of Waterton.

Follow the Cameron Lake trail for a little more than a kilometre then take the
trail to the right to Akamina Pass (trail
sign). It is a moderate climb from here
to the pass on a wide trail. The trail runs
through the trees with little in the way
of views. On the left a cut line marks
the boundary of the park. The trail now
becomes the Akamina Road where there
is a possibility of meeting snowmobiles.
Descend gently down the B.C. side to the
Forum Lake trail branching off to the left
after about 1 km.

Forum Lake There is a trail sign at this
point which may be visible. Follow
the trail for a short distance to a ranger
cabin which is passed on the left. Just
beyond there is another trail junction.

Keep left and climb two steep hills to
a levelling below the headwall. Here it
becomes impossible to follow the trail.
Work your way up the headwall (open
forest and meadow) following the best
line possible, then when it begins to
level, continue across to the lake which
will be below you in a deep hollow.
The run back down to the ranger cabin
is superb.

Wall Lake Continue past the Forum
Lake trail, to the next trail branching off
to the left which goes to Wall Lake (sign
post). The route from here is obvious
except at one point where a trail sign
points up the ridge to Wall Lake. Do
not take this cutoff but continue straight
ahead along the obvious trail to the lake.
The trail cuts the corner and climbs over
the ridge then runs along the creek to the
lake. There is an impressive mountain
wall behind the lake with many frozen
waterfalls hanging on it.

MOUNT ASSINIBOINE PROVINCIAL PARK

Mount Assiniboine Provincial Park is a very popular ski destination. The meadows below Mount Assiniboine offer some of the finest ski touring in the Rockies. There is always plenty of snow, the terrain is open and rolling and the scenery is outstanding.

For information about Mount Assiniboine Provincial Park you should visit the website www.bcparks.ca.

Access The park cannot be accessed by motor vehicle. The usual methods of approach are either by helicopter or on skis. The helicopter is quick, comfortable but costly. As a compromise many parties fly in and ski out. For helicopter information or reservations contact Mount Assiniboine Lodge (403) 678-2883.

There are three ski access routes described in this guidebook. The route from Shark Mountain is the shortest and most popular. The route from Sunshine Village Ski Resort is somewhat longer and more difficult but still sees some traffic. The route from Banff over Allenby Pass, although the historic approach route, is now rarely used.

Facilities There are several overnight possibilities of varying degrees of comfort and cost: Mount Assiniboine Lodge, the Naiset Huts or camping. The lodge is privately managed and is the luxurious place to stay. The Naiset Huts are much more affordable although very rustic. There is a designated camping area for the truly penurious.

Regulations Helicopter access to the park is restricted to landings at Mount Assiniboine Lodge or at the Naiset Huts, three days of the week only, Wednesdays, Fridays and Sundays. On long weekends flights are allowed on Mondays instead of Sundays. If you are skiing to Mount Assiniboine Park and are planning on spending a night at the Bryant Creek Shelter you will need a permit from Banff National Park.

Dinner time at Mount Assiniboine Lodge.

Skiing across the meadows below Mount Assiniboine.

History The meadows below Mount Assiniboine and the mountain itself have been a destination for adventure seekers for over 100 years. Mount Assiniboine was first climbed in 1901 by British clergyman James Outram, led by his Swiss guides Christian Bohren and Christian Hasler Sr. Their ascent was a remarkable tour de force—in only five days they travelled from Banff via Sunshine Meadows, traversed the mountain (up the south face and down the north ridge), and returned to Banff.

In 1922 the B.C. government created Mount Assiniboine Provincial Park. In 1925 A.O. Wheeler (founder of The Alpine Club of Canada) built several cabins (now the Naiset Huts) which he used for his walking tours for several years. Eventually these cabins were sold to The Alpine Club of Canada for a minimal amount.

In March of 1928, a young Norwegian ski adventurer, Erling Strom, and his aristocratic partner, the Marquis d'Albizzi, led four clients to Mount Assiniboine over Allenby Pass. After spending a month skiing in the meadows below the striking tower of Mount Assiniboine, Strom was hooked. He returned that summer and built Mount Assiniboine Lodge which opened for business the following spring. If you visit the lodge today you can see the names of the early guests carved into the logs high over the main entrance to the dining room.

The 1930s was the golden decade of skiing in the Canadian Rockies and folks came from all over North America to experience the beauty and grandeur of the area. In those days guests and their guides would ski 45 km from Banff, staying at two smaller huts along the way (Ten Mile and Halfway). Fresh supplies were packed in the same way but staples were brought in on horseback the previ-ous autumn and stored in the cellar. In these days if you came to Assiniboine you were there for 2,3 or even 4 weeks. You could relax and adjust to a wilderness pace of life. Today, however, with the helicopter and satellite telephone, skiers come for two or three days on tight schedules. Your stockbroker, your lawyer or your kids can phone you now as easily as phoning across town. 'Civilization' does indeed have mixed blessings.

Strom operated the lodge he had lovingly built for many years but the winter trade never became a large part

Mount Assiniboine Lodge

Mount Assiniboine Lodge is what one imagines the post card picture of the ski lodge in the Canadian Rockies should look like. This historic log building sits beneath the impressive tower of Mount Assiniboine one of the most spectacular peaks in the world.
Location In the meadows along the NE shore of Lake Magog (GR 972403).
Map Mount Assiniboine 82 J/13
Facilities A central lodge surrounded by six guest cabins. Outdoor plumbing but propane heating. Large sauna. The lodge is equipped with a telephone.
Capacity About 30
Hosts Sepp and Barb Renner
Season Mid February to Mid April
Cost About $150 per person which includes guiding and all meals. Beer and wine are available for purchase.
Reservations Write Mount Assiniboine Lodge, Box 8128, Canmore, Alberta T1W 2T8 Email: assinilo@telusplanet.net Website: www.canadianrockies.net/assiniboine
Phone 403-678-2883
Fax 403-678-4877

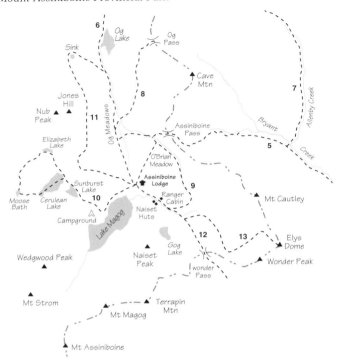

of the operation, likely because the travel distance from Banff or Sunshine Village was so far. Eventually Strom sold the lodge to the province of British Columbia who then leased it out to commercial operators. Since 1983 Swiss born mountain guide Sepp Renner and his wife Barb have operated the lodge. With the advent of helicopter access ski traffic has picked up and now forms a major portion of the yearly business.

Meanwhile the ACC Cabins, which came to be known as the Naiset Huts, fell into disrepair over the years. In 1971 they were sold to the B.C. government who completely refurbished them and now operate them charging a minimal fee.

Naiset Huts

Four small, rustic cabins nestled in the trees near Mount Assiniboine
Location In the trees above the east end of Lake Magog (GR 973402).
Map Mount Assiniboine 82 J/13
Facilities These are simple cabins with wooden bunks and foam pads. There are wood heating stoves but no cooking stoves, pots or eating utensils.
Capacity Two cabins for 5 and two cabins for 8.
Water From Magog Creek
Reservations Phone Mount Assiniboine Lodge 403-678-2883

5 SHARK TO ASSINIBOINE VIA BRYANT CREEK   Ski touring 1

Grade Intermediate/advanced
Distance 25 km one way
Time It is a very full day to ski to Mount Assiniboine and many parties take two days. Most parties can ski back out to the Shark Mountain parking lot in one day if they get an early start.
Height gain 440 m
Max elevation 2180 m
Maps Mount Assiniboine 82 J/13
Spray Lakes Reservoir 82 J/14

Facilities There are toilets at the Shark Mountain trailhead. The Bryant Creek Shelter is located about half way along this tour. The Naiset Huts and Mount Assiniboine Lodge are located near Lake Magog.

Hazards The slopes above the trail below Assiniboine Pass present some avalanche hazard.

Access The trail to Mount Assiniboine starts from a large parking lot at the Shark Mountain Cross Country Ski Trails. To reach this parking lot drive through the town of Canmore and follow the Smith-Dorrien/Spray Trail up the hillside and through the narrow pass. After 38 km turn right at the turn off for Engadine Lodge. Drive past the entrance to the lodge and continue down the road for 5 km to the parking lot.

Most parties who ski to Mount Assiniboine use this route and it is usually well packed. Often skiers will fly to Assiniboine then ski back out to their cars via this trail. The only real difficulty is the descent from Assiniboine Pass. It is very steep and it is often best to remove your skis and walk down the trail.

From the Shark Mountain parking lot follow the Watridge Lake trail (see page 44). It is a wide trackset trail with many signs marking the way. After about 3 km the trail climbs for a short distance. This is about as far as the trail will be trackset. It then descends steeply for about 100 vertical metres, crosses some flats then crosses the Spray River on a bridge. From here the trail climbs briefly then meanders through the forest for 0.5 km until it crosses Bryant Creek on another bridge.

From Bryant Creek climb for a short distance up the hillside to join the Bryant Creek trail. Turn left along the trail. Soon there is another trail junction and here you stay right (the left fork goes down to a warden cabin). For the next 10 km the trail stays on the right side of the valley and is very easy and clear to follow as it runs through the forest. After about 2 km the trail crosses a bridge over a creek then continues for another 2 km when it begins to climb. The grade is gentle at first but gradually the trail steepens. Just before reaching the Bryant Creek Shelter the trail climbs a steep, open hillside, continues a short distance through forest then descends to a meadow. The Bryant Creek Shelter is located about 600 m across the meadow to the left.

Cross the right flank of the meadow and enter the trees again. Ski past the Bryant Creek Warden Cabin. Follow the trail along the edge of the trees on the right side of the valley for about 3 km then ski out left into the valley. Cross the meadows to the left-centre of the valley then continue for about 4 km to the hillside below the pass, sometimes following bits of trail through the trees and sometimes open meadow.

Bryant Creek Shelter

A rustic cabin which is often used as an overnight stop on the way to Mount Assiniboine.

Location At the far corner of a meadow, 600 m SW of the warden cabin, on the west side of the trail along Bryant Creek (GR 043392).

Map Mount Assiniboine 82 J/13

Facilities Wood heating stove, axe and woodpile. No cooking stove, pots or eating utensils. Bare wooden bunks with no foamies.

Capacity 18

Water From Bryant Creek

Reservations Phone Banff National Park Information Centre 403-762-1550

The climb to Assiniboine Pass is steep and gains about 200 vertical metres. The trail follows the left side of the valley and eventually makes several switchbacks near the top. It works its way between two cliffbands then traverses out right to the lowest point in the pass.

Ski through the pass and climb a small, steep hillside through the trees to a higher point. From here the trail descends a long slope out into O'Brians Meadow. Cross the meadow and climb the hillside on the opposite side, then ski around a little pond before entering the trees. From here the trail heads south to the lodge crossing meadows and traversing sections of forest.

If it is early in the season and there has not been much ski traffic the direct trail to the lodge will not be well broken and will be hard to follow. In this case it is sometimes easier to ski through the lowest point in the pass then descend gently for several hundred metres in a westerly direction until you reach a meadow. On your left along here is a steep wooded hillside—do not attempt to ski across it. Follow the meadow which soon begins to curve to the left (southwest) then ski through some trees for a short distance to O'Brians Meadow. Ski out to the right into expansive Og Meadows, angle left and ski across these meadows then finish through a draw to the lodge.

Assiniboine Lodge is situated on a bench above Lake Magog. The Naiset Huts and the Rangers Cabin are about 300 m to the south of the lodge along Magog Creek.

Bryant Creek shelter.

6 SUNSHINE TO ASSINIBOINE VIA CITADEL PASS Ski touring 2

Grade Advanced
Distance 30 km one way
Time Although this tour can be done in one very long day many parties will take two days
Height gain 730 m
Height loss 760 m
Max elevation 2390 m
Maps Banff 82 O/4
Mount Assiniboine 82 J/13

The approach to Mount Assiniboine from Sunshine Village Ski Resort is not often used nowadays. It is hard for most of us to resist the appeal of the helicopter and, if we do, we usually opt for the shortest route from Shark Mountain via Assiniboine Pass. However, if you are looking for some adventure and a long hard tour, this trip is for you.

Facilities There are two cabins located at Police Meadows about halfway along this tour (GR 907486). Note that these cabins are incorrectly marked on the topo map. The cabins are in good shape and the stove is in working order. These cabins are privately owned, but are left open for use in emergency.

Hazards There are a number of hazards on this tour. First of all you need good visibility to find your way across Sunshine Meadows to Citadel Pass. The descent from the pass to the Simpson River is subject to avalanche hazard and good route finding skills are required. If you plan to stay at the Police Meadows cabins you will find them tricky to locate so leave yourself some daylight to get settled in. Finally, the route up Golden Valley and Valley of the Rocks is famous for bottomless depth hoar and tricky route finding, so be prepared for hard trail breaking. This tour will challenge all ski tourers.

Access Begin at the Sunshine Village Ski Resort (see Citadel Pass page 71).

Ski 10 km from Sunshine Village to Citadel Pass. From the pass the route descends 600 m to the headwaters of the Simpson River. This descent is subject to avalanche threat from both sides, but the route itself is reasonably safe if you follow the best line. It is possible to stay on lower angled or treed slopes virtually all the way.

From the pass the route descends very gently for the first kilometre, past a lake, then climbs briefly to the brow of a steep hill. As you descend from Citadel Pass be sure to follow the drainage out to the left and not get drawn off to the right by an obvious line of meadows. Descend the steep hill using the safety of the trees wherever possible. There is some avalanche hazard at the top of the hill. From the bottom of this steep hill the remainder of the descent to the valley bottom stays in the centre of the drainage. However, there are serious avalanche paths on both sides, so exercise caution.

As you descend you can look directly south across the valley to a side valley (actually named the Simpson River on the map), where you will see a large meadow. This is Police Meadows and you can likely spot the cabin on the right flank of the meadow. If you intend to stay at the cabin, the best approach route in winter is to follow the left bank of the creek downstream (serious bushwhacking) until it joins the Simpson River, then

31

Looking up toward Citadel Pass from Police Meadows. Photo Art Longair.

turn left and ski upstream along the river for about 1.5 km to reach the meadow.

It is possible to avoid the descent to the valley bottom by traversing left, high above Golden Valley, to reach Valley of the Rocks directly. If conditions are perfectly stable this traverse is an option but you must cross some very large avalanche slopes and the risk is high. If you chose to do this traverse you must be very sure that the snow is stable.

The route up Golden Valley is a frustrating series of hills and sinks. You are continually climbing rolls only to descend again on the other side. There is no proper drainage to follow. It is recommended that you work along the left (northeast) side of the valley and attempt to ski near the edge of the trees as much as possible. Higher up in Valley of the Rocks the going gets easier: the trees spread out, the terrain is uniform and it is possible to make some headway.

About 1.5 km before Og Lake the trail leaves the trees behind and from here to Lake Magog traverses open meadows. The route passes Og Lake and heads due south passing through a narrow gap then continues for about 3 km across flat open meadows. The last 0.5 km ascends an open draw through the forest then pops over the hill just 100 m to the west of the lodge.

Of historical interest In 1974 Don Gardner, Chris Shank and Larry Mason left Sunshine Village Ski Resort at midnight on a ski marathon. At 7:00 am they arrived at Mount Assiniboine Lodge where Lizzie Rummel fed them breakfast. From here they continued over Assiniboine Pass, down Bryant Creek to Spray Lake then along the road to a waiting car at Three Sisters Dam. An impressive feat indeed: over 80 km in 17 hours.

Opposite: Mount Assiniboine Lodge.

7 BANFF TO ASSINIBOINE VIA ALLENBY PASS   Ski touring 2

Grade Advanced
Distance 44 km one way
Time 2 days are normally required for this tour
Height gain 1070 m over Allenby Pass 260 m over Assiniboine Pass
Height loss 500 m from Allenby Pass to Bryant Creek
Max elevation 2440 m at Allenby Pass
Maps Banff 82 O/4
Mount Assiniboine 82 J/13

This is the original route to Mount Assiniboine; the route followed by Erling Strom and his party in 1928. It was used for many years afterwards by guides and their guests but has today fallen into disuse. It is a long way.

Facilities Banff Sundance Lodge (403-762-4551) is located along Brewster Creek (GR 935614) and is open in winter. Halfway Cabin is located along the creek, 3 km north of Allenby Pass (GR 995496). It is marked incorrectly on the map and is on the opposite side of the creek.

Access Park your car 0.8 km along the Sunshine Village Ski Resort access road at the start of the Old Healy Creek Road to Sundance Lodge (see page 60).

Follow trail #1 along the Old Healy Creek Road for about 2 km to its junction with Brewster Creek Road. Turn right and work your way along the trail up Brewster Creek to Banff Sundance Lodge. To this point the skiing is easy and the trail will quite likely be packed. Beyond here, however, this is a back

country route and you should be prepared to break trail.

The trail continues up Brewster Creek for about 12 km then turns right up a side valley. Several kilometres up this side valley you will find Halfway Cabin. From here the trail climbs steeply through the trees to the high meadows of Allenby Pass. Follow Allenby Creek down from the pass then descend to Bryant Creek where the route joins the Shark Mountain Trail to Mount Assiniboine.

Looking across Lake Magog to Mount Magog, Mount Assiniboine and Mount Strom. Photo Vance Hanna.

8 OG PASS

Ski touring 1

Grade Easy/intermediate
Distance 10 km return
Time 4-5 hours return
Height gain 300 m
Max elevation 2300 m
Map Mount Assiniboine 82 J/13

A pleasant day trip through varied terrain. There are excellent views of Mount Assiniboine and a fun run down from the pass.

The trail starts just 100 m northwest of Mount Assiniboine Lodge. Descend the draw for about 0.5 km until the trail breaks out into Og Meadows. Ski across the meadows heading north for about 2 km then, just before the meadows narrow into a short 'canyon', turn right. From here follow the drainage up to Og Pass.

On your return you can ski back down the creek from the pass, then, for variation, just before reaching the meadows turn south and follow another drainage to Assiniboine Pass. From Assiniboine Pass work your way back through the meadows and forest to Mount Assiniboine Lodge (see page 27).

9 DEAD HORSE CANYON

Grade Easy
Distance 5 km loop
Time 2-3 hours
Height gain 120 m
Max elevation 2290 m
Map Mount Assiniboine 82 J/13

A short and varied tour offering some climbing, a bit of a downhill run and some travel through the forest.

Hazards The walls of the creekbed can be potentially dangerous during unstable snow conditions.

From Mount Assiniboine Lodge ski southeast past the cabins. Cross the little creek and ascend the hillside in front of the ranger cabin. Continue climbing up the open hillside above and after about 0.5 km angle left through some open trees to gain the bench at the edge of treeline. Ski across this bench for a short distance until you reach a prominent drainage which descends the hill to the north. The tour now follows the creekbed losing about 120 m in elevation. It is a fun run but never too steep. Continue down the creek bed until you reach O'Brians Meadow. Cross the meadow in a northwest direction then follow the trail from Assiniboine Pass heading south to Mount Assiniboine Lodge (see page 27).

10 MOOSE BATH

Grade Easy/intermediate
Distance 8 km return
Time 4 hours return
Height gain The trail climbs 140 m as far as the pass above Elizabeth Lake, then descends 150 m to Moose Bath. On the return the trail climbs about 100 m to reach Cerulean Lake.
Max elevation 2290 m
Map Mount Assiniboine 82 J/13

Facilities The tour passes by the Sunburst Lake Cabin but it will be locked. There is an outhouse here.

Hazards The hillside descending to Elizabeth Lake has glades in the trees which could pose an avalanche threat in certain conditions. Straying too far to the right as you climb from Moose Bath up to Cerulean Lake could expose you to avalanche from the slopes of Sunburst Peak.

From Mount Assiniboine Lodge work southwest along the brow of the hill above Magog Lake. After a bit more than 1 km work your way right through some trees into a shallow drainage. Follow this drainage northwest for about 0.5 km until it pops over the crest of a hill to reach Sunburst Lake. About 100 m along the right shore of the lake you will find the Sunburst Lake Cabin tucked in the trees. This is a pleasant spot for a break.

Continue northwest along the edge of the lake then cross a short neck of land to the shore of Cerulean Lake. Traverse the east (right) edge of this lake for a short distance, then climb the hillside directly above its north corner. About 100 vertical metres of reasonably steep climbing through the trees brings you to the top. Down the other side you will see Elizabeth Lake. Descend to the lake taking a line a bit to the left. There is an opportunity for a few turns here, so have some fun. Cross Elizabeth Lake and descend the creek that runs southwest. For most of the descent stay on the left

bank of the creek, then work your way left (south) to a small pond shown on the map (Moose Bath!).

Cross the pond and work your way up the hillside above, through the trees, to reach Cerulean Lake. Cross the lake to the northeast to rejoin your earlier tracks which are then followed back to the lodge.

Of Historical Interest The Sunburst Lake Cabin was owned and operated by Lizzie Rummel for 20 years, from 1951 to 1970. As well as the cabin there were several tent cabins and her famous tipi. Lizzie became a legend in the Canadian Rockies and eventually had a school, two lakes and a street in Canmore named for her. People would journey from around the world to spend time with her on the shores of Sunburst Lake. She could always remind us of what was really important and beautiful in life.

Opposite: Jones' Cabin is one of the Naiset Huts.

11 JONES BENCH

Grade Easy
Distance 10 km loop
Time 4-5 hours
Height gain 180 m
Max elevation 2350 m
Map Mount Assiniboine 82 J/13

This is a superb ski tour. It ascends quickly above timberline and traverses high above the meadows for several kilometres. The views are excellent and there is opportunity to make a few turns along the way. Highly recommended!

From Mount Assiniboine Lodge ski west across the meadows for about a kilometre until they begin to pinch out in the trees. Follow the drainage that curves up to your right toward a small peak called The Nublet (GR 950417). Climb at a gradual angle up the creek bed gaining about 120 vertical metres until you reach the edge of treeline. From here work your way out right to a rounded shoulder. Above you now is The Nublet and the adventurous can climb on skis or perhaps on foot to its rounded and gentle summit. The leeward (southeast) side of this shoulder offers an excellent place to make a few turns.

Carry on traversing the bench in a northerly direction for 3 km. After you pass beneath Jones Hill (on your left)

you begin to descend gradually. To reach the valley bottom near Og Lake it is necessary to ski all the way to a sink that is marked on the map (GR 951444) before descending to your right. Do not cut down into the valley before this point as you will encounter very steep terrain. Just beyond the sink you can descend easily to the valley floor.

Return to the lodge across the meadows along the valley bottom. Just before reaching the lodge it is necessary to ascend a draw, ski through a section of trees then pop through a little pass to the lodge.

Of Historical Interest Ken Jones was the first home-grown Canadian to receive all the National Parks guides badges—for skiing, mountain climbing, river and bush craft. For years he guided at Skoki, Lake Louise and Mount Assiniboine. He was also a professional log builder who worked on Skoki Lodge in 1936 and built the central building of Num-ti-jah Lodge on the Icefields Parkway in 1948 and 49. From 1967 to 1974 he was the Ranger at Mount Assiniboine Park. One of the Naiset Huts is, in fact, his old ranger cabin and is now called Jones' Cabin.

Jones Hill, Jones Bench and Jones Pass (at Skoki) are all named for Ken. For the last two decades of his life he was often found at Mount Assiniboine Lodge, chopping wood, shovelling snow and telling stories.

Skiing across Lake Magog below Mount Assiniboine. Photo Alf Skrastins.

12 WONDER PASS

Ski touring 1

Grade Easy
Distance 7 km return
Time 3 hours return
Height gain 210 m
Max elevation 2360 m
Map Mount Assiniboine 82 J/13

Wonder Pass is a very pleasant, short ski tour, perfect for a lazy day. The trail leads you high above the trees into beautiful alpine terrain where the views are excellent.

Facilities The trail passes by the rangers cabin where you can stop for a chat and a check on the snow conditions. Across from the rangers cabin are the Naiset Huts.

Options The tour can be extended beyond Wonder Pass. You can carry on southeast, along a bench, to a promontory high above Marvel Lake. There are excellent views from here.

From Mount Assiniboine Lodge ski southeast past the cabins then cross the little creek. Ascend the hill past the ranger cabin and continue up the hillside above. The trail follows open terrain along the left bank of Magog Creek. After crossing the creek (where the creek turns east), the route stays high on the left for the last kilometre and traverses into the pass. On the return trip you can come back the same way if you choose, or you can take a more direct line down the drainage below Wonder Pass. Both routes offer the opportunity to make a few turns.

13 ELYS DOME

Grade Intermediate/advanced
Distance 8 km return
Time This is a full day tour
Height gain 650 m
Max elevation 2830 m
Map Mount Assiniboine 82 J/13

A wonderful tour for a sunny spring day. It takes you to the top of the unnamed peak (GR 012389) between Mount Cautley and Wonder Peak. The skiing can be excellent and there are marvellous views of Mount Assiniboine.

Hazards There is avalanche potential on this tour so use caution.

Ski up the hill past the rangers cabin and then work your way left across the meadows toward the peak. The route up the peak ascends a ramp which traverse from right to left. If you choose a good line the tour can be done in reasonable safety however, there are steeper slopes nearby which can be dangerous in certain conditions. The descent offers excellent skiing.

Of Historical Interest Elys Dome is named for the sister of Sam Evans, a packer and guide who worked at Skoki and Assiniboine in the 1930s and 40s. He came from Montana and was reputed to be enormously wealthy. They say he was an heir to the Dupont fortune but he worked along with the rest of the guides and never let on.

TELEMARK AREAS

The Nublet
Some excellent terrain for making turns can be found on the shoulder below The Nublet. These southeast facing slopes are set at a reasonable angle, are protected from the wind and are in the sun all day. Highly recommended! See the Jones Bench tour (page 37) for the approach.

The Cerulean Lake Hillside
The hillside above the north shore of Cerulean Lake offers some good terrain for turns. This is glade skiing, in the trees, so it is excellent for those snowy and cloudy days. See the Moose Bath tour (page 36) for the approach.

Of Historical Interest Erling Strom was born in 1897 in Norway and emigrated to the United States in 1919. For years he was a ski instructor at Lake Placid and ran a lodge in Stowe, Vermont. He is noted for having made the second ascent of Denali (Mount McKinley, North America's highest peak) in 1932. Skis were used on this ascent. Strom, however, will always be associated with Mount Assiniboine and the beautiful lodge that he built in the meadows below.

KANANASKIS COUNTRY

14 Chester Lake	inter/advanced	p. 41
15 Burstall Pass	inter/advanced	p. 43
16 Watridge Lake	easy	p. 44
17 Ribbon Creek to Skogan Pass	intermediate	p. 45
18 Ribbon Creek Ski Trails	easy/intermediate	p. 46
19 Peter Lougheed Provincial Park Trails	easy/intermediate	p. 47
20 Smith-Dorrien Ski Trails	easy/intermediate	p. 48
21 Mount Shark Ski Trails	easy/intermediate	p. 48

Kananaskis Country encompasses 4000 square kilometres of superb mountain terrain in the front ranges of the Rocky Mountains, directly west of Calgary. Peter Lougheed Provincial Park and Spray Valley Provincial Park are located in the heart of Kananaskis Country. This wonderful region has always been a favourite with Calgary hikers, climbers and skiers. The recreational potential was vigorously developed by the provincial government during the 1970s and 1980s, most notably the wonderful ski trail complex at Kananaskis Lakes.

The area can be approached from Calgary via the Trans Canada Highway (Highway 1) and Highway 40 (Kananaskis Trail) or from Canmore via the Smith-Dorrien/Spray Trail. Both these roads are maintained in good winter driving condition.

There is not a lot of commercial development in Kananaskis Country. There are two downhill ski resorts—Fortress Mountain and Nakiska. Kananaskis Village has several hotels and restaurants, as well as a grocery store and sports shop. Gas and some groceries can be purchased at Fortress Junction, 42 km along Highway 40 from Highway 1.

For pleasant accommodation try Engadine Lodge (403-678-4080) along the Smith-Dorrien/Spray Trail. The Ribbon Creek Hostel is located near Kananaskis Village and offers excellent low cost accommodation.

There is a Visitor Information Centre at Barrier Lake along Highway 40 which is open in winter, 9:00 am to 4:00 pm, seven days a week. There is another Visitor Information Centre in Peter Lougheed Provincial Park which is open 9:30 am to 4:00 pm, seven days a week.

There are four outstanding trail systems in Kananaskis Country: the Ribbon Creek Ski Trails, the Peter Lougheed Provincial Park Ski Trails, the Mount Shark Ski Trails and the Smith-Dorrien Ski Trails. They offer excellent skiing for novice and expert alike and are hugely popular on the weekends. You can ski for a few hours on these trails or all day if you like. I have included a little information about each system to get you started. For more information stop at the Visitor Information Centres at Barrier Lake or Peter Lougheed Provincial Park. Here you can purchase excellent maps of these trail systems for a nominal fee.

14 CHESTER LAKE

Grade Intermediate/advanced
Distance 8 km return
Time 3-4 hours return
Height gain 310 m
Max elevation 2220 m
Map Spray Lakes Reservoir 82 J/14

The snow comes early to Chester Lake making this a very popular early season trail. It gets you up high into beautiful mountain terrain and provides an exciting run on the way back down.

Facilities There are toilets at the parking lot. There is an outhouse on the left just before you reach the lake.

Hazards Be careful of other skiers coming down the steep trail. Ski with caution.

Access There is a parking lot along the east side of the Smith-Dorrien/Spray Trail 40 km from Canmore or 20 km from the Kananaskis Lakes Trail junction.

The trail starts at the top left hand corner of the parking lot and follows a wide road, rising gradually, for about 100 m to a trail junction. Stay left and continue another 300 m to another trail junction. Stay left again and continue along the wide trail for about 0.5 km when it begins to climb more steeply. (It is also possible to take the right hand fork which climbs steeply. The two trails eventually join up in about 2 km). The trail swings to the right for a ways, then back to the left. It traverses right a second time then back to the left again.

Finally the wide trail swings right for a third time and climbs steeply to a trail sign. At this point you are about 2.5 km from the parking lot. (The alternate trail joins up at this point.) Beyond here the trail climbs steeply up the hill for a short distance then angles out right. The wide road ends and the trail narrows through the forest. After several hundred metres the trail curves left, levels through the forest for a ways, then climbs steeply over a hill and out into the open. Cross a meadow then ascend a trail through the forest for about 0.5 km. Eventually you break out of the trees and ski across open meadows to reach the lake which is tucked way back in the cirque below Mount Chester.

Burstall Pass with Mount Birdwood in the background. Photo Gillean Daffern

15 BURSTALL PASS

Grade Intermediate/advanced
Distance 8 km one way
Time This is a full day tour
Height gain 500 m
Max elevation 2380 m
Maps Spray Lakes Reservoir 82 J/14
Kananaskis Lakes 82 J/11

This is one of the finest ski tours in the Rockies. The snow comes early (late November) and builds up deep over the winter. There are excellent opportunities for making turns nearby.

Facilities Toilets at the parking lot.

Hazards A large avalanche path crosses the trail near Burstall Pass. Move quickly across this spot. There is avalanche potential in the area if you stray from the trail, so take all safety precautions if you go looking for turns.

Options You can extend your tour by skiing to South Burstall pass.

Access The trip begins at the Burstall Pass parking lot located on the west side of the Smith-Dorrien/Spray Trail, 40 km from Canmore or 20 km from the Kananaskis Lakes Trail junction.

From the parking lot follow the well packed trail across Mud Lake Dam and up a hill to the French Creek trail junction. Keep right and follow the main Burstall Creek trail for several kilometres until it descends to the right, through the trees, to reach the gravel flats of Burstall Creek.

Angle across the gravel flats to a point just left of West Burstall Creek, where you will find the trail again. Most folks put on their skins here. Climb steeply up through the forest for about 150 vertical metres to where the angle lays back and you ski out into open glades. Ski across meadows (don't linger in the huge avalanche path), then ascend a draw. As you rise above treeline you will see excellent ski slopes off to the right. From Burstall Pass itself (GR 146244) there is an excellent view of Mount Assiniboine to the west.

On the way back down, rather than descend the steep trail through the trees to the gravel flats, it is best to descend the drainage of West Burstall Creek. It offers a good little ski run.

16 WATRIDGE LAKE

Grade Easy
Distance 6.5 km to Watridge Lake return
Time 2-3 hours return
Height gain 50 m
Max elevation 1800 m
Map Spray Lakes Reservoir 82 J/14

This is a very pleasant tour along a wide easy trail which will likely be track set all the way. There are plenty of trail signs so it is almost impossible to get lost. Along the way you may see heavily laden skiers on their way to or from Mount Assiniboine.

Facilities Toilets at the trailhead.

Option 1 Beyond the turn off to Watridge Lake you can continue for about 1 km to the bridge over the Spray River. The trail is level at first then descends steeply for about 120 vertical metres. Be sure to zip up your jacket for the thrilling descent. Watch for descending skiers on the way back up the hill.

Option 2 You can ski about 1 km to Karst Spring where a natural underground stream flows out of the mountain.

Access Turn west off the Smith-Dorrien/ Spray Trail about 33 km from Canmore or 28 km from the Kananaskis Lakes Trail junction onto the road signed for Mount Engadine Lodge and Mount Shark. Continue past the turn off for Mount Engadine Lodge and drive for about 5 km to a large parking lot at the Mount Shark Ski Trails.

This trail is actually a wide road which cuts through the Mount Shark Ski Trail complex. It starts from the information board in the corner of the parking lot where the access road comes in, descending 50 m through the trees to the right to reach the wide snow covered road. Continue 0.5 km along the road through the forest, then descend a short hill to a creek. Ascend the other side and ski out into the open (old cut blocks). Continue for about 1 km, rolling up and down, then angle right down into the forest again. After several hundred metres the wide trail crosses a bridge over Watridge Creek and enters the open again. Ski along the trees around the left

(south) edge of the cut block for about 0.5 km. The trail then begins to climb, enters the trees again and narrows. After gaining about 50 vertical metres the trail levels off. Here you will see a trail sign for Watridge Lake which is a short distance down to your left. Descend a short, steep hill to the Lake.

Karst Spring Ski around the left (east) side of Watridge Lake then follow a trail through the forest in a southerly direction. After about 300 m the trail reaches the stream flowing from the Karst Spring. To see the actual outlet, which is very interesting, ski through the trees along the right side of the stream for about 400 m then, at the end, it is necessary to climb quite steeply, gaining about 75 vertical metres up to the stream outlet where the water rushes from the mountain. The water is warm from its journey beneath the earth and never freezes. The moss is vibrant green and stands out beautifully in its white setting.

17 RIBBON CREEK TO SKOGAN PASS

Ski touring 1

Grade Intermediate
Distance 21 km to pass return
Time This is a full day tour
Height gain 625 m
Max elevation 2075 m
Map Spray Lakes Reservoir 82 J/14

This is one of the classic ski tours in the Ribbon Creek area. It gets you up high and has great views. Unfortunately, the noise of the Nakiska Ski Resort and the jet aeroplanes

overhead, on their way to Vancouver, detract from the enjoyment somewhat.

Facilities There are toilets at the trailhead and a camp shelter.

Options It is possible to ski across the pass and descend the other side to Dead Mans Flat. In fact this trail can be skied in either direction or as a traverse.

Access Drive down Kananaskis Trail for 23 km from the junction with the Trans Canada Highway and take the turn right to Kananaskis Village and Nakiska Ski Resort. Turn first left, then keep right before you cross the bridge to reach the Ribbon Creek parking lot.

There are actually two parking lots at Ribbon Creek and the trail to Skogan Pass starts at the camp shelter between the two lots. Ascend a wide gradual trail for about 0.5 km then cross the Nakiska Road. Descend a short distance to a junction and take the left hand fork. The trail now goes along the brow of the hill for about 1 km, with great views out over the valley to the right, to a four way trail junction. Carry on straight ahead and wind your way uphill for about 1 km to an intersection with a road (snowmobile traffic). Stay right for a short distance then keep right again on a broad trail, while the snowmobile road curves up to the left. Here there is a barrier across the trail. Continue past the barrier for a short distance to another intersection. Take the right hand fork and immediately cross a creek. The trail now starts to climb again for over a kilometre, eventually reaching the powerline. Cut

back sharply left and climb steeply for a ways. The trail then levels off, crosses an open area, then curves right and climbs steeply to another intersection. Turn sharply left and climb at a moderate angle. Ignore two roads which branch off right. After about 0.5 km the road comes out of the thick trees into an area

Skogan Pass trail below first junction with Skogan Loop. Photo Gillean Daffern.

45

of low trees and climbs straight up the hillside. The road then enters the forest again and in about 100 m comes to another trail junction. From here there are two choices:

1. You can carry on straight ahead through the forest along a level trail until it reaches the power line. Turn left up the power line and climb at a moderate angle for about 0.5 km until the road angles left into the woods. In about 300 m the road crosses the power line into the woods on the right. Continue along the road through the woods on the right of the power line for about 0.5 km until it comes out at the power line again. Continue up the power line for about 100 m to a trail intersection.

2. It is also possible to turn left and ski the 3.5 km Skogan Loop. This trail winds leisurely uphill through cutblocks and offers incredible panoramas. It eventually rejoins trail #1 at the powerline. This is the end of the groomed trail.

To continue to the pass, ski at an angle into the trees on the left and carry on through the forest on a road that rolls up and down for about 1.5 km. Pass under the power line again and ascend moderately steeply through the trees for the last 0.5 km to the pass. If you are heading for Dead Mans Flat continue straight ahead through the lowest point in the pass. To get a great view angle up left, climbing steeply for about 100 m, to the powerline.

18 RIBBON CREEK SKI TRAILS   Nordic skiing 1

Grade Most trails are easy/intermediate
Distance There are 50 km of trails
Max elevation 2075 m
Map Spray Lakes Reservoir 82 J/14

This was the first ski trail system developed in the Kananaskis Valley—by Don Gardner in 1972. When there is adequate snow it provides exceptional cross country skiing. Ranging across the lower slopes of Mounts Collembola, Allan and Kidd there are plenty of outstanding

viewpoints. Most of the trails are wide and are regularly groomed and track set.

Facilities There are plenty of amenities in the vicinity of the Ribbon Creek Ski Trails, at Kananaskis Village and at the Nakiska Ski Resort. There are toilets at the Ribbon Creek trailhead.

Note Trail maps are available at information centres.

Access Drive along Kananaskis Trail for 23 km from the junction with the Trans Canada Highway and turn right for Kananaskis Village and Nakiska Ski Resort. You can park at three different lots to access these trails:
1. Keep right for Nakiska Ski Resort.

2. For Kananaskis Village turn left then cross Ribbon Creek bridge.
3. For Ribbon Creek parking lot keep left initially, then turn right before you cross Ribbon Creek bridge.

19 PETER LOUGHEED PROVINCIAL PARK TRAILS Nordic skiing 1

Grade Most trails are easy/intermediate
Distance There are 98 km of ski trails
Max elevation 2125 m
Map Kananaskis Lakes 82 J/11

This is a truly excellent system of Nordic ski trails, one of the best in Western Canada. It was designed and built in the mid to late seventies under the direction of Don Gardner. The trails are varied, often 4 m wide with two tracks and a skating track but sometimes narrow through the woods. They are well maintained and are regularly groomed. On a sunny weekend, you will find hundreds of skiers of all abilities enjoying themselves on these trails.

Note Trail maps are available at information centres.

Facilities There are ten parking lots from which you can access these ski trails: Pocaterra, Canyon, Visitor Information Centre, Elkwood, William Watson Lodge, Boulton Creek, Boulton Bridge, Lower Lake, Elk Pass and Upper Lake. Four parking lots have something to offer other than washrooms:
1. Pocaterra has a hut.
2. The Visitor Information Centre has indoor washrooms, telephones, interpretive films and displays and a deluxe lounge with fireplace and comfy chairs and couches.
3. William Watson Lodge has low cost accommodation for handicapped persons and senior citizens.
4. Boulton Creek has the Trading Post Cafe serving light meals at reasonable prices.

Access Drive down Kananaskis Trail for 50 km from the junction with the Trans Canada Highway then turn right onto the Kananaskis Lakes Trail. The ten parking lots are scattered along the left and right sides of this road over the next 13 kilometres—Pocaterra, Visitor Information Centre, Elkwood, Boulton Creek, Boulton Bridge, Elk Pass and Upper Lake will be found a short distance off the road to the left and Canyon, William Watson Lodge, and Lower Lake will be found a short distance off to the right.

Elk Pass trail in Fox Creek. Photo Gillean Daffern.

47

20 SMITH-DORRIEN SKI TRAILS

Grade Intermediate/advanced
Distance There are 29 km of ski trails
Max elevation 2110 m
Maps Spray Lakes Reservoir 82 J/14
Kananaskis Lakes 82 J/11

This network of trails offers many hours of enjoyable skiing. The trails are all old logging roads and occasionally have long leg burning downhills. The trails are rarely groomed so you may be breaking trail.

Facilities Toilets at the trailheads.

Note Trail maps are available at information centres.

Access These trails can be accessed from two parking lots. At the south end the Sawmill parking lot is located on the east side of the Smith-Dorrien/Spray Trail, 14 km from the Kananaskis Lakes Trail junction or 47 km from Canmore.

At the north end the Chester Lake parking lot is located on the east side of the Smith-Dorrien/Spray Trail 20 km from the Kananaskis Lakes Trail junction or 40 km from Canmore.

21 MOUNT SHARK SKI TRAILS
Nordic skiing 1

Grade Most trails are easy/intermediate
Distance There are 18 km of trails
Max elevation 1810 m
Map Spray Lakes Reservoir 82 J/14

Due to their high elevation these trails get lots of snow, offering great skiing from late November to May. They were designed and built in 1984 under the direction of Tony Daffern and members of the Foothills Nordic Ski Club. These trails are usually groomed and trackset. There are outstanding views all around of Tent Ridge, Mount Shark, Cone Mountain, Mount Engadine and even the tip of Mount Assiniboine.

Facilities Toilets at the parking lot.

Note Trail maps are available at information centres.

Access Turn west off the Smith-Dorrien/Spray Trail, about 33 km from Canmore or 28 km from the Kananaskis Lakes Trail junction onto the road signed for Mount Engadine Lodge and Mount Shark. Continue past the turn off for Mount Engadine Lodge and drive for about 5 km to a large parking lot at the Mount Shark Trails.

BANFF/CANMORE AREA

Banff is located in Banff National Park along the Trans-Canada Highway 130 km west of Calgary. It is a town of about 6000 permanent residents and is the major mountain resort in Canada. Canmore, a town of about 11,000 is located just outside the park, along the Trans Canada Highway, 20 km to the east of Banff. It is rapidly becoming a major tourist destination and due to the presence of the Canmore Nordic Centre is now Canada's premier centre for Nordic skiing. Canmore was host to the Nordic events at the 1988 Olympic Winter Games. Both these towns are located in the Bow River Valley which runs from Bow Pass to Calgary. There are two major highways along the valley: Highway 1 (the Trans Canada Highway), a major 4 lane freeway, and Highway 1A (also known as the Bow Valley Parkway where it runs through Banff National Park) a narrow, two lane highway intended largely for sightseeing.

Facilities You will find everything that you are likely to need on a ski trip in Banff. There are many stores and shops with all manner of goods. There are several gas stations, some of which remain open 24 hours. There are two major equipment stores: Mountain Magic (403-762-2591) and Monod Sports (403-762-4571). In the unlikely event that they cannot help you, try Mountain Equipment Co-op (403-269-2420) in Calgary. All modern amenities are also available in Canmore. There are numerous restaurants, shops and gas stations. For your equipment needs phone Altitude Sports (403-678-0832) or Valhalla Pure Outfitters (403-678-5610).

Accommodation Banff and Canmore have accommodation to suit all budgets, ranging from small bed and breakfast establishments to grand hotels like the Banff Springs Hotel. There is a large modern hostel located in Banff

(403-762-4122) and The Alpine Club of Canada runs an inexpensive and comfortable clubhouse (403-678-3200) in Canmore which is open to the public.

Information/Permits Information about snow conditions, weather and trails as well as back country permits and registration may be obtained from the Park Information Centre at 224 Banff Avenue (403-762-1550). The centre is open 10:00 am to 6:00 pm in winter.

Wardens The Banff Warden Office (403-762-1470) is located just east of town on the north side of Banff Avenue in the industrial compound.

Banff Sundance Lodge

This is the historic Ten Mile Cabin which was used by skiers in the 1930s to reach Mount Assiniboine.
Location Along Brewster Creek, 11 km SW of Banff (GR 935614).
Map Banff 82 O/4
Facilities Sundance Lodge has been completely refurbished and now has indoor plumbing, hot showers and solar electric power.
Capacity 20 in ten private rooms.
Cost About $100 per person. All meals provided.
Reservations Write: Warner Guiding and Outfitting Ltd., Box 2280, Banff, Alberta, T0L 0C0 Email: warner@horseback.com, Website: www.xcskisundance.com Phone: 1-800-661-8352 or 403-762-4551 Fax: 403-762-8130

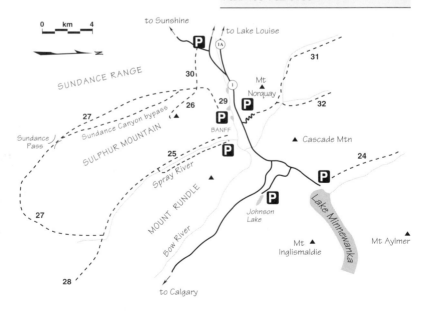

22 CANMORE NORDIC CENTRE

Grade All grades
Distance There are many kilometres of trails
Time You can spend a few hours here or all day
Height gain From minimal to 100 m
Max elevation 1500 m
Maps Canmore 82 O/3

The Canmore Nordic Centre is a world class system of Nordic ski trails. It was created for the XV Winter Olympics in 1988. There are recreational trails and trails of the most advanced difficulty. All trails are groomed and track set.

Facilities There is a day lodge with washrooms, lockers, showers, food and beverage service, waxing rooms and meeting rooms. A full service ski shop is located on site providing rentals, lessons and equipment.

Information At the day lodge you can acquire a map of all the trails and information on what is currently in the best condition.

Note There is a daily fee for use of the Canmore Nordic Centre.

Access The Canmore Nordic Centre is located on a bench above the northwest end of the town of Canmore, under Mount Rundle. From the centre of Canmore drive west along 8th Avenue, cross the bridge over the Bow River, then continue for a few blocks along Rundle Drive. Turn left onto Three Sisters Drive, ascend the hill, then take the right hand exit onto Spray Lakes Road. The Nordic Centre is on the right about 1 km along this road (large signs).

Competitive skiing at Canmore Nordic Centre. Photo Gillean Daffern.

23 DEAD MANS FLAT TO SKOGAN PASS

Ski touring 1

Grade Intermediate
Distance 9.5 km one way
Time This is a full day ski tour.
Height gain 670 m
Max elevation 2070 m
Maps Canmore 82 O/3
Spray Lakes Reservoir 82 J/14

An excellent trail with a great view at the top. It is uphill all the way to the pass but there is a great run down at the end of the day.

Hazards In low snow years there may not be adequate snow for this tour.

Options You can traverse the pass in either direction, between Dead Mans Flat and Kananaskis Village (see page 45). It will be necessary to leave a second car at one end.

Access Turn off the Trans Canada Highway at Dead Mans Flat and drive south up the hill for about 1 km towards the Alpine Haven Resort. Just before the resort turn right into a parking lot.

The trail starts at the far end of the parking lot. Ski down a road thorough the trees for several hundred metres to the powerline. Turn left and start up the hill following the powerline. After about 200 m angle left into the trees along a road. Do not attempt to ski directly up the powerline as the way ahead is blocked by a deep canyon. After about 1.5 km the road comes out of the trees onto the powerline again. Follow the powerline for about 1.5 km then angle briefly to the left into the trees again. After about 200 m the road comes out onto the powerline again. Continue along the powerline—almost immediately it drops steeply into a dip then it climbs steadily up the hill. After about 2 km, just before the powerline levels off, turn up sharply to the left on a road into the trees.

The road makes three switchbacks up the hill then makes a long rising traverse right, eventually breaking out of the trees into meadows at treeline. There is a great view of the four peaks of Mount Lougheed to the southwest at this point. Continue across meadows and open trees gradually gaining elevation until the trail enters the trees again. The angle now lays back and the trail continues for a ways through the trees. The trail then curves right and begins climbing at a moderate angle, then it lays back again for a ways. Finally it curves to the left and climbs at a moderate angle up to the pass (about 0.5 km before reaching the pass a road cuts to the right—do not take it, but continue straight ahead).

The road crosses the low point in the pass. If you are traversing over to Kananaskis Village you just continue straight ahead down the road. For an excellent viewpoint turn sharply to the right and climb a short, steep hill up to the powerline. Here you will have a great view back down to Dead Mans Flat.

The author getting an early start on the season along the Cascade Fire Road.

24 CASCADE FIRE ROAD

Nordic skiing 1

Grade Easy
Distance The road is normally track set for 13 km to Stony Creek
Time A few hours or all day
Height gain 180 m
Max elevation 1480 m
Maps Banff 82 O/4
Castle Mountain 82 O/5

This is one of the most popular trails in the Rocky Mountains. The snow is usually good and this is one of the first trails to be trackset. Highly recommended!

Access Drive east from the town of Banff for several kilometres, pass under the Trans Canada Highway, and continue up the Lake Minnewanka Road. This road is soon blocked off (to protect wolf habitat) and you must run right at the Johnson Lake turn-off. Continue along this road for about 10 km to the large parking lot at Lake Minnewanka.

The trail begins a few metres back along the road. Go under or around the road barrier and ski along the snow covered road (the old Lake Minnewanka Road) for a short distance to reach the start of the Cascade Fire Road which cuts off to the right. From here you can ski along the fire road for as far as you like. The road climbs a bit but only enough to give you a little cool air in your hair on the way down.

25 SPRAY RIVER TRAIL

Nordic skiing 1

Grade Easy
Distance 10 km return
Time 3-4 hours return
Height gain 200 m
Max elevation 1390 m
Map Banff 82 O/4

This is one of the most popular ski tours in Banff Park. The trail is always well groomed and, because it is along an old fire road, it requires little snow. It makes a pleasant outing for all levels of ability.

Facilities At the end of the trail, where it crosses the Spray River, there are picnic tables.

Options The Spray River Trail serves as an integral part of two other trails: the Goat Creek Trail and the Sundance Pass/Spray River Trail.

Access Drive up Spray Avenue to the Banff Springs Hotel. Go past the statue of the gentleman pointing very seriously (Cornelius Van Horne) then carry on underneath the CPR version of the Arc de Triomphe. Continue past the parkade to a small parking lot.

The trail sets off from the end of the parking lot along a wide road usually with a trackset trail. There are lovely views of Mount Rundle and the Spray River Valley along the way and a few hills, but they are all quite manageable even for the novice. After about 5 km the trail reaches some picnic tables and this is an excellent spot to stop for lunch and a cup of tea.

From here you can return to your car the way you came or cross the river and make your way back along a trail on the far side. This trail is narrower and likely not track set. It gains some elevation then skis along a bench with views out to the left of Sulphur Mountain. Eventually it descends a moderately steep hill to the Banff Springs Golf Course. To find your way back to your car follow a trail back along the Spray River, cross a bridge to the west bank then climb a steep little hill to join the Spray River Fire Road. Turn right and continue about 0.5 km to the parking lot and your car.

Along the Spray River trail.

26 SULPHUR MOUNTAIN ROAD

Ski touring 1

Grade Intermediate
Distance 5 km one way
Time 3 hours up, 30 minutes down
Height gain 850 m
Max elevation 2290 m
Map Banff 82 O/4

This is hardly a Nordic tour but is included because some folks still ski this trail. There is an excellent view from the top and, in good conditions, the run down is lots of fun.

Hazards In icy conditions the ski down can be very fast and in cold weather the wind chill on the long descent may

Access Park at the Cave and Basin lot at the end of Cave Avenue. Walk around the Cave and Basin and follow Sundance Road for 2 km to where the Sulphur Mountain Road joins it from the left.

The tour simply follows the road all the way to the top. Put on good grip wax or skins and start climbing. Take a long rest at the top then bundle up well for the chilling descent.

27 SUNDANCE PASS

Ski touring 1

Grade Advanced
Distance 28 km loop
Time A very full day
Height gain 350 m
Max elevation 1740 m
Map Banff 82 O/4

Pass down to the Spray River is tricky and the skiing is not easy. There should be at least 60-70 cm of snow to make this trip enjoyable, so wait until later in the season. Due to the north/south orientation of the valley it gets lots of sun during the day.

This is a long and challenging tour which is not often skied, so you might be breaking trail. Although it starts at the outskirts of Banff townsite it is not long before you feel as though you are really in the wilderness. The routefinding from Sundance

Facilities There are camp shelters and picnic tables at Sundance Canyon, near the start of the tour, and there are picnic tables along the Spray River.

Access Park at the Cave and Basin parking lot at the end of Cave Avenue. A second car should be left at the Spray River Trail parking lot (near the Banff Springs Hotel, see page 54). Otherwise it is a long walk back to the Cave and Basin at the end of the day.

From the parking lot walk around the Cave and Basin to the start of Sundance

Road. Put on your skis here and ski along the road. The skiing is easy and the views across the Bow Valley are excellent. There are two options for negotiating the canyon itself. You can ski up Sundance Road then follow the summer trail directly up Sundance Canyon. This trail starts by crossing a foot bridge to the left bank of the creek, then climbs without difficulty for a short distance.

Descending the Sulphur Mountain Fire Road can be exciting. Photo Alf Skrastins.

The terrain steepens and it is necessary to take your skis off. For the next 50 vertical metres you climb some steps with a railing, cross a little bridge, then climb steeply above to reach easier ground. Beyond here you put on your skis again and follow the creek and the trail. Just beyond the end of the right-hand cliffs, you cross to the right side of the creek. The trail climbs a short distance through the trees before it begins to turn right, back towards Banff. At this point leave the trail to the left and carry on straight up the valley. The way through the woods is quite open. Carry on trending slightly left until you reach the creek again. Follow the creek for 4 or 5 km until near the area of the pass. Following the creek is occasionally difficult and it is necessary to travel through the woods on the right or left bank for a distance, until it is possible to return to the creek again. When you are near the pass there is a large meadow off to your right which is a scenic place to sit in the sun and have lunch. Above you is the summit of Sulphur Mountain and to the west is the Sundance Range.

Alternatively you can follow the canyon bypass trail which avoids Sundance Canyon completely. It starts on the left side of Sundance Road between the Old Healy Creek Road and Sundance Canyon itself.

The bypass trail is an excellent alternative. After a steep start it climbs gradually through the forest and is clear to follow. It soon levels out and runs back into the valley for several kilometres. Eventually it becomes more difficult to follow the trail as the forest opens. If you lose the trail traverse out to the right to the creek bed and continue along the valley bottom to the meadow near the pass.

Not far beyond this meadow, the creek peters out and it is necessary to ski through the forest. There is a great deal of deadfall here and it is absolutely imperative to work your way to the left (east) side of the valley bottom, until you locate the trail which runs through the woods. This is the only reasonable way through the forest so take a little time to search for it. Follow the trail for 2-3 km.

Eventually the trail breaks out into a series of long, thin clearings. Follow the clearings, trending downhill and staying on the left side. At the end of the clearings it is necessary to find the trail again. A creek also appears at this point and for the next kilometre the trail is never far from the creek. The trail initially starts on the left bank of the creek then quickly it crosses to the right bank. It climbs high on a ridge then drops steeply down and swings back left again into the creek. The trail cross the creek one more time to the left bank and climbs very steeply up a hill. From the top of this hill the rest of the descent becomes more reasonable. The trail now stays in the forest and does not return to the creek. The descent begins steeply but soon becomes more moderate. It is a fun glide down the trail to the Spray River Road.

Turn left and ski along the Spray River Road. It is 2.2 km to the junction with the Goat Creek tour (Canmore to Banff, see page 58) and then an additional 9.5 km to the Spray River Trail parking lot (see page 54).

28 CANMORE TO BANFF VIA GOAT CREEK

Ski touring 1

Grade Intermediate
Distance 18 km one way
Time 4-5 hours one way
Height loss 270 m
Max elevation 1640 m
Maps Canmore 82 O/3
Banff 82 O/4

This trail is usually skied one way from Canmore to Banff as a downhill run. Leave a second car at the Spray River

Access There is a large parking lot at the Goat Creek trailhead which is located on the right (west) side of the Smith-Dorrien /Spray Trail about 8 km from Canmore. To reach it drive through the town of Canmore and follow the signs for the Nordic Centre (see page 51). Do not turn into the Nordic Centre but continue up the steep hill to the pass. Follow the road around a little lake and down a short hill. The parking lot is on your right.

Leave a second car at the Spray River Trail parking lot (see page 54).

From the Goat Creek trailhead ski down a few metres to the creek and cross a small bridge. The trail then angles up onto the right bank and contours around the hillside for about 1.5 km, entering Banff National Park. From here the trail gradually descends towards Banff for another 5 km, until it cross Goat Creek. The trail is wide and the skiing is easy. The last part of this section of the trip is a short, moderately steep descent to Goat Creek.

Trail parking lot in Banff, then drive back to Canmore.

Facilities There are washrooms at the parking lot at the trailhead at the Canmore end and picnic tables at the bridge across the Spray River, 5 km from Banff.

Hazards The descents to Goat Creek and later to the Spray River can be tricky if icy.

Cross the creek on a footbridge and climb the hill on the other side. The trail then ascends for about 50 vertical metres, contours around the hillside and in about 1 km descends to the Spray River. Cross the Spray River on a small bridge and ski a short distance to join the Spray River Road. Turn right on the road and ski up the hill. From the top of this hill you get a long and gentle downhill for several kilometres to the Spray River picnic site. Continue along the Spray River Road to your car at the parking lot near the Banff Springs Hotel.

29 CAVE AND BASIN TRAILS

Grade Easy
Distance 6 km of trails
Time These trails make a pleasant half day outing.
Height gain Nil
Max elevation 1470 m
Map Banff 82 O/4

These trail are readily accessible, offer some pleasant skiing and do not require a lot of snow to be skiable. The views across the Bow Valley towards Mount Norquay and Mount Edith and west towards Mount Borgeau and Mount Brett are excellent.

Facilities At Sundance Canyon there is a camp shelter and picnic tables where it is possible to have lunch and a warm fire (bring an axe).

Options The trails link up with the Sundance Pass tour, Sulphur Mountain Road and the Old Healy Creek Road.

Access Parking is available at the Cave and Basin at the end of Cave Avenue or at the recreation grounds near Martin Stables (turn right about halfway along Cave Avenue).

There are two trails in this network and you can be creative in how you ski them.

Trail #1 begins at the recreation grounds and over 4.6 km of easy skiing works its way to Sundance Canyon (one way). The trail starts by skiing back for a short distance on the right side of the entrance road to reach the trail beside Cave Avenue. It continues through the trees along the right side of Cave Avenue, beneath the Cave and Basin parking lot, then through a fascinating area of gurgling hotsprings and singing birds! The trail then meets Sundance Road which it follows to Sundance Canyon. Along here the views are great but for much of the way the road can be windblown and bare of snow. About 1 km before reaching Sundance Canyon you will see, on the right, the start of the Old Healy Creek Road.

Trail #2 is really a branch which swings off trail #1 at the Cave and Basin parking lot and heads north along an old dike to reach the Bow River. It continues pleasantly along the edge of the river for another kilometre until it reaches the Sundance Road. This trail can be skied as a loop of 2.7 km (incorporating a portion of trail #1) from the Cave and Basin Parking lot. It can also be incorporated into a ski along trail #1 to Sundance Canyon, either on the way there or the way back.

Of Historical Interest The Cave and Basin Hot Springs have long been known to the native people. In 1883 three railway workers William and Tom McCardell and Frank McCabe explored the springs and built a shack on the site, hoping to exploit the commercial possibilities. The Canadian Government however, declared a ten square mile area around the springs as Canada's first national park in 1885. Two years later the park was enlarged to 260 square miles and named Rocky Mountain Park. From these beginnings has grown world famous Banff National Park.

Banff/Canmore Area

30 OLD HEALY CREEK ROAD/SUNDANCE LODGE   Ski touring 1

Grade Trail #1 along Old Healy Creek
Road is easy and trail #8 to Banff Sun-
dance Lodge is intermediate
Distance Old Healy Creek Road is 4.8
km one way. Trail #8 to Banff Sundance
Lodge is 12 km one way
Time You can ski for a few hours or all
day if you wish. The tour to Sundance
Lodge will take about 3-4 hours one way
Height gain Minimal on the Old Healy
Creek Road and 150 m up to Banff
Sundance Lodge
Max elevation 1580 m
Map Banff 82 O/4

These two trails offer very pleasant skiing
and the Old Healy Creek Road may even
be track set. The trail to Banff Sundance
Lodge will likely be well packed by the
snowmobiles taking supplies to the lodge.

Access These trails can be reached in two
different ways. You can park at the Cave
and Basin (see page 59) and follow trail
#1 along the Sundance Canyon Road to its
junction with the Old Healy Creek Road.
There is also a parking lot 0.8 km along
the Sunshine Village Road. To reach the
latter drive west of Banff for 9 km along
the Trans Canada Highway and take the
turn-off to Sunshine Village Ski Resort.
The parking lot will be 0.8 km along this
road on your left.

The Old Healy Creek Road can be skied one
way if you leave a car at each end or return.
It is a broad road and is often trackset. It
crosses Healy Creek on a bridge not far
from the Sunshine Village Road.

Trail #8 to Banff Sundance Lodge is also
a wide road and the trail will likely be
well packed. It cuts off the Old Healy
Creek Road 1.8 km from the parking lot
at the Sunshine Village Road. You might
consider staying overnight and enjoying
the stars and smell of wood smoke.

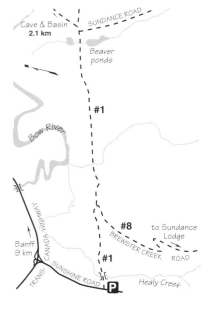

60

31 FORTY MILE CREEK

Grade Intermediate
Distance 10 km return to Edith Pass fork, 34 km return to Mystic Warden Cabin
Time 4-5 hours return to the Edith Pass fork. All day to the Mystic Warden Cabin and back
Height loss 120 m to Forty Mile Creek
Height gain 120 m to Edith Pass fork 270 m to Mystic Warden Cabin
Max elevation 1830 m
Maps Banff 82 O/4
Castle Mountain 82 O/5

This is a very interesting and pleasant ski tour. You can ski a short distance along the creek or take the day to ski as far as the Mystic Warden Cabin. Leave yourself plenty of time for the return trip—it is a long way.

Facilities Food, toilets and telephones at the Mount Norquay Ski Resort. Outhouse at the Mystic Warden Cabin.

Options Beyond the Mystic Warden Cabin you can ski another 3 km to Mystic lake. You can also carry on over Mystic Pass (see page 63) and down Johnston Creek to the Bow Valley Parkway.

Access Drive up the road to the Mount Norquay Ski Resort from the Trans Canada Highway. Park in the large parking lot on the right.

From the parking lot ski past the big day lodge, then down and across the ski slopes passing below the lower terminals of the Cascade Chair, the Spirit Chair and the Pathfinder Express Chair. The trail starts just beyond and a few metres below the terminal of the Pathfinder Express Chair.

Very soon a steep trail branches down to the right. Do not take this trail. Instead take the left hand branch which climbs uphill for a ways. Then the trail descends gradually down the hill for about 2 km to Forty Mile Creek, losing about 120 m in elevation. It is generally wide and has no sharp corners.

Turn left and ski along the left side of the creek on a narrow trail that works its way up and down through the trees for about 1.5 km until it reaches a bridge across the creek. Although the views are good here, this is not the place to stop for lunch, as you are below a giant avalanche path. Cross the bridge and continue up the right side of the creek for another 1.5 km until you reach the Edith Pass Trail fork. The very impressive mountain that you have been admiring along the trail is Mount Louis, one of the great climbs in the area.

Follow the right branch which continues up Forty Mile Creek. For the next 12 km the trail stays on the right side of the creek and climbs very gradually as it works its way up the valley. It is generally easy to follow. Sometimes it is a few metres above the valley bottom and sometimes it drops down near the creek. The trail crosses some small creeks which can be a nuisance early in the season. It also crosses some large slide paths—do not linger here. Toward the end the trail descends to the left for a short distance to a fork. Follow the branch to the left which descends to the creek. Cross the bridge to the Mystic Warden Cabin on the far side. The cabin steps are a great place to sit and have lunch.

Return the same way to your car at the Mount Norquay Ski Resort.

32 ELK LAKE SUMMIT

Grade Intermediate/advanced
Distance 20 km return
Time A full day tour
Height loss 120 m to Forty Mile Creek
Height gain 500 m from Forty Mile
Creek to Elk Lake Summit
Max elevation 2060 m
Maps Banff 82 O/4
Castle Mountain 82 O/5

A challenging trail, particularly on the
return trip. It does however, offer an entertaining ski tour without having to drive
too far from Banff.

Options It is possible to carry on beyond
Elk Lake Summit to the Cascade Fire
Road. This trail is rarely skied and there
is not much of a trail to follow. It is a long
trip so get an early start. The route basi-
cally follows the creek bed north for 5 km
beyond the summit then turns east and
follows a gap in the mountains down to the
Cascade River. It may be a problem getting across the river to reach the fire road.
Ski south along the fire road for 13 km to
Lake Minnewanka (see the Cascade Fire
Road, page 53).

It is also possible to visit Elk Lake. The
best bet is to continue through the pass,
down to the drainage which flows from
Elk Lake, then climb up the drainage to
the lake.

Access This tour begins at the Mount
Norquay Ski Resort and follows the
Forty Mile Creek trail to the point where
it meets the creek (see page 61).

After you descend the trail from the
Mount Norquay Ski Resort and reach
Forty Mile Creek, cross the creek on
a footbridge in an easterly direction
towards Cascade Mountain. Follow the
trail on the other side then begin climbing in steep switchbacks for several
hundred metres until you reach a junction. Follow the branch which heads
left, up the valley. The trail now climbs
at a much more moderate angle and is
quite enjoyable. It continues for 6 km
without difficulty along the hillside to
Elk Lake Summit.

*The Mount Norquay Ski Resort began as a hum-
ble log cabin. It was built in the autumn of 1928
and officially opened during the Banff Winter
Carnival, February 3, 1929. It was destroyed by
fire in January 1938. Courtesy Whyte Museum of
the Canadian Rockies.*

33 MYSTIC PASS

Grade Advanced
Distance 13 km from Forty Mile Creek over the pass to Johnston Creek. The circuit from the Mount Norquay Ski Resort to the Bow Valley Parkway, near Johnston Canyon, is 37 km.
Time Most parties will require 2 days to ski the entire circuit
Height gain 430 m from Forty Mile Creek to Mystic Pass
Height loss 730 m from Mystic Pass to Johnston Creek
Max elevation 2250 m
Map Castle Mountain 82 O/5

This tour begins at the Mystic Warden Cabin and connects Forty Mile Creek with Johnston Creek. It is a long adventure and it is likely that you will be breaking trail most of the way. Only very strong skiers will do this tour in one day. If visibility is poor it will be tricky to find your way over the pass so be sure to bring your map and compass.

Hazards Much of this tour is threatened by avalanche slopes. It is recommended that you undertake this adventure only when the hazard is low.

Access This tour starts at the Mystic Warden Cabin (see the Forty Mile Creek trail, page 61)

The trail begins on the north side of the cabin. After a short, flat section through the woods, the trail climbs steeply for about 75 vertical m then levels off and heads left into the valley. It runs along horizontally for several kilometres, crossing some large avalanche slopes. Eventually at a huge avalanche slope you angle down left to the creek where you will find a camping area and some picnic tables. It is also possible to ski along the creek for much of this section and avoid the avalanche hazard.

From here the way to the pass is tricky. It is possible to follow the trail most of the way, if you have sharp eyes. The trail begins straight up the hill above the campsite. It is also possible to work your way up the drainage coming down from the pass. Either way it is not easy and requires good route finding skills.

From Mystic Pass descend a groove which soon steepens into a creek drainage. The slope continues to steepen and

it is best to traverse left and descend open timber to the valley below. Once you are in the valley, work your way along as best you can, following the creek at times, or through the open woods and even skirting the forest on the right or left flank.

After 1.5 km the valley bottom opens up beneath a large rock tower high on your right. After another kilometre the trees begin again but the way is easy down the creek or through open timber on either side of the creek. At the point where a large avalanche path descends from the left (south) side of the valley, the summer trail climbs up on the right bank of the creek and traverses along about 60 m above the creek. It is possible to follow the trail or else carry on down the creek bed. The last kilometre of descent down the creek is easy, either along the creek itself or following the trail along the right bank. Continue past the junction with the Johnston Creek trail and follow the creek for several hundred metres down to Johnston Creek. Turn left and continue toward the Ink Pots (see Johnston Creek trail, page 87).

BANFF TO CASTLE JUNCTION

The section of the Bow Valley between Banff and Castle Junction offers some excellent ski touring. Trailheads are located along the two parallel highways which run along the valley, the Trans Canada Highway and the Bow Valley Parkway (Highway 1A) and along the Kootenay Highway (Highway 93). The Sunshine Village Ski Resort is also a major trail head. The turn-off for Sunshine Village is along the Trans Canada Highway 9 km west of Banff.

Bow Valley Parkway

This is the 'Old Highway' along the Bow Valley and is perfect for sightseeing. The road is narrow and curvy and a 60 km/hr. speed limit is in effect. It is well maintained but during storms it is advisable to drive the Trans Canada Highway as it will be plowed and sanded more promptly. The only facilities along this road in winter are at Castle Junction and Baker Creek. To protect wildlife the road is closed between the hours of 6 pm and 9:00 am, from March 1 to June 25.

Facilities

The Castle Mountain Hostel is located at Castle Junction. Just across the road are the Castle Mountain Chalets (403-762-3868) which offer more upscale accommodation, a gas station and a small general store. Ski trails start right at the front door. Farther west along the road are the Baker Creek Chalets (403-522-3761) which offer cosy cabins, a fine restaurant and lounge and ski trails just across the highway.

Egypt Lake Shelter. Photo Art Longair.

Backcountry Accommodation

There are two possibilities for backcountry accommodation in this area: the Egypt Lake Shelter which is primitive with no equipment apart from a heating stove, woodpile and axe, and Shadow Lake Lodge which offers fine food and deluxe accommodation in 12 heated cabins.

Egypt Lake Shelter

A rustic cabin in a delightful setting at the base of the Pharaoh Peaks, near Egypt Lake.

Location In a meadow just above the right bank (true left) of Pharaoh Creek, 0.5 km NE of Egypt Lake (GR 772621).

Map Banff 82 O/4

Facilities Wood heating stove, axe and woodpile. No cooking stove, pots or eating utensils. Bare wooden bunks with no foamies.

Capacity 18

Water Snowmelt/Pharaoh Creek

Reservations Banff National Park Information Centre 403-762-1550

Skiing across the meadows toward the twin peaks of Quartz Hill. The nearest peak (on the right) is the one you can ski up. Photo Clive Cordery.

Sunshine Village Ski Resort

The meadows near Sunshine Village Ski Resort provide a wonderful opportunity for ski touring. They are large, stretching 10 km out to Citadel Pass and on a sunny day it is paradise up here. The terrain is open and rolling, perfect for ski touring. However, when the clouds roll in and visibility becomes poor, navigation is difficult. So save this area for that beautiful spring day when you can sit in the sunshine and marvel at the tower of Mount Assiniboine in the distance.

Access

Access to the meadows is now difficult. It is no longer possible to purchase a one ride ticket for the gondola to the Ski Resort. The only alternatives are to either ski up the ski out or purchase a full day ski ticket for about $60.

To reach the Sunshine Village Resort turn off the Trans Canada Highway about 9 km west of Banff and drive up the Sunshine Village access road to the Borgeau Parking Lot. If you chose to ski up the 'Ski Out' the trail begins just in front of the gondola terminal building. The climb takes 2-3 hours and gains 480 vertical metres over 4 km. If you can afford it you can always purchase a lift ticket and take the gondola up the hill. Then you can combine a ski tour with a few runs on the lifts.

History

The Sunshine area had become popular as a summer destination long before its merits as a ski centre were discovered. One of the earliest visitors to the Sunshine Meadows was the legendary Bill Peyto who led

his guests to Mount Assiniboine via this route. Among these was James Outram who made the first ascent of Mount Assiniboine in 1901. A.O. Wheeler (of Alpine club of Canada fame) and the Brewsters also used this route to conduct their guest into the Mount Assiniboine area. In 1928 the Canadian Pacific Railway built a cabin at Sunshine for the Trail Riders of the Canadian Rockies.

Cliff White and Cyril Paris were amongst the first to show an interest in the area as a winter destination. They skied through Sunshine in 1929 on they way to Assiniboine via Citadel Pass. They were looking for a location for a ski lodge and the next year struck upon Skoki. In 1933 Jim and Pat Brewster, Jim's wife Dell, Austin Standish and several others skied to Sunshine from the Bow Valley via Egypt Lake. They were impressed with the area, particularly the depth of snow, and the following winter they leased the cabin from the CPR and Sunshine Village hosted its first paying guests. In 1936 Brewster Transport bought the cabin for $300.

In the early days skiing at Sunshine Village was ski touring. Waxes, climbing skins and hard work were used to get up the hill. In 1942 the first rope tow was built at Sunshine Village and since then the area has undergone continuous development—the Strawberry Platterpull in 1957, the WaWa T-Bar in 1961 and the Standish Chairlift in 1965. Nowadays the beauty that once attracted the ski adventurer must be found by skiing well beyond the resort, out into the silence and peace of the meadows.

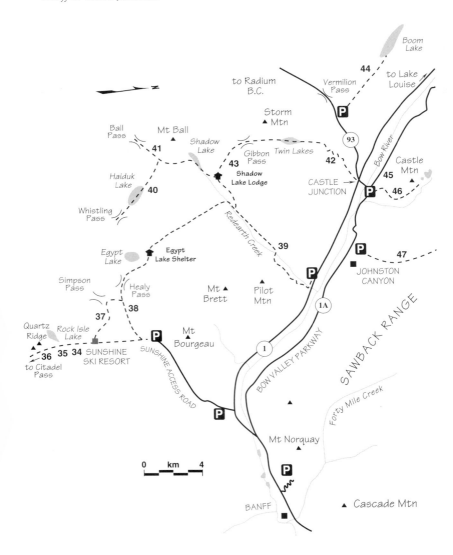

Looking out over Rock Isle Lake toward Quartz Hill with Mount Assiniboine in the distance.

Photo Gillean Daffern.

---

34 ROCK ISLE LAKE

Ski touring 1, 2

Grade Easy
Distance 4 km return
Time 2 hours return
Height gain 110 m
Max elevation 2290 m
Map Banff 82 O/4

The tour to Rock Isle Lake is a perfect introduction to the joys of ski touring. It is hard not to notice the change; leaving the hectic pace of the ski resort behind and skiing out into the solitude and peace. Many have discovered themselves and the mountains on the Sunshine Meadows.

Facilities There are washrooms, telephones and restaurants both at the lower terminal of the gondola and at the resort.

Hazards The meadows are not recommended when visibility is poor, unless you are expert at map and compass navigation. The hillside just to the south of Rock Isle Lake offers good skiing but the slopes present avalanche potential. Ski with caution.

Options From Rock Isle Lake you can carry on to Quartz Hill (see page 70) or Citadel Pass (see page 71).

Access See the introduction page 66 for access to Sunshine Village Ski Resort.

The trail to Rock Isle Lake begins at the bottom of the Strawberry Chairlift. Ski up the run to the left of the lift (Rock Isle Road), then continue through the broad pass out into the meadows. There is a good view from here of Mount Assiniboine straight ahead. There will often be a snowmobile track along here. The lake is about 0.5 km ahead and down slightly to the right. From the lake you can carry on farther or simply spend the day exploring where you chose.

35 QUARTZ HILL

Grade Intermediate
Distance 10 km return
Time 5 hours return
Height gain 350 m
Max elevation 2530 m
Map Banff 82 O/4

A tour up Quartz Hill is special indeed. The trail takes you high above the meadows and the view is outstanding. Clear visibility is required to do this tour safely. The tour described takes you up the lower peak only. The higher peak is more challenging.

Facilities There are washrooms, restaurants and telephones at the bottom terminal of the gondola lift. All of these facilities are also available at Sunshine Village Ski Resort.

Hazards Be sure to follow a safe line throughout this trip as there are little slopes and rolls along the way which can be deceptive and which offer avalanche potential.

Options This trip can be combined with a tour to Citadel Pass (see page 71).

Access See introduction page 66 for access to the Sunshine Village Ski Resort.

The first section of the trail to Quartz Hill is identical to the tour to Rock Isle Lake (see page 69). When the trail turns down

to the right to Rock Isle Lake, carry on straight south towards the twin summits of Quartz Hill which can be seen clearly on the horizon. From this point you can reach Quartz Hill by two routes.

You can ascend the small hill on the right, above Rock Isle lake, then

Skiing over sastrugi near the summit of Quartz Hill. Photo Gillean Daffern.

continue along the crest of the ridge, rounding problem areas on the left, over to the base of Quartz Hill.

Alternatively, you can follow a groove on the left side of this ridge crest until near Quartz Hill, then turn up to the right to gain the start of the mountain. Either way you end up at the base of the broad open slope on the north side of Quartz Hill. Work your way up easily for about 200 vertical metres to the top of the hill. Skis can be worn right to the top.

To return to Sunshine Village Ski Resort you can head back down the same trail or, if you feel adventurous, you can descend carefully down the other side of the peak to the notch between the two summits of Quartz

Hill. It may be easiest to take your skis off and walk the short distance down to the notch. The climb to the higher summit of Quartz Hill is steep, step kicking is required and there are large drops down the west face. This climb is ski mountaineering and is recommended only for those with some climbing experience. However, the descent from the notch down the northeast side of Quartz Hill is fun and not too steep. Stay right to avoid steeper slopes lower down. From the bottom of this descent you can work your way back north across the meadows to rejoin your trail from earlier in the day. This necessitates a short climb through a notch where you may have to herringbone or wax up.

36 CITADEL PASS
Ski touring 2

Grade Easy/intermediate
Distance 20 km return
Time This is a full day tour
Height gain 430 m
Max elevation 2390 m
Map Banff 82 O/4

This is a perennial favourite amongst local skiers. On a sunny day the tour across the

meadows to Citadel Pass with the summit of Mount Assiniboine on the horizon is highly recommended.

Options It is possible to carry on to Mount Assiniboine (see page 31).

Hazards If visibility is poor, route finding can be very difficult.

Access Begin at Sunshine Village Ski Resort

Ski up the run to the left of the Strawberry Chairlift (Rock Isle Road). At the top the angle lays back and you ski through a broad, gentle pass. Far to the south Mount Assiniboine can be seen on the skyline. Beyond the pass the tour heads out due south across the meadows. The route that most skiers follow stays on the right side of the meadow. It passes under

the lower quartz Hill and then climbs for about 100 vertical metres to cross a ridge that runs out from the higher Quartz Hill. This is the high point on the tour. Descend the other side of the ridge for about 2 km, losing about 150 m and passing Sundown Lake. The trail then levels out, crosses a drainage and begins to climb again, gaining about 120 m over the next 1.5 km to Citadel Pass.

Pioneer Banff skier Norm Knight rests in the Sunshine Meadows in the 1930s.
Courtesy Whyte Museum of the Canadian Rockies.

TELEMARK AREAS

Ski touring 2

The slopes around the Sunshine Meadows offer some short but very pleasant skiing. Here are two of the best spots to ski.

Twin Cairns

The peak just west of the top of the Standish Chairlift is Twin Cairns. It is an entertaining ski ascent and on the way back down you can make a few turns. It is not possible to ski right to the top; you must scramble up the rocks the last few metres along the ridge.

Quartz Hill

The northeast slopes of Quartz Hill offer excellent skiing. In some places the slopes are gentle and in others the angle is quite steep. The whole slope is open and you must ski with caution. At the highest point the run would be about 200 vertical m.

Opposite: Approaching Healy Pass.

72

Access Take the turn-off about 9 km west of Banff on the Trans Canada Highway for the Sunshine Village Ski Resort. Drive another 9 km to the Borgeau Parking Lot and park with the crowds of downhill skiers. Walk beyond the terminal of the gondola lift to the trailhead which is the bottom of the old ski-out trail (most everyone uses the new ski-out trail now).

If you intend to ski to Healy Pass or Egypt Lake and return the same way to your car, then you will need only one car. However, many people make a two day trip of this, staying overnight at the Egypt Lake Shelter, then skiing down Pharaoh and Redearth Creeks on the second day to the Trans Canada Highway. In this case you will need to leave a second car at the Redearth Creek parking lot (on the southwest side of the highway, 20 km west of Banff).

Begin by skiing up the old ski-out above the Borgeau Parking Lot. Be sure you have good grip wax on your skis because it is pretty much uphill all the way to the pass. Some people even like to use climbing skins to make it a little easier. The trail climbs up the broad ski-out for about 0.5 km, then turns off on a smaller trail to the right. Along this section of trail you can admire the frozen waterfall on the cliff on the right side of the valley. It is called Borgeau Left Hand and is a well known and popular ice climb.

The trail descends for a short distance then crosses a creek. It now climbs steadily for several kilometres until it reaches Healy Creek. This section of the trail is narrow, fast and tricky to negotiate on the way down.

Cross the creek and continue along the north bank through the woods, gradually gaining height. The trail crosses several large avalanche paths where it is not advisable to stop. After about 4 km there is a camping area on the left with some picnic tables and an outhouse. A short distance farther along the trail branches; the left fork heads up to Simpson Pass and the right fork heads up to Healy Pass. Beyond this point the trail climbs steeply again and after some distance climbs almost straight up the hill. Just as the trail reaches tree line it begins to level off, making a traverse to the left out into the open where the drainage comes down from the pass.

If it is a cold, blustery day this is your last point for shelter so it is a good place to have a drink and a bite to eat before heading up to the pass. Once into the drainage you can follow it straight west to the pass. On a sunny day this section in the meadows, high above the valley, is very beautiful. Looking back you can see the striking tower of Mount Assiniboine on the horizon.

If you are returning to the Borgeau Parking Lot the ski down is steep and tricky. It is an advanced trail. Stay in control and ski safely.

If you are going on to Egypt Lake it is best to head directly down the meadows ahead of you and through the trees until you gain the valley. It is likely you will reach Pharaoh Creek upstream from the shelter. Turn right and ski down the creek for a short distance until the creek opens up dramatically into a broad meadow. There is a very obvious bridge across the creek, sticking up out of the snow in the meadow. The shelter is on a bench on the left (west) bank, in the direction of the Pharaoh Peaks, about 20 m above the creek.

Skiing the Redearth Creek Fire Road. Photo Alan Kane.

39 REDEARTH CREEK

Nordic skiing/ski touring 1 & 2

Grade The trail along the fire road, as far as the turn off to Shadow Lake, is easy. The short section up to Shadow Lake is very steep and is difficult to descend. The section up Pharaoh Creek from the warden cabin to Egypt Lake is intermediate, but is fast and tricky on the way back down.

Distance 11 km to the turn-off to Shadow Lake, 2.5 km from the turn-off to Shadow Lake and 9 km from the turn-off to the Egypt Lake Shelter.

Time For most people it is a full day to get to the Egypt Lake Shelter (one way) via Redearth and Pharaoh Creeks. The trip to Shadow Lake and back out again is usually a full day. For a shorter day you can ski to the picnic site about 6 km up the fire road, where the road crosses the creek.

Height gain 425 m to Shadow Lake
600 m to Egypt Lake

Max elevation 1820 m at Shadow Lake
1995 m at Egypt Lake

Map Banff 82 O/4

The Redearth Creek trail is very popular. The first part is a fire road and is easy and often trackset. It is a good place to practice your skills in a safe environment. The tour all the way to Shadow Lake is popular as well. The full tour up to Egypt Lake, with an overnight at the shelter, is a great adventure and is highly recommended.

Hazards The descent down Pharaoh Creek has some sharp turns at the bridges. Ski carefully! The climb towards Shadow Lake, from the turn-off, is difficult, particularly to descend. If it is at all icy it is advisable to walk down.

Options You can ski to Egypt Lake then continue over Healy Pass to the Borgeau Parking Lot near Sunshine Village. Most people ski this tour in the opposite direction. One can also ski over Gibbon Pass and exit via Twin Lakes.

Facilities There are toilets at the Redearth Creek parking lot. Picnic tables and an outhouse can be found at the 6 km bridge, where the fire road crosses Redearth Creek. There is a deluxe, full service lodge at Shadow Lake and a rustic shelter at Egypt Lake.

Access There is a large parking lot on the south side of the Trans Canada Highway about 20 km west of Banff. It is located 200 m west of the animal overpass which crosses the highway. When approaching from the east use caution as you must turn left across two lanes of oncoming traffic.

Cross through the metal animal fence by using the gate provided, then ski west along the trail, up the hillside. After about 300 m the trail swings left through the forest and soon joins the fire road. The road is wide and the skiing easy.

After 6 km the road descends gently to the creek and crosses it. There are picnic tables and an outhouse on the far side.

The road continues up the right bank of the creek for another 5 km to the Shadow Lake turn-off. From here it is challenging to get to Shadow Lake. The trail climbs very steeply for about 100 vertical metres before it levels off and turns to the left for another 2 km to Shadow Lake Lodge. A few hundred metres before the lodge the trees begin to open up into a meadow. The lodge is on the right at the edge of the trees.

Once you leave the trail to Shadow lake, Parks Canada considers the Avalanche Terrain Rating to be a 2.

If you are going to Egypt Lake then stay on the fire road for several hundred metres beyond the Shadow Lake turn-off. The road descends to Redearth Creek and crosses it to a warden cabin and a corral. The road ends here and a trail crosses Pharaoh Creek to the far side and heads up the left bank. For about 5 km the trail follows next to the creek, sometimes on one bank and sometimes on the other, crossing the creek perhaps eight times on small bridges. After 5 km the trail crosses to the east (left) bank of Pharaoh Creek and begins to angle up the hillside. For the next 2-3 km the trail stays on the east bank of the creek and climbs perhaps 100 vertical metres above the creek before descending to the creek again.

For the rest of the way the valley bottom is wide and open and it is best to follow the creek bed. After about 1.5 km a warden cabin can be seen in the edge of the trees on the left. Just a few hundred metres beyond, on a bench on the right above the creek, is the Egypt Lake Shelter. Beyond this point the creek pinches off and becomes quite narrow, so it should be easy to decide if you have missed the shelter.

Shadow Lake Lodge

A modern log lodge in a beautiful setting.
Location About 0.5 km NE of Shadow Lake (GR 736687)
Map Banff 82 O/4
Facilities Two central lodges surrounded by 12 guest cabins. There is outdoor plumbing but propane heating.
Capacity 32
Season December 27 to January 2, and January 31 to March 31
Cost About $130-$145 per person. All meals provided.
Reservations Write Shadow Lake Lodge and Cabins, Box 2606, Banff, Alberta, T0L 0C0 Email: shadow@telusplanet.net Website: www.brewsteradventures.com Phone: 403-762-0116 Fax: 403-760-2866

Shadow Lake Lodge

40 HAIDUK LAKE

Grade Intermediate
Distance 14 km return from Shadow Lake Lodge
Time A moderate day trip
Height gain 250 m
Max elevation 2060 m
Map Banff 82 O/4

This is a popular tour with visitors at Shadow Lake Lodge. The tour takes you to a lovely lake tucked away in the mountains.

Options If you wish to continue to Whistling Pass, ski across Haiduk Lake then climb steeply, gaining about 100 vertical metres, to reach a higher bench. Soon the trees disappear and you can ski straight up the valley to the pass, avoiding a small band of cliffs on the left.

From the pass it is possible to descend a short distance to Scarab Lake.

The descent to Egypt Lake is steep and difficult and is not recommended.

Access This tour begins at Shadow Lake Lodge.

From the lodge follow the right bank of the river up to Shadow Lake. Ski along the left side of the lake to the point where Haiduk Creek enters the lake (this point is normally obvious because the incoming stream melts a pool out into the lake).

From here the route follows Haiduk Creek upstream for about 2.5 km. At the start the ascent is a bit steep and forested but it soon opens up into meadows. After about 1 km you reach a large meadows. Angle out to the right corner where the way continues up the open drainage of the creek.

After another 2 km you cross a second large meadow to its end where a huge avalanche path can be seen sweeping down. Just before reaching the end of the meadow look for a trail on the left (GR 724654) normally marked with flagging, which climbs to Haiduk Lake.

The trail now climbs steeply for about 150 vertical metres then meanders through forest for a short distance until it breaks out into more open country. Continue skiing along the right side of the creek. It is sometimes hard to stay on the trail as it makes its way through meadows, glades and open forest. The way is often marked with flagging.

Eventually you arrive at a large, open meadow which you cross to reach the lake about halfway along its left shore.

Note: Many people turn up left from Shadow Lake before they reach the true creekbed. They follow a false creekbed which appears to be the obvious way. However, the forest soon pinches in and the way becomes very narrow. After about 1 km this route pops over a hill and descends to the meadow mentioned above.

41 BALL PASS

Grade Advanced
Distance 12 km return from Shadow Lake Lodge
Time An easy day trip
Height gain 380 m
Max elevation 2200 m
Map Banff 82 O/4

An adventurous trip that takes you to a high and remote pass.

Access This tour begins at Shadow Lake Lodge.

Follow the Haiduk Lake Trail to RE21 (GR 724654) along the west fork of Haiduk Creek (where the Haiduk Lake Trail leaves the creek and begins to climb steeply through the trees) (see page 79). To ski to Ball Pass continue

Facilities There are picnic tables before the trail begins its steep climb to Ball Pass.

Hazards The final part of the climb up to the pass is subject to avalanche risk. Retreat if you doubt the stability of the snowpack.

Options It is possible to descend the other side of Ball Pass, down Hawk Creek to the Kootenay Highway.

southwest along the right bank of the creek. At times the route follows the creek itself. After about 0.5 km the angle eases and after 1.5 km a band of cliffs looms straight ahead. Ski along the creek which curves to the right under the cliffs. Gradually the cliffs peter out and after 0.5 km disappear completely.

Preparing for the run down from Ball Pass. Photo Gillean Daffern.

Swing left and begin climbing the treed slope above the creek. Soon another set of cliffs will appear straight ahead. Climb diagonally up and to the left under the base of the cliffs to the highest larch trees,

then climb the slopes above, angling to the right into the pass. This last section of about 75 vertical metres, above the final larch trees, is steep and potentially dangerous. Use caution!

42 TWIN LAKES

Ski touring 1

Grade Advanced
Distance 15 km return
Time This is a full day tour
Height gain 630 m
Max elevation 2060 m
Maps Banff 82 O/4
Castle Mountain 82 O/5

A very steep and challenging trail which can often be icy.

Hazards The descent from Twin Lakes can be very difficult. Take care!

Options This makes a good, long tour when combined with Gibbon Pass and Redearth Creek.

Access There is a small parking area along the off ramp from the Kootenay Highway onto the Trans Canada Highway eastbound. Climb through the gate in the fence and put your skis on.

Ski several metres down a wide road to a clear area with a trail bulletin board on the left. Continue straight ahead for about 50 m, cross a bridge over the creek then continue ahead for 50 m to a junction. Turn right and ski about 1 km along a wide trail through the trees, parallel to the creek. Go through an open meadow with a cliff above on the left then enter the trees. Continue another 3-400 m along a narrow trail then cross a bridge over the creek.

From the bridge make several switchbacks up the steep hillside above, then continue along over rolling terrain high above the right bank of the creek. The trail is hard to follow as it climbs and descends and meanders along. After about 0.5 km the trail begins to climb steeply. It does not switchback much but just climbs straight up the hillside. Over the next few kilometres the trail gains about 400 vertical metres.

At the 2000 m level the angle lays back and over the next 2 km the trail traverses left (south), climbing gradually into the Twin Lakes drainage. Ski up the creekbed for another 2 km to reach the southern (lower) Twin Lake.

Crossing lower Twin Lake beneath an unnamed peak.

Crossing Gibbon Pass.

43 GIBBON PASS

Grade Advanced
Distance 5 km from Twin Lakes to Shadow Lake
Time 3-4 hours one way
Height gain 230 m
Max elevation 2290 m
Map Banff 82 O/4

This pass can be traversed in either direction. The Shadow Lake side is easy to ascend as the trail is easy to follow but it is difficult to find your way down if you are going the opposite direction.

Hazard There is some avalanche hazard off the slopes of Storm Mountain.

Access This trail connects the Twin Lakes tour and the Redearth Creek/ Shadow Lake tour.

Ski south across south Twin Lake to the far end then work your way up through the trees to the southeast. There is an open draw to the right but this is very exposed to avalanches and not recommended. The going through the forest is not too difficult as the trees are fairly far apart. After about 100 vertical metres the angle lays back and the trees open up into meadows. Then it steepens again for about 100 vertical metres through open trees (this is a very nice ski slope). Eventually you break out into open meadows which are followed to the pass. From here there are great views of Mount Assiniboine to the south.

From the pass head across open meadows towards the southeast. The trees begin very quickly and you must follow the best line possible, dropping straight down the hillside below for 460 vertical metres to Shadow Lake Lodge. The hill is steep and skiing is tricky—many switchbacks will be necessary. At times it may be possible to follow the summer trail but normally it will be hard to find. The lodge is located on the edge of a meadow right at the bottom of the hill.

If you are doing this tour from Shadow Lake the trail up the hill to Gibbon Pass will be found behind the cabins at Shadow Lake Lodge. Put your skins on for the climb.

44 BOOM LAKE

Nordic skiing 2

Grade Easy/intermediate
Distance 10 km return
Time 3-4 hours return
Height gain 180 m
Max elevation 1890 m
Map Lake Louise 82 N/8

The Boom Lake trail is one of the most popular in the Rocky Mountains. Due to its high location near Vermillion Pass it gets snow early and keeps the snow well into the spring. It takes little snow to make the trail skiable and you can often find keen skiers here in November. This is a very pleasant outing.

Facilities Toilets located at the trailhead.

Hazards The steep initial sections of this trail can prove difficult for beginner skiers on the way back down. Beware!

Access A large parking lot is located on the north side of the Kootenay Highway 6 km southwest of Castle Junction.

The trail starts at the north end of the parking lot. It immediately crosses a bridge and soon starts to climb. For the next 0.5 km the trail climbs fairly steeply, then for another kilometre it continues to climb but at a lesser angle. For the next 3 km, until just short of the lake, the trail rolls up and down through mature forest. The last several hundred metres is a downhill run to the lake, arriving on the lakeshore about one quarter of the way along the north bank. The trail is usually well packed and sometimes groomed.

Boom Lake.
Photo Alan Kane.

45 TRAILS NEAR CASTLE JUNCTION

Grade Easy
Distance There are 8.7 km of trails
Time You can ski here for a few hours or all day if you chose
Height gain Nil
Max elevation 1450 m
Map Castle Mountain 82 O/5

You can spend some pleasant hours skiing here. The three trails are normally track set by the management of Castle Mountain Chalets.

Options You can also ski the trail to Tower and Rockbound Lakes from here (see page 86).

Facilities The Castle Mountain Hostel is located within a few metres of these trails. Just across the road are the Castle Mountain Chalets, which offer deluxe accommodation, gas pumps, a general store and telephones.

Access All three trails begin at Castle Mountain Junction where the connector road from the Trans Canada Highway intersects with the Bow Valley Parkway. Just east of the junction on the north side of the Bow Valley Parkway you will find a parking lot. You can leave your car here and make your way to the trails either on skis or on foot. More detailed maps are available from the store at the Castle Mountain Chalets.

Trail #1 starts from the junction and runs west along the north side of the highway. Just beyond Castle Mountain Chalets the trail angles right and gets away from the road. This trail is 10 km return if you follow it to the end.

Trail #2 is short and easy. From the parking lot it heads northwest through the woods for a short distance and crosses a bridge over Silverton Creek. It works its way east and reaches a campground where it does a loop. This is a 1.5 km loop.

Trail #3 makes a 2.2 km loop on the south side of the highway. It begins near the access road into the hostel and heads south until it reaches the power line which it follows to the east for about 1 km. The trail then turns north and works its way back to Castle Junction.

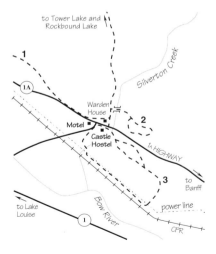

85

Rockbound Lake. Photo Alf Skrastins.

46 TOWER LAKE AND ROCKBOUND LAKE   Ski touring 1

Grade Intermediate/advanced
Distance 17 km return
Time A full day trip
Height gain 760 m
Max elevation 2200 m
Map Castle Mountain 82 O/5

This is a steep climb much of the way but you are rewarded at the top with a beautiful valley tucked in behind Castle Mountain. The two lakes are in a lovely setting and the views are exceptional. The ski down at the end of the day can be very hard on the legs, particularly if the trail is icy.

Access The parking lot is situated on the north side of the Bow Valley Parkway next to the wardens house, just a few metres east of Castle Junction.

The trail heads straight into the woods from the parking area. It begins climbing immediately and it is best to either wear skins or have a very good climbing wax on your skis. As you work your way up through the trees there are occasional views over the Bow Valley. Over the

next 4 km the trail climbs 500 vertical metres. About half way up the climb the trail splits. Follow the branch that swings steeply up to the right. Eventually the trail reaches the shoulder of Castle Mountain and begins to lay back. It swings to the left quite sharply and heads northwest into the valley behind the mountain. For another 3 km, as far as Tower Lake, the trail rolls pleasantly up and down, gradually gaining elevation. On your left are impressive views of

Eisenhower Tower looming high above. The open meadow near Tower Lake is a lovely place to stop and have lunch, however, the sun leaves this valley early so bundle up.

If you want to continue up to Rockbound Lake the way is not too difficult. Skins will be a real asset. The route climbs treed slopes through the cliffs directly across from you on the other side of Tower Lake. Although the route looks unlikely it is actually quite reasonable and there is only 100 vertical metres of steep climbing. Just over the top of the hill the route descends a short distance

to Rockbound Lake where you will be surrounded by impressive scenery. An outstanding viewpoint can be found over to the right, where the stream leaves the lake and plunges over a cliff. From the edge of the chasm cut by the stream there is a great view down the Bow Valley, all the way to Banff.

The return trip to your car can be a real challenge. It follows the exact same route but now is almost all downhill. Keep your speed under control. The trail down from the shoulder is quite wide but in icy or crusty conditions can be dangerous.

47 JOHNSTONS CREEK

Ski touring 1

Grade Intermediate/advanced
Distance 10 km to the Ink Pots return
34 km to Luellen Lake return
Time 4-5 hours to the Ink Pots return
A full day to Luellen Lake and back
Height gain 200 m to the Ink Pots
520 m to Luellen Lake
Max elevation 1620 m at the Ink Pots
1950 m at Luellen Lake
Map Castle Mountain 82 O/5

This trail offers a moderately steep ascent, then crosses a high shoulder before descending steeply to the Ink Pots. If

conditions are icy or crusty the skiing will be challenging. The Ink Pots are a lovely destination. The continuation up Johnston Creek to Luellen Lake is not a difficult tour but it is long, so leave yourself lots of time for the return journey.

Options For the really adventurous you can continue up Johnston Creek beyond Luellen Lake to Pulsatilla Pass, then down Wildflower Creek to Baker Creek. You can descend Baker Creek to the highway or even carry on to Baker Lake, Skoki and Lake Louise.

Access There is a parking lot at Moose Meadow, on the north side of the Bow Valley Parkway, 2 km west of Johnston Creek Resort. (Note: There is another parking lot on the south side of the road, 1 km further west, and it is also called Moose Meadow).

The trail climbs up and right from the parking lot (do not take the trail that heads off left along the valley floor). It climbs very gradually through the trees

for the first 2 km, working its way back to the east towards Johnston Canyon to join the summer trail. From this point the grade begins to steepen and after another kilometre climbs at a steep angle up to the shoulder. You are now high above the creek and there is an excellent view down the Bow Valley. Up to this point the trail is very wide but beyond here the trail narrows.

The trail now descends, sometimes quite steeply, down to the valley bottom.

Skiing down toward the Ink Pots. Photo Gillean Daffern.

It emerges from the trees and the Ink Pots are right there. On a sunny day this is a lovely spot to sit and contemplate.

If you chose to continue farther up the valley, ski a short distance and you will see a bridge crossing the creek. You can either cross the creek and ski through the meadow along the right bank or just follow the creek itself (if it is frozen and snow covered). After a kilometre both trails join and the route now follows the creek bed. Continue along the creek for another kilometre to where a small creek enters from the right (east). This is where you turn if you wish to ski to Mystic Pass (see page 63).

To continue up to Luellen Lake you have two choices. You can turn up the small side creek for several hundred metres until you see a trail sign on the left bank. At this point you join up with the summer trail which continues up the valley through the forest. It is also possible to continue up Johnston Creek for 2 km, then at some clearings on the right side of the creek, work your way several hundred metres up to the right, through the forest, to join the summer trail. From here just keep following the trail. It is never particularly steep but keeps climbing steadily. After a few kilometres it passes a warden cabin. Carry on up the trail beyond the warden cabin for another 4-5 km to the cutoff for Luellen Lake. To this point the trail has stayed in the forest on the right (northeast) side of the creek.

To reach Luellen Lake turn left at the cutoff and ski straight downhill, following a trail, for a short distance to the creek. Cross the creek and climb a steep bank on the far side. Find the summer trail again which climbs the hill above. There are many blazes. The trail climbs steeply up the hill for about 0.5 km, angles left and pops over a ridge, then descends a short distance to the lake.

KOOTENAY NATIONAL PARK

Kootenay National Park is the forgotten treasure amongst our wonderful Rocky Mountain Parks. Here you can find skiing in a quiet and beautiful setting. It is unlikely that you will run into many folks on these ski trails.

Access The park is traversed from the northeast to the southwest by the Kootenay Highway (Highway 93). Along the way there are only two facilities which are open in winter: the Kootenay Crossing Warden Station and the Dolly Varden Campground. The highway has a fair amount of traffic but it is all headed for the Columbia Valley, the Panorama Ski Resort and other destinations in B.C. The highway is well maintained and is rarely closed in winter due to snow or avalanches.

The original Fay Hut, built in 1927 and destroyed by a forest fire in 2003. Photo Hans Fuhrer.

Facilities Radium, which is located just a few kilometres west of the park gates, is a bustling little town where it is possible to find whatever you require. There are service stations, restaurants, grocery stores, motels, a liquor store and a post office. The famous Radium Hot Springs are located just east of town along the highway, just inside the park.

The Kootenay National Park Administration Office (250-347-9615) is located in the town of Radium, on the hill above the Husky service station. The Warden Headquarters (250-347-9361) are just inside the park gates, on the hillside across the road from the Radium Hot Springs Aquacourt.

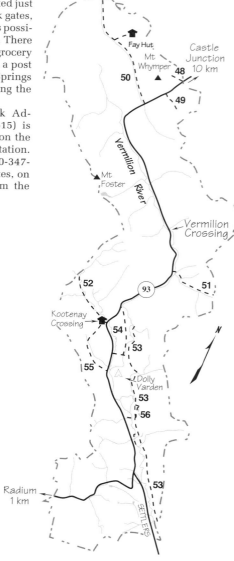

48 CHICKADEE VALLEY

Grade Intermediate
Distance 10 km return
Time 3-4 hours return
Height gain 200 m
Max elevation 1860 m
Map Mount Goodsir 82 N/1

This is a pleasant half day outing. Good snow cover is required in the creek bed, so wait until after Christmas. The scenery at the head of the valley is alpine and impressive. For those interested in making a few turns there are opportunities in this valley.

Hazards Several large avalanche paths reach the valley bottom.

Access Park at the Great Divide parking lot, located on the south side of the Kootenay Highway 10 km southwest of Castle Junction.

From the parking lot cross the highway and walk west a few metres until just level with the end of the parking lot. Put your skis on and head up into the woods. There is an opening in the trees here. Follow glades in the trees for several hundred metres, angling left, until you reach the open area of the creek bed. Follow the creek for 4 km until the end of the valley. The trail is moderately steep for the first kilometre, then it lays back for the rest of the tour. At the end of the valley there is a large open area where the view is terrific.

There are excellent opportunities for making turns on the slopes above this valley and it is a popular destination for this purpose.

Skiing in Chickadee Valley. Photo Alf Skrastins.

Skiing through the maturing new growth forest on the Stanley Glacier trail. Photo Hans Fuhrer.

49 STANLEY GLACIER VALLEY

Ski touring 3

Grade Intermediate
Distance 10 km return
Time 4 hours return
Height gain 275 m
Max elevation 1850 m
Map Mount Goodsir 82 N/1

This tour is best later in the season. With a good base of snow there is excellent potential for making turns at the head of the valley. The steep switchbacks at the start of the tour are a little daunting so you should have a good wax that really works or perhaps even use skins. The run back down to the car, following the creek bed rather than the trail, is excellent. The good skiing through the burned out forest that we have enjoyed in the past has now disappeared as the new growth matures.

Hazards A number of large avalanche paths descend to the valley and you should not stop where exposed to the threat from above. There is a lot of deadfall on this tour, resulting from the fire, so be careful of hitting a half buried tree.

Access Park on the south side of the Kootenay Highway 13 km from Castle Junction.

The trail leaves the parking lot and immediately crosses the Vermilion River via a footbridge. From here it switchbacks steeply up the hillside above. Usually it is not too hard to follow but often has deadfall across it (old burned trees) which can be a nuisance on the way up and a real danger on the way down (later in the season the deadfall will be well covered). After about 180 vertical metres the angle eases off and the trail meanders for 0.5 km across the flats, then dips down left to reach Stanley Creek.

Cross the creek on a small footbridge then head back into the valley on the left side of the drainage. Toward the end of the treed valley the trail climbs a few metres up onto the left (northeast) flank and is a bit hard to follow. Continue up the valley to the end of the trees. For those interested in making turns there are good slopes nearby.

On your return follow the trail back down as far as the crossing of Stanley Creek. From here there is an excellent descent straight down the creek bed. However, this should only be done later in the season when there is good snow cover and the creek is well frozen. Follow the creek down until almost at the valley bottom, then cut over the left bank and follow the hillside back down to the junction with the up trail.

50 TOKUMM CREEK (PROSPECTORS VALLEY) Ski touring 3

Grade Easy/intermediate
Distance 14 km to Kaufmann Lake junction one way
Time It normally takes a full day to ski to the Kaufmann Lake junction and return, or to ski one way to the Fay Hut with full packs.
Height gain 340 m to Kaufmann Lake junction
Max elevation 1830 m at Kaufmann Lake junction
Map Mount Goodsir 82 N/1
Lake Louise 82 N/8

This is a long tour up a wild valley. You can make a short day of it or ski as far as you like. This trail is not recommended early in the season as there are many creek crossings which are bridged by single logs only (slippery!!!).

Facilities Toilets at the parking lot.

Hazards There are many avalanche paths which descend to the valley floor. Do not linger in these areas. A forest fire swept through Prospectors Valley in the summer of 2003. Deadfall across the trail will be a hazard for many years to come.

Options The adventurous can continue up the valley, beyond Kaufmann Lake turn-off, to the Eagle Eyrie near Opabin Pass. There is no trail much of the way and you should follow the creek bed when possible. Travel is not too difficult if you wait until later in the year when the creek is well frozen and covered with snow.

This tour is often done in reverse by strong skiers in a long hard day. You begin by skiing up the road to Lake O'Hara (see page 141), then continue to Opabin Pass (see page 145) and finally complete the tour by skiing down Tokumm Creek to the Kootenay Highway. Get an early start and carry a headlamp.

Access Park at the Marble Canyon parking lot on the north side of the Kootenay Highway, 7 km west of the Alberta/B.C. border.

Begin by skiing parallel to the highway back northeast, through a large swath in the trees, for about 150 m, to gain the Tokumm Creek trail which is found up on the left bank. This route bypasses the Marble Canyon portion of the trail. Due to the forest fire of the summer of 2003 there may be changes to the route of the trail. Follow the trail through thick forest with a few short climbs. After about 3 km the trail emerges from the trees onto the open flats beside Tokumm Creek. For the rest of the way follow the trail which is found along the right bank of the creek. The ski up to Kaufmann Lake is sometimes done but is not highly recommended—it is steep and narrow.

Fay Hut approach (elevation gain 430 m) The turn-off to the Fay Hut is sometimes difficult to locate. After about 9 km along Tokumm Creek you cross a large, obvious drainage coming in from the right. Shortly after this drainage Tokumm Creek starts to narrow (either ski along the creek or along the trail which is up on the right bank). In another 1.5 km there is another open area, with a large avalanche path on the left and a creek coming in from the right. This is the turn-off.

From the turn-off ski up the drainage along the left side or, if there is enough snow, along the creek itself. In about 1.5 km a wall of grey and black streaked rock about 20 m high and 50 m wide is encountered where the stream turns left. Cross the stream to the right bank. The going gets steep here. Trend up and right, zigzagging through light trees. You are heading towards a cliff band with an obvious break just to the right of straight above you. The route lies through this break and is a skis-off affair. It can be a strenuous struggle but there is a thick rope hanging down to help you.

Fay Hut

The original Fay Hut, built in 1927 and the oldest of the ACC huts, was destroyed by a forest fire in August 2003. A beautiful new log hut was built to replace it in the summer of 2005. This hut also, unfortunately, burned down in the winter of 2009. The Alpine Club of Canada is now considering whether to replace the hut once again.

51 SIMPSON RIVER

Ski touring 1

Grade Easy
Distance 8 km one way to the park boundary
Time A full day tour
Height gain 120 m
Max elevation 1370 m
Map Mount Assiniboine 82 J/13

Facilities The Surprise Creek Cabin (GR 826468) in Mount Assiniboine Provincial Park is 2 km beyond the Kootenay National Park boundary.

Options The Simpson River can be followed all the way to Simpson Pass then down Healy Creek to the Borgeau parking lot at Sunshine Village Ski Resort.

Access Park 0.7 km north of the Simpson Monument, 6 km south of Vermilion River Crossing.

From the parking lot cross a foot bridge over the Vermilion River. Ski into the woods straight ahead for about 200 m, then turn right and continue for about 1 km through the forest to the Simpson River. Beyond here the trail follows the left bank of the river as far as the Park boundary. Note! The start of this trail may have been affected by the forest fire of 2001.

52 WEST KOOTENAY

Ski touring 1

Grade Easy
Distance 13 km one way to park boundary
Time A full day to the park boundary and back
Height gain 40 m
Max elevation 1230 m
Map Spillimacheen 82 K/16

The West Kootenay ski tour follows an old fire road winding through mixed coniferous forest to the park boundary.

Access Park at the Kootenay River Crossing Warden Station, 61 km from Castle Junction.

The trail starts between the warden's house and the office. Walk about 100 m past another house then put your skis on. Cross a short open space then enter the woods following a wide road. Ski about 400 m through the woods, then about 400 m up a reasonably steep hill. Continue another 300 m to a trail junction. The lefthand fork is the Dolly Varden trail and the righthand fork is the West Kootenay trail. Turn right and continue for about 12 km to the Park boundary. Beyond this point there are logging roads and it is said to be possible to ski to Golden.

53 EAST KOOTENAY

Grade Easy
Distance 30 km
Time You can ski for a few hours or all day if you like
Height gain nil
Max elevation 1210 m
Maps Spillimacheen 82 K/16
Mount Assiniboine 82 J/13
Tangle Peak 82 J/12

A pleasant, easy ski following the fire road on the east side of the Kootenay River. The northern section is a pleasant valley bottom road, winding through pine forests, while the southern section stays close to the river with its broad alluvial flats.

Access Park at the McLeod Meadows picnic area, on the east side of the Kootenay Highway, 16 km south of Kootenay River Crossing.

Start skiing from the north end of the parking lot where it loops around. Skirt along the edge of a meadow, next to the trees, for about 50 m. Just after a small wooden bridge, turn right into the trees. Follow the trail through the trees for about 300 m. On your left you will see a big building (McLeod Meadows Theatre). Cross the campground road and continue another 300 m to the Kootenay River. Cross two large footbridges in succession to the far shore. The trail now angles steeply up left for about 200 m to reach the East Kootenay fire road.

You can turn right and ski for about 17 km to the park boundary (the trail is maintained only as far as Pitt Creek). Or you can turn left and ski about 14 km to the Split Peak Junction (the trail is maintained only as far as Daer Creek).

Note There is now only the one crossing over the Kootenay River so you will have to return the way you came.

54 HECTOR GORGE
Ski touring 1

Grade Easy
Distance 22 km return
Time You can ski for a few hours or all day if you like
Height gain 150 m
Max elevation 1280 m
Maps Spillimacheen 82 K/16
Mount Assiniboine 82 J/13

A pleasant tour along a wide road through thick forest.

Access There is a small plowed pull-out on the east side of the Kootenay Highway 5.5 km south of Kootenay River Crossing and 1 km north of the Dolly Varden Winter Campground.

From the parking lot ski straight east along a road through the forest. After 200 m you cross a bridge over the Kootenay River. Continue another 1.3 km through the forest to the Simpson River, turn left and continue along the road. You can ski for another 10 km (or as far as you like) till the trail reaches the highway between Kootenay Pond and Hector Gorge.

55 DOLLY VARDEN
Ski touring 1

Grade Easy
Distance 11 km one way
Time An easy day one way or a full day return
Height gain 100 m
Max elevation 1310 m
Map Spillimacheen 82 K/16

This is a very pleasant tour. It follows the southern section of the West Kootenay fire road through mature forest from Kootenay River Crossing Warden Station to Crooks Meadow.

Access Park at the Kootenay River Crossing Warden Station, 61 km from Castle Junction. If you want to ski this trail one way only, a second car can be left at Crooks Meadow along the Kootenay Highway, 8.5 km south of the Crossing.

The trail starts between the warden's house and the office. Walk about 100 m past another house and put your skis on. Cross a short open space then enter the woods following a wide road. Ski about 400 m through the woods, then about 400 m up a reasonably steep hill. Continue another 300 m to a trail junction. The broad trail that heads out left is the Dolly Varden Trail. From here the trail rises and falls gently through the woods. After about 3 km another trail branches right up to Luxor Pass. Beyond here the skiing can be a little less pleasant early in the season as the snow pushes the alder trees across the trail but does not completely cover them. You can continue along this trail for another 8 km to the Kootenay Highway at Crooks Meadow.

56 DOG LAKE

Grade Intermediate/advanced
Distance 6 km return
Time 3 hours return
Height gain 75 m
Max elevation 1210 m
Maps Mount Assiniboine 82 J/13
Tangle Peak 82 J/12

This is a delightful and interesting tour. The trail is a little steep and in icy conditions could be tricky. It is possible to ski this tour as a loop, ascending to the lake via route #1 and descending via route #2.

Access Park at the McLeod Meadows picnic area on the east side of the Kootenay Highway, 16 km south of Kootenay River Crossing.

Follow the description for the East Kootenay tour (see page 96) until it crosses the Kootenay River and climbs the hill to reach the East Kootenay Fire Road. From here there are two ways to reach Dog Lake.

1. Cross the East Kootenay Fire Road and take the Dog Lake trail that climbs into the forest straight ahead. The trail climbs moderately steeply for the first 0.5 km so be sure you have a good wax. It then lays back but continues to gain elevation for another 0.5 km. The last 0.5 km is a steep downhill to the lake. The trail reaches the lake mid way along the south shore.

2. A more moderate way to reach Dog Lake is to turn left and ski along the East Kootenay Fire Road for 2 km. At a trail sign turn off to the right. From here the trail climbs gradually for about 1.2 km to reach the lake at its outlet. Much of the way this trail follows the stream which drains Dog Lake along the right bank (true left bank).

Dog Lake. Photo Hans Fuhrer.

LAKE LOUISE AREA

57 Taylor Lake	advanced	p. 101
58 Baker Creek	intermediate	p. 103
59 Baker Creek Powerline Trail	easy	p. 103
60 Moraine Lake Road	easy	p. 105
61 Paradise Valley	intermediate	p. 106
62 Fairview Loop	easy	p. 107
63 Tramline Trail	easy	p. 109
64 Telemark Trail	intermediate	p. 110
65 Lake Louise Shoreline Trail	easy	p. 111
66 Great Divide Trail	easy	p. 113
67 Bow River (Riverside) Loop	easy	p. 114
68 Plain of Six Glaciers	intermediate	p. 115
69 Whitehorn Trails	easy/intermediate	p. 116
70 Pipestone Trails	easy/intermediate	p. 117
71 Hidden Bowl	easy	p. 119
72 Purple Bowl	intermediate	p. 120
73 Bath Creek	easy/intermediate	p. 121

Lake Louise is known world wide as a mountaineering centre and as a downhill ski resort. It also offers extensive opportunities for cross country skiing—Nordic skiing along set tracks or ski touring in a wilderness setting. The scenery is outstanding and the area gets lots of snow. It is the perfect centre for a ski holiday.

Facilities The facilities at Lake Louise are spread out. There are three distinct centres which are collectively referred to as Lake Louise. These are: the Lake Louise townsite, Upper Lake Louise and the Lake Louise Ski Resort. All amenities that you might require can be found at these locations.

Lake Louise Townsite There are two service stations here, two major hotels, the Post Hotel (403-522-3989) and the Lake Louise Inn (403-522-3791), and numerous restaurants and lounges. The Lake Louise Alpine Centre (403-522-2200) offers excellent low cost accommodation with a lovely ambiance. Wilson's Sports (403-522-3636) can help you with your equipment needs. In addition there is a post office, liquor store, art gallery, book store, grocery store and an outstanding bakery called Laggans.

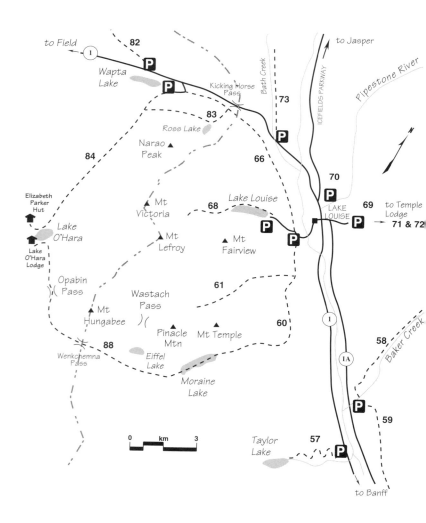

Most of these are located at the Samson Mall. There is also a medical centre and a parks information centre.

Upper Lake Louise On the shores of Lake Louise itself, about 3 km up the hill from the townsite, is the famous CPR Hotel, The Chateau Lake Louise. It is very luxurious but, during the winter, is not as expensive as it looks. Just a short distance down the road is Deer Lodge which is a little less grand but perhaps more homey. Many trails begin near here and are referred to collectively as the Upper Lake Louise Trails.

Lake Louise Ski Resort Is located across the other side of the valley from the lake, about 2.5 km northeast of the townsite. Lifts begin from the Lodge of the Ten Peaks. The Whitehorn Trails are located near here and the access to Skoki begins nearby.

History Lake Louise was not the original home of mountaineering in Canada—that honour rests with Rogers Pass, where there was a luxurious hotel called Glacier House. However, the focus shifted over the years and, when Glacier House closed in autumn 1925 (the railway had been re-routed), Lake Louise became the alpine centre of Canada.

For years illustrious mountaineers from around the world would meet at the Chateau to climb the glittering peaks and to prepare for their trips into the backcountry. Today Lake Louise is still a great climbing centre—the massive north face of Mount Temple, the airy ridge of Mount Victoria and the steep quartzite cliffs at the end of the lake draw adventure seekers from around the world.

Lake Louise has also grown in stature as a ski destination. Skoki Lodge opened its doors in the spring of 1931 and has now grown into the downhill skiing giant known as Skiing Louise.

An extensive array of Nordic ski trails has developed all around the valley. The Chateau, which for years was open only in summer, now does a healthy business in the winter and the once-rustic Post Hotel has grown into the sophisticated operation we see today.

57 TAYLOR LAKE

Ski touring 1

Grade Advanced
Distance 10 km return
Time 5-6 hours return
Height gain 600 m
Max elevation 2070 m
Map Lake Louise 82 N/8

Steep and tricky this is hardly a cross country ski trail at all. However, many people still ski it. To be avoided when conditions are icy.

Options It is possible to traverse southeast to reach O'Brian Lake.

Access A parking lot is located on the southwest side of the Trans Canada Highway, 8 km west of Castle Junction.

The first 2 km of this trail are reasonable as they work their way up the hill through the trees. The trail then steepens and is a continuous climb to the lake. Be careful on your way back down as the trail is narrow and the corners tight.

The upper end of Paradise Valley. Photo Leon Kubbernus.

58 BAKER CREEK

Ski touring 1

Grade Intermediate
Distance 12 km to the meadows return
Time 4-5 hours
Height gain 210 m
Max elevation 1700 m
Map Lake Louise 82 N/8

A popular trail with pleasant views of Protection and Lipalian Mountains. The meadows make a superb place to sit in the sun and have lunch.

Facilities Toilets at the parking lot.

Options You can continue skiing farther up this valley. The trail crosses the meadow, gradually climbing and staying above the creek, then continues another 5 km to a campground. Really keen skiers can carry on for another 12 km to Baker Lake then descend via Boulder Pass to Lake Louise.

Access Park across the road from the Baker Creek Chalets on the Bow Valley Parkway about 14 km west of Castle Junction. The parking lot is on the south side of the bridge.

From the far left end of the parking lot ski about 75 m along the creek then cross a bridge to the north side. From here ski back to the left, under the hill, away from the creek, for about 100 m, then turn right into a draw and start climbing. The trail

climbs steeply for a short distance angling up to the left, then makes a long switchback to the right and crosses under the powerlines. It continues to climb through a mature forest of lodgepole pines at a moderate angle for several kilometres. Keep your eye open for some viewpoints on the right, high on the hillside above Baker Creek. Eventually the trail flattens out for several more kilometres as far as a beautiful meadow under the slopes of Lipalian Mountain.

59 BAKER CREEK POWER LINE TRAIL

Nordic skiing/ski touring 1

Grade Easy
Distance 7 km return
Time 2 hours
Height gain Nil
Max elevation 1480 m
Map Lake Louise 82 N/8

Although not one of the most scenic trails it does have one good view of the peaks surrounding the Bow Valley. It is an easy ski, accessible and may be packed or trackset.

Facilities Toilets at the parking lot.

Access Park across the road from the Baker Creek Chalets on the Bow Valley Parkway about 14 km west of Castle Junction. The parking lot is on the south side of the bridge.

From the far right hand corner of the parking lot head straight back into the woods. The trail may be marked occasionally

with signs with a #2. After about 100 m it reaches a clearing, turns right and for the next few kilometres follows the power lines. Eventually the power lines run up a steep hillside to the left and the trail turns down right into the trees. Ski through the trees to a campground where you can do a circuit on the roads, then return to your car the way you came.

Lake Louise Area

UPPER LAKE LOUISE TRAILS

There are seven trails in this network. They are all well maintained and are normally either packed or trackset. They provide wonderful Nordic skiing opportunities for all levels of ability. They are easy to access and are located in the heart of beautiful country. There are amenities nearby such as washrooms, telephones and restaurants. These trails are perfect for a pleasurable day of fresh air and exercise for families or for those who are new to the sport. After a day of skiing it is pleasant to visit the Chateau for a cup of hot chocolate in luxurious surroundings.

These trails are in the process of being renumbered so this guide does not contain trail numbers. The trails are also in the process of being reorganized in light of animal movement patterns and there may be some changes in the near future. Check with the Park Information Centre in the Samson Mall for more up to date information.

Many of these trails are accessed from the large parking lot on your left just before you reach the Chateau Lake Louise. There are heated washrooms at the west end of the lot (nearest to the Chateau).

Credit must go to volunteers from the Calgary Ski Club for their work on these trails over the past 10 years.

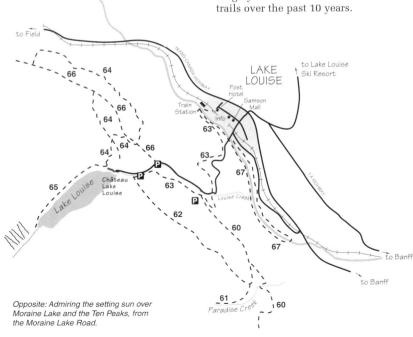

Opposite: Admiring the setting sun over Moraine Lake and the Ten Peaks, from the Moraine Lake Road.

60 MORAINE LAKE ROAD

Grade Easy

Distance 22 km to Moraine Lake return
16 km to viewpoint return

Time This tour can vary from an hour or two, if you are fast, to a full day outing if you choose.

Height gain On the way out 250 m (to viewpoint), on the way back 60 m (from the lake to the viewpoint)

Max elevation 1880 m

Map Lake Louise 82 N/8

The trail follows a paved road which is not plowed in the winter. Consequently it requires little snow to be in condition and is one of the first trails to be skiable each season. The grade is always gentle and it is a perfect trail for beginners. It also is a popular trail for more experienced skiers to get a good workout and to push their heart rate up a bit. Because the trail contours around the shoulder of Mount Temple, high above the valley, the views down the Bow Valley and then later, into Consolation Valley and the Valley of the Ten Peaks, are excellent.

Facilities At Moraine Lake there are picnic shelters and tables.

Hazards Be sure to leave enough time and energy for the return trip. Do not stop while crossing the avalanche paths near Moraine Lake.

Options This tour links up with more advanced tours such as the traverse of Wenkchemna Pass and Opabin Pass to Lake O'Hara.

Access A large parking lot is located on your left about half way up the hill from the townsite of Lake Louise, at the turn-off for the Moraine Lake Road.

From the end of the parking lot, ski around the road closure gate, then simply head up the road. The trail is usually track set and on the weekend there will be plenty of company on this trail. After about 2.5 km the trail crosses Paradise Creek, then it climbs gently for another kilometre. The trail now levels out as far as the viewpoint overlooking Consolation Valley. This is a good place to stop for lunch and is as far as most people go. For the more adventurous another 3 km of skiing, gently downhill, takes you to Moraine Lake (this portion of the trail crosses major avalanche paths and should be traversed without stopping).

In Paradise Valley beneath the immense north face of Mount Temple.

61 PARADISE VALLEY

Ski touring 2

Grade Intermediate
Distance 20 km return from the Moraine Lake Road trailhead
Time A full day trip for most parties
Height gain 410 m to the meadow at the head of the valley
Max elevation 2090 m at the meadow
Map Lake Louise 82 N/8

A popular ski tour offering interesting skiing and some of the most impressive mountain scenery in the Canadian Rockies.

Hazards Do not linger in the slide paths which descend from Mounts Haddow and Aberdeen.

Options The traverse through Wastach Pass, to the west of Eiffel Peak, is possible. Some parties combine this pass with Wenkchemna and Opabin Passes when they do the traverse from Lake O'Hara to Lake Louise, finishing their adventure along Paradise Valley.

Access The tour begins along the Moraine Lake Road. There is a large parking lot on the left side of the road about halfway up the hill between the townsite of Lake Louise and the Chateau.

From the parking lot ski around the road closure barrier and head up the road. After about 2 km angle right and climb up a hill through the woods. After a short distance another trail (the Fairview Trail) will branch off to the right and curve back to the northwest. Do not follow this trail. Instead, carry on ahead and climb a steep bank to gain the crest of a forested ridge. Continue climbing through the trees for about 0.5 km, until the trail intersects with the main summer trail between Lake Louise and Moraine Lake.

Turn to the right towards Lake Louise and ascend for a short distance to another trail junction. Now turn left into Paradise Valley. The trail climbs for a short distance then makes a long descent into the valley, breaking out of the trees at Paradise Creek. This is a good spot to rest and admire the impressive north face of Mount Temple towering 1500 m above.

The trail now crosses the creek on a bridge and continues over rolling terrain along the south bank. After 0.5 km the trail again crosses the creek to the north side and continues working its way up the valley through mature forest. After several kilometres the trail makes its way back to the left to the creek.

The trail now works its way up a steep hillside, in the area between the two arms of the creek, eventually following along the north bank of the south arm to a large meadow. There are good views of the great face of Mount Hungabee at the end of the valley and high above you, to the south, can be seen the solitary needle called the Grand Sentinel.

62 FAIRVIEW LOOP

Nordic skiing 1

Grade Easy
Distance 7.5 km to complete the loop
Time 2 hours
Height gain 50 m
Max elevation 1730 m
Map Lake Louise 82 N/8

Highly recommended, this trail traverses through forests and clearing giving a nice open feeling, variety and good views. There are moderate little uphills, downhills and turns which help to make the trail entertaining and interesting.

Facilities There are heated washrooms at the west end of the parking lot, nearest the Chateau. Full services are available at the Chateau Lake Louise.

Options This trail forms a pleasant alternate start to the tour along the Moraine Lake Road. It can also be combined with the Tramline Trail to the lower townsite of Lake Louise.

Access A large parking lot is located on the left, just before reaching the Chateau. Park at the east end of lot C (farthest from the Chateau) for the start of this trail.

From the east end of the parking lot the trail goes up to the right for a short distance, then turns left into the trees. It rolls up and down for several kilometres below Fairview Mountain before reach-

ing an exhilarating downhill run, which is enjoyable even for beginners. After about 3 km the trail turns sharply to the left and descends to the Moraine Lake Road. Turn left again and follow the road to the junction with the Tramline Trail at the edge of the parking area for the Moraine Lake Road. Turn left and ski up the gradual grade of the Tramline Trail back to the parking lot.

Enjoying the falling snow on the Fairview Trail.

63 THE TRAMLINE TRAIL

Grade Easy
Distance 4.4 km one way
Time 30-45 minutes downhill, 1.5 hours uphill
Height gain 180 m
Max elevation 1730 m
Map Lake Louise 82 N/8

A fun trail and an interesting way to connect upper and lower Lake Louise. It is entertaining to ski the trail in one direction, have a cup of tea and a rest, then return along the trail to your starting point. The trail is downhill (or uphill) all the way so it can be a lot of fun to ski down but a bit of a grind to ski back up again. The trail is wide and has a gentle grade all the way. Halfway down the trail there is a beauti-ful view along the Bow Valley. A portion of this trail is excellent to start young children on—they can ski easily downhill from parking lot C and you can have a car waiting to pick them up at the Moraine Lake Road parking area.

Facilities There are heated washrooms at the west end of the parking lot, nearest the Chateau. All services are available at both ends of the trail (the Chateau or the Post Hotel/Samson Mall).

Hazards The trail can be challenging when it is icy. Beware!

Options This trail links up very nicely with the Bow River (Riverside) Loop.

Access A large parking lot is located on the left, just before reaching the Chateau. Park at the east end of lot C (farthest from the Chateau) for the start to this trail.

From the end of parking lot C the trail heads gently downhill, parallel to the road. After 1.6 km it crosses the Moraine Lake Road then descends into the forest. After a short distance it curves around left, to the Lake Louise road. You must take off your skis and cross the road (Be careful!!). The trail crosses Louise Creek and descends to the Bow River, directly across from Laggan Station (the VIA Rail Station). From here the trail is a little complex and contrived but it can be skied almost all the way. Cross the Bow River on a footbridge then turn right and follow a trail along the river. After about 0.5 km the trail crosses a road to the left then continues down to the right (east) parallel to the railway tracks. Finally the trail goes underneath the railway tracks at the railway bridge over the Pipestone River. You are now on the doorstep of the Post Hotel and the Samson Mall is just a few hundred metres east.

Of Historical Interest

The Tramline Trail is an old tram railway bed. During the period from 1912 to 1930 this tramway was the means of access for guests from the railway station up to Chateau Lake Louise.

Page 110 The Telemark Trail is the site, every March, of the Lake Louise Loppet (formerly called the Telemark Loppet) cross country ski race. This citizen's race has been held every year since 1973.
Photo Gillean Daffern.

Lake Louise Area

64 TELEMARK TRAIL

Grade Intermediate
Distance 9.3 km loop
Time 2-3 hours
Height gain 120 m
Max elevation 1760 m
Map Lake Louise 82 N/8

This trail is really composed of two distinct parts—the upper trail above the old 1A Highway (now the Great Divide Trail) and the trail below the 1A Highway. The upper trail is steep, tricky and in many places confusing. There are several trails in this area and sometimes it is difficult to know which one to choose. The lower trail is excellent offering varied, rolling terrain with hills, turns and open meadows. It is ideal for beginners. The two components are combined to form a figure-8.

Facilities There are heated washrooms at the west end of the parking lot, nearest the Chateau. Full services are available at the Chateau Lake Louise.

Hazards The upper Telemark Trail can be tricky to follow. It can also be very challenging when icy. Ski with caution!

Options This trail could be combined with a tour along the Great Divide Trail.

Access On the left side of the road, just before the Chateau Lake Louise, is a large parking area. Park at the west end of the lot, nearest the Chateau.

Walk along the path in front of the Chateau to just beyond the building. The Telemark Trail turns up immediately behind the Chateau and then makes a sharp turn at Hillside Cottage. From here it winds its way through open forest then makes a steep descent, crosses a junction and rounds a sharp bend to the snow covered 1A Highway. Cross the highway and ski along an old access road for a few hundred metres. The trail then turns into the woods and follows lovely, rolling terrain for about 4 km. The trail makes a sharp turn to the left on the brow of a hill and ascends to the 1A highway.

Turn left and ski back along the highway for 1.7 km. Turn right into the woods and climb gradually up a winding trail to the junction you crossed on the way down from the Chateau. Continue straight up an old road to where the trail ends near the Chateau staff quarters. From here you can carry your skis back to your car.

65 LAKE LOUISE SHORELINE TRAIL

Nordic skiing 1

Grade Easy
Distance 6 km return
Time 2 hours return
Height gain 30 m
Max elevation 1760 m
Map Lake Louise 82 N/8

A pleasant trail in beautiful surroundings. Well suited to beginners.

Facilities There are heated washrooms at the west end of the parking lot, nearest the Chateau. Full services are available at the Chateau Lake Louise.

Hazards Do not ski across the lake unless it is well frozen and covered with a substantial cushion of snow.

Options This trail joins up with the Plain of Six Glaciers trail (see page 115).

Access On the left side of the road just before the Chateau Lake Louise is a large parking area. Park at the west end of the lot, nearest the Chateau.

From the parking lot walk around to the front of the Chateau. Cross in front of the Chateau and just beyond the building take the trail up to the right towards Lake Agnes. After only 100 m turn left onto a trail through the trees. This trail parallels the lake about 20-40 m up the hillside. It climbs very gently for a ways, then descends for the second half to join the main trail just beneath the prominent waterfall which can be seen up on your right. Look closely and you might see some ice climbers. You can carry on for another 0.5 km beneath the very impressive quartzite cliffs. Beyond this the trail becomes more challenging. You can return to your car the same way or for variety you can ski across the lake.

111

Banff skier Dolly Pike along the shores of Lake Louise sometime in the 1930s or '40s.
Courtesy Whyte Museum of the Canadian Rockies.

Setting off along the Great Divide Trail.

66 GREAT DIVIDE TRAIL

Nordic skiing 1

Grade Easy
Distance 15 km return
Time 3-4 hours
Height gain 30 m
Max elevation 1670 m
Map Lake Louise 82 N/8

This trail is actually a snow covered highway. It is flat and usually trackset and is an excellent place for novice skiers to practice or for expert skiers to train. The snow comes early here and the road requires only 20-30 cm to be skiable.

Facilities At the Great Divide there are toilets, picnic tables and camp shelters.

Access Follow the road which climbs from the lower townsite of Lake Louise towards the Chateau. After several kilometres the road takes a sharp turn to the left to make its final climb up to the Chateau. At this point proceed straight ahead and park in the plowed lot.

Hazards Commercial dogsled operators also use this trail but the teams are well controlled and organized. They run in a separate track from the skier's track.

Options It is possible to carry on beyond the Great Divide for another 3 km to the start of the Lake O'Hara Fire Road (see page 141). You can leave a car here and ski just one way (11 km) or for the really hardy you can ski return (22 km). An enjoyable combination is to ski the Great Divide Trail for 3.6 km to the turn-off onto the lower Telemark Trail (see page 110) and then return to your car along this lovely trail.

Put your skis on and ski down the road straight in front of you. You can ski as far as you like. The road is almost all flat except for a short hill just before the Great Divide.

67 BOW RIVER (RIVERSIDE) LOOP

Nordic skiing 1

Grade Easy
Distance 7 km loop
Time 2 hours
Height gain Nil
Max elevation 1550 m
Map Lake Louise 82 N/8

This trail follows the edge of the Bow River and the views are excellent. There are numerous self guiding information displays which are fun to stop and read. The drawback of this trail is that it crosses several roads and this requires

the removal of skis. Because the trail is so near to town there will likely have been pedestrian traffic, causing damage to the ski track.

Facilities Amenities can be found nearby at the Samson Mall.

Hazards Be careful crossing roads—take your skis off!

Options The Tramline Trail and the Bow River Loop make a good combination.

Access Parking is available at the Samson Mall, the Post Hotel, the tent and trailer campground and Laggan Station (the VIA Rail Station). The trail is accessible from any of these locations. The trail is described starting from Laggan Station.

From Laggan Station cross the Bow River on the footbridge. Turn left and continue east along the river. Several cleared paths follow above the river, but the trail actually drops below these into the trees in an un-obvious way and follows a trail close to the river. Take off your skis and cross the upper Lake Louise access road, then continue along the edge of the river. The next section down to what is called the Island Bridges is 2.5 km and crosses another road at the campground, then skirts the trailer village. At the Island Bridges the trail crosses the river then returns along the northwest bank. This section crosses another road and may be beat up by pedestrian traffic. Back at the upper Lake Louise access road you can cross the bridge over the Bow River and return along the previously described trail to Laggan Station

or you can cross the road and work your way on foot through bits of civilization into the Samson Mall.

Of Historical Interest
Lake Louise was discovered by Tom Wilson in 1882. In 1885 the railway was completed and the CPR saw tourism as an integral part of their business. Over the years they have constructed a succession of chalets and grand hotels on the shore of Lake Louise.

The first chalet was constructed in 1890 but was destroyed by fire in 1893. In 1894 a more luxurious chalet was built and a second story was added about 1898. The chalet was substantially enlarged between 1904 and 1911. By 1920 the first concrete wing was added. In 1924 a fire consumed all of the wooden structure, leaving only the concrete wing standing.

The nucleus of the present structure was built on the ruins. In the 1970s it was renovated to allow opening in winter. In more recent years a new wing, entrance, parking structure and conference centre have been added.

68 PLAIN OF SIX GLACIERS

Ski touring 3

Grade Intermediate
Distance 10 km return
Time 4-6 hours
Height gain 200 m
Max elevation 1900 m
Map Lake Louise 82 N/8

This is an outstanding tour that takes you into the heart of one of the most impressive mountain settings in North America. The skiing is not difficult and the tour is not long. The last half of the tour follows a creekbed so wait until after Christmas when there should be adequate snow.

Facilities Heated washrooms are available at the west end of the parking lot, nearest the Chateau. A hot drink at the end of the day in the Chateau Lake Louise is a real treat.

Hazards Beyond the end of the lake you should not follow the summer trail which is located high on the northwest side of the valley as it is extremely exposed to avalanches from above. The valley bottom is crossed by several large avalanche paths. Care should be taken in choosing rest stops so that you are not on one of these paths. This tour is not recommended when the avalanche hazard is high.

Access On the left side of the road just before the Chateau Lake Louise is a large parking lot. Park at the west end of the lot, nearest the Chateau.

From the parking lot walk or ski to the front of the Chateau. You can either follow the Lake Louise Shoreline Trail (see page 111) or head directly across the lake (be certain that it is well frozen). At the end of the lake the trail passes beneath some large quartzite cliffs on the right. Just beyond this point the summer trail starts to climb steeply, angling up to the right. It is best not to follow this trail and instead make a short jog a few metres to the left into the creek bed. Follow the creek for about 2 km, climbing gently most of the time, until you reach a large, open, flat spot surrounded by impressive mountains. It is best to stop here since travel any further will take you into terrain that

requires glacier travel experience. This is a lovely place to break out the thermos and sandwiches and enjoy the view. Skiing back down the creekbed is fun but the plod across the lake at the end of the day can be a little tedious.

Of Historical Interest
The Plain of Six Glaciers sits in the centre of some of the greatest mountain scenery in Canada. Above you tower Mounts Lefroy and Victoria. These two peaks were first climbed in August, 1897 by a strong international team of climbers led by Swiss guide Peter Sarbach. This was the beginning of the long tradition of mountain guiding in Canada. The upper walls of Lefroy and Victoria are hung with glaciers and ice walls. Perhaps you will be lucky enough to see an ice avalanche thunder its way to the valley bottom.

69 WHITEHORN TRAILS

Grade Easy/intermediate
Distance 6.4 km of trails
Time The loops can be skied in a few hours
Height gain 75 m
Max elevation 1670 m
Map Lake Louise 82 N/8

These trails meander through the forest and are short and pleasant. Unfortunately, the noise emanating from the ski resort spoils the experience somewhat.

Access From the Trans Canada Highway at Lake Louise follow the signs for the Lake Louise Ski Resort (Skiing Louise). Park at the farthest end (the northeast corner) of parking lot #4.

The trail starts at the extreme right hand (northeast) end of the parking lot next to the complex of maintenance sheds and trailers. It initially descends for a few metres then divides into two branches. It makes little difference whether you chose the right or left hand branch. You can do the loop of trail #1 which is an easy trail or you can combine this loop with trail #2 to make a longer tour. Trail #2 is only marginally harder. The trail is almost completely in the trees and only occasionally does one get a glimpse of Mount Whitehorn above. The trails are well marked with numbers but care should be taken in following them, particularly after a heavy snowfall, as it would be easy to get lost once you are in the woods. The trails are usually packed and sometimes trackset.

Facilities The Lodge of the Ten Peaks at Skiing Louise is nearby providing washrooms, telephones and restaurants.

Hazards Be careful not to lose your bearings in the woods as it all looks much the same once you get started. Note that Parks Canada is completely revamping their cross country ski trails near Lake Louise and the trail numbers may change in the near future.

Of Historical Interest

The roots of the mammoth ski development now know as Skiing Louise began when Skoki Lodge opened in the spring of 1931. The first guests skied all the way from the train station at Laggan (about 20 km). Temple Lodge hosted its first guests in 1939 and the following year the Lake Louise Ski Lodge (now called the Post Hotel) opened its doors. Up to this point skiing at Lake Louise was a self propelled affair.

In the 1950s this all began to change. In 1952 the first ski tow was installed near Temple Lodge and two years later the Larch Pomalift was built. In 1959 the gondola lift to Whitehorn was opened and since then the growth of the ski area has been phenomenal. It is heartening to note that it now requires an Act of Parliament to extend the boundaries of ski resorts within the National Park.

70 PIPESTONE TRAILS

Grade Mainly easy with one intermediate trail
Distance There are 21 km of trails
Time You can ski for a few hours or all day if you like
Height gain 120 m between the low point and the high point of the trail system.
Max elevation 1670 m
Map Lake Louise 82 N/8

The Pipestone Trails offer good skiing for beginner and expert alike. It is a great place to get a few hours of fresh air if you have limited time. The trails are all easy with the exception of trail #5 which has some steep hills and is graded intermediate. Note that Parks Canada is in the process of revamping the ski trails around Lake Louise and the number system may be changed in the near future. Contact the Park Information Centre for up to date information.

Hazards Trail #5 should be avoided if you are not a strong skier or if conditions are icy. It is easy to get turned around when you are skiing these trails so keep a close check on your progress at each intersection.

Access Turn north off the Trans Canada Highway 0.7 km west of the Lake Louise overpass and follow the signs. The road climbs uphill for several hundred metres then turns right into a parking lot.

The Pipestone network comprises five numbered trails. Trail #1 is 12.6 km, trail #2 is 2.8 km, trail #3 is 2.1 km, trail #4 is 1.9 km and trail #5 is 1.5 km. The trails run through a mix of forest and meadows. The open area around the unnamed lake along the west arm of trail #1 is an excellent spot for a sunny lunch break. There are few hills of any steepness on trails #1-4, however, the way the trails are laid out it is almost continually uphill when skiing north (away from the parking lot) and then a thrilling downhill run on the way back. The last portion of trail #1 (west branch) is a little confusing where it works its way through the horse barns. The view of the Lake Louise peaks across Mud Lake on trail #5 is excellent.

Skiing the Pipestone Trails. Photo Alf Skrastins.

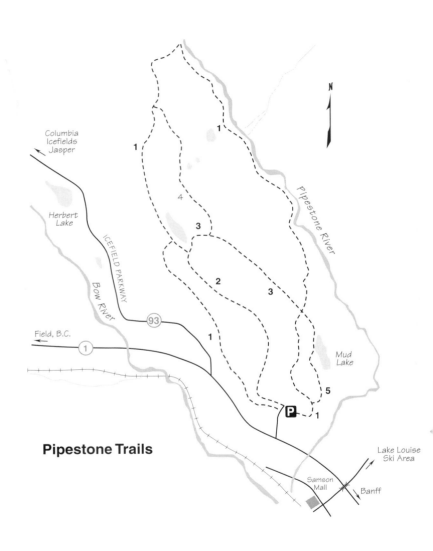

Columbia
Icefields
Jasper

Herbert
Lake

Pipestone River

Bow River

ICEFIELD PARKWAY

93

Field, B.C.

1

Mud
Lake

P

1

5

1

Pipestone Trails

Lake Louise
Ski Area

Samson
Mall

Banff

N

1

1

4

3

2

3

71 HIDDEN BOWL

Grade Easy
Distance 8 km return (from Temple Lodge)
Time 4-6 hours return (from Temple Lodge)
Height gain 250 m to Hidden Lake
Max elevation 2270 m
Map Lake Louise 82 N/8

The tour to Hidden Bowl is a delightful trip in beautiful surroundings. It passes the historic Ptarmigan Hut, sometimes known as Halfway Hut. Once in Hidden Bowl there is opportunity to make a few turns on the slopes of Richardson Ridge. The view down the valley to the Lake Louise peaks is outstanding.

Facilities Washrooms, telephones and restaurants can be found at Temple Lodge.

Access Take the exit from the Trans Canada Highway at Lake Louise and proceed up the hill towards the Lake Louise Ski Resort. After 1.5 km turn right and drive 1 km to the Fish Creek parking lot. If you are a guest at Skoki Lodge you can catch a bus to Temple Lodge. If not you will have to ski up the 'ski out' for 3 km to Mount Temple Lodge. This 'ski out' trail crosses the road beside the Fish Creek parking lot. As an alternative it is possible to buy a one trip lift ticket which will take you from the Lodge of the Ten Peaks to the top of Mount Whitehorn and from here you can ski down to Temple Lodge.

The trail starts just beyond the bus drop off point at the Temple Ski Area, about 100 m up the hill from the lodge. It heads northeast, through the trees, along the east flank of the valley. The trail is usually well packed because the

snowmobile travels along here taking supplies to Skoki Lodge. The trail runs for about 2 km through the trees then it breaks out into the open valley bottom. After a short distance the Halfway Hut can be seen about 100 m off to your left across the other side of Corral Creek (the hut is marked incorrectly on the map—it is really on the north side of Corral Creek, in the angle formed with Hidden Creek).

From the hut head northwest directly up Hidden Creek. After about 0.5 km the terrain starts to open up and there is some pleasant skiing on moderate angled slopes to your left. From these slopes (called Richardson Ridge) you can get good views of Mount Richardson, Pika Peak and Ptarmigan Peak.

The return trip is a fun downhill run. You can make it all the way back to your car at the Fish Creek parking lot with only the occasional section of uphill work.

72 PURPLE BOWL

Ski touring 2

Grade Intermediate
Distance 6 km return (from Temple Lodge)
Time 4-6 hours
Height gain 500 m
Max elevation 2500 m
Map Lake Louise 82 N/8

The Purple Bowl tour is an excellent way to get away from it all and up into alpine terrain for a few hours. This is the original Purple Bowl which was popular with skiers back in the 30s and 40s. Nowadays lift addicted folks often refer to the bowl between Larch Hill and Silvertip Ridge as 'Purple Bowl' because that is the bowl that

they can access from the top of the Larch Chair without having to walk. But it is not the true Purple Bowl and was originally called Wolverine Bowl and Wolverine Valley by the early ski pioneers.

Facilities Washrooms, telephones and restaurants are available at Temple Lodge.

Hazards The slopes of Silvertip Ridge on the southwest side of Purple Bowl are attractive and can offer some good skiing. However, they are sufficiently large and steep enough to offer serious avalanche potential. They should be treated with respect.

Access The trail begins at Temple Lodge. See Hidden Bowl (page 119) for details on how to reach the lodge.

The route begins about 100 m up the hill from Temple Lodge, along the trail which goes to Halfway Hut and on to Skoki. Follow the trail for several hundred metres then angle up to the right on a man made cut through the trees (there are often tracks here and the trail may be packed). The trail angles up and curves to the right, heading almost due east into Purple Valley. It runs high above a stream and after about 1 km breaks out of the trees into the open. You can now meander up the open valley, with Silvertip Ridge on your right, towards the high alpine terrain of Purple Bowl at the end. It is possible to ski several kilometres to attain a high pass from where you can look down on Baker Creek far below. There are some gentle slopes up here to make turns on. This is indeed a glorious spot on a sunny day.

On the ridge above Purple Bowl.
Photo Alf Skrastins.

73 BATH CREEK

Ski touring 1

Grade Easy/intermediate
Distance 14 km return
Time A full day tour
Height gain 210 m
Max elevation 1820 m
Map Lake Louise 82 N/8

This tour follows a creek bed and so requires a good cover of snow. Save it for later in the year. There are good views of Mounts Bosworth and Daly.

Access The parking lot is located on the north side of the Trans Canada Highway, 9 km west of Lake Louise, just before the highway cross a bridge over Bath Creek.

From the parking lot head north toward the railway tracks, skiing just beside Bath Creek. Take off your skis and cross both sets of tracks. From here you have two

Early season along Bath Creek.

choices for the first portion of this tour. You can either follow a trail along the bank of the creek, just in the edge of the trees, or you can follow the trail which heads through the forest straight ahead. After about 100 m take the branch to the left which brings you down to the creek. Both trails connect here and continue along the edge of the forest, beside the creek, for about 1 km. The trail now breaks out into the creek bed and for the next 3 km travels easily and pleasantly up the creek. It then opens up and the tour continues up the gravel flats for another 2 km.

Gradually, the flats narrow in and the route takes to the right bank of the creek for a short distance before crossing to the left bank where it stays for the remainder of the tour. About 1 km up the creek from the gravel flats you reach a canyon. This can be avoided by climbing up on the left into the trees, then descending back to the creek after a short distance. Follow the creek for another kilometre until it becomes a canyon again. This is a good place to stop for lunch and end the tour.

Fossil Mountain from just above Deception Pass. Photo Alan Kane.

SKOKI AREA

Skoki is one of the most popular areas for cross country skiing in the Rockies. There are plenty of trails, outstanding scenery and good snow. In the heart of it all is historic Skoki Lodge, a delightful place to relax for a few days and enjoy the Canadian backcountry ski experience.

Access From the overpass at the Lake Louise townsite on the Trans Canada Highway drive 1.6 km towards the Lake Louise Ski Resort. Turn right onto the Temple Lodge access road and continue for 1 km to the Fish Creek parking lot.

If you are a lodge guest a small bus will take you from here to Temple Lodge. Otherwise you will likely have to ski 3 km up the 'ski out' which passes right by the Fish Creek parking lot.

From Temple Lodge it is possible to ski to Skoki in the morning, have a cup of tea, then return to your car before dark. It is a better idea to stay overnight at the lodge and savour the old time ambiance.

History Skoki Lodge was one of the earliest ski lodges in the Canadian Rockies. It was built in the autumn of 1930 by Earl Spencer for Cliff White and Cyril Paris and opened for business the following spring. The lodge was enlarged to its present form in 1936. During its heyday, in the 1930s and 40s, the world came to Skoki to experience the magic of winter in the Canadian Rockies. In those days people skied all the way from Laggan Station (at the Lake Louise townsite) to Skoki, sometimes overnighting at Halfway Hut.

There is a magic world of ski history associated with Skoki Lodge. The first ski guides in the region, Vic Kutschera and Herman Gadner worked here. The first avalanche fatalities in the region occurred near Skoki: Raymond 'Kit' Paley was killed on Fossil Mountain in 1933 and Herman Gadner on Mount Richardson in 1945. Their ghosts are said to play cards at night in Halfway Hut.

Read all about this fascinating story in *Skoki: Beyond the Passes* by Kathryn Manry, published by Rocky Mountain Books, 2001.

Breakfast at Skoki Lodge.

Skoki Lodge.

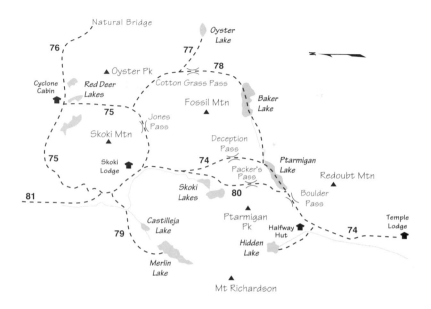

Skoki Lodge

A delightful log lodge which has been in continuous operation since 1931.
Location Beneath the west flank of Skoki Mountain along the right bank of Skoki Creek (GR 642082).
Map Hector Lake 82 N/9
Facilities A central lodge surrounded by several guest cabins. Not much has changed at Skoki since the thirties and this is a great place to step back in time and experience our romantic past. Heating is still by wood and coal stoves (supplemented by propane) and, after dark, lighting is provided by coal oil lamps and candles. Outdoor plumbing. There is a small, rustic sauna. Radio telephone for emergency use.
Capacity 22
Hosts Leo and Katie Mitzel
Cost About $140 per person. All meals provided.
Reservations Write: Skoki Lodge, Box 5, Lake Louise, Alberta, T0L 1E0 Email: skoki@skilouise.com Website: www.skilouise.com/skoki Phone: 403-522-3555 (best to phone between 1:00 pm and 5:00 pm when the rush of skiers is over for the day) Fax: 403-522-2095
Note! A minimum stay of two nights is required.

74 SKOKI VIA BOULDER AND DECEPTION PASSES   Ski touring 1

Grade Intermediate
Distance 11 km one way (from Temple Lodge)
Time 4-5 hours one way
Height gain 540 m
Max elevation 2510 m
Maps Lake Louise 82 N/8
Hector Lake 82 N/9

The tour to Skoki is a classic and local skiers find that they repeat this trip over and over as the years pass by. The scenery is outstanding, the trail is interesting but not too difficult and the lodge at Skoki is a marvellous place, rich in history. You can get a hot drink here before skiing back to your car. It is highly recommended that you stay several nights and discover the roots of our skiing heritage.

Facilities There are toilets, telephones and a restaurant at Temple Lodge. Halfway Hut is located several kilometres up the trail from Temple Lodge. It is a bare bones structure with no stove. It can provide shelter on a windy day but is not intended for overnight

use. Skoki Lodge has a radio telephone for emergency use.

Hazards This tour takes you through avalanche country. Although there is little danger if you stay on the correct trail, you must be careful not to stray onto surrounding terrain which may not be safe. This is backcountry skiing and you should be prepared to deal with emergencies. Crossing Ptarmigan Lake on your return journey can be difficult if the wind is blowing in your face.

Options There are a number of lovely trails in the vicinity of Skoki Lodge.

On the return trip it is a pleasant alternative to ski through Jones Pass and around Fossil Mountain, through Cottongrass Pass and across Baker Lake to regain the trail at Ptarmigan Lake.

If you are really ambitious it is possible to descend Skoki Creek to Little Pipestone Creek and then down to the Pipestone River which can be followed back to Lake Louise (see page 134).

Halfway Hut is located at the entrance to Hidden Valley. It was built in 1931 and is now rumoured to be the home of the ghost of Raymond 'Kit' Paley who was one of the first ski fatality in the Rockies. He was avalanched on the slopes of Fossil Mountain in 1933.

Skiing from Temple Lodge toward Boulder Pass. In the distance Mount Temple and Valley of the Ten Peaks.

Access Park at the Fish Creek parking lot. This can be reached by taking the exit from the Trans Canada Highway and proceeding up the road towards the Lake Louise Ski Resort. After 1.6 km turn right onto the Temple Lodge access road. Follow this for 1 km to the Fish Creek parking lot which will be on your right. If you are a lodge guest a small bus will take you to Temple Lodge. Otherwise you will likely have to ski up the 'ski out' which passes by the parking lot. This will add another 3 km each way to your tour.

From the bus drop-off point near Temple Lodge continue up the snow covered road and across the Larch Run, about 100 m up the hill from Temple Lodge. The trail to Skoki heads into the woods on the far side. Just a few metres after starting along the trail another trail branches down to the left. Do not take this trail. Continue straight ahead, crossing some open areas, for about 2 km gradually gaining height. The trail is normally well packed and easy to follow because of the passage of the snowmobile transporting supplies to Skoki. Eventually the trail breaks out of the woods into a large open meadow with beautiful views all around. Over on the left, on a small hill above the creek, is Halfway Hut.

Continue up the valley, staying generally toward the left side and at the end climb a moderately steep hill to Boulder Pass. It is best to stop for a last bite to eat and a drink in the trees before Boulder Pass as there is no protection from the wind beyond here for a long ways.

Cross the lake then climb 180 vertical metres to Deception Pass which is above to the left. It is a good idea to stop and put your skins on unless your wax is working really well.

From Deception Pass it is a fun run down to Skoki Lodge. The trail is well marked at the start with large stakes. From the pass the trail continues north across the slopes of Fossil Mountain following open terrain, then angles left down into the trees. The trail through the trees to the lodge is often packed by the snowmobile and is easy to follow. The lodge is located on the right bank of Skoki Creek beneath the slopes of Skoki Mountain.

75 SKOKI MOUNTAIN LOOP

Grade Intermediate
Distance 9 km loop
Time 4-5 hours
Height gain 80 m
Max elevation 2200 m
Map Hector Lake 82 N/9

This is an interesting trail that can be started after a leisurely breakfast and still bring you back to the lodge in plenty of time for afternoon tea. The trail can be skied in either direction, the prime consideration being the steep hill rounding the northwest side of Skoki Mountain. It is challenging and is a personal choice whether you want to struggle up it or swoop down it. One can always take the skis off and walk.

Facilities The Cyclone Warden Cabin can be visited on this trip, however, it will be locked. Unfortunately the historic old cabin was removed by Parks Canada and this modern one left in its place.

Options This trail can be combined with a trip to the Natural Bridge (see opposite page).

Access The trail begins and ends at Skoki Lodge.

From the lodge head south, up the valley. Within a hundred metres the trail curves round to the left and climbs slightly through the trees up to Jones Pass. Descend the other side at a gentle angle, staying to the left. Do not linger on these large avalanche paths. Continue down the draw for about a kilometre then through the trees to reach a large open meadow at Red Deer Lakes. The Cyclone Cabin is across the far side of the meadow up against the forest. This is a good spot to relax and enjoy a cup of tea and a sandwich.

You can return to Skoki Lodge around the north side of Skoki Mountain. From the Cyclone Cabin ski west along the meadows staying at first on the right (north) side of the valley. The trail then crosses the open meadow and enters the forest on the south side of the valley. This spot is a little tricky to spot so watch closely for a piece of flagging hanging from a tree. From here the trail makes its way through trees and open glades on the north side of Skoki Mountain. It then descends steeply down to Skoki Creek near the campground. From here it is a gentle uphill ski through the forest to Skoki Lodge.

Returning to Skoki Lodge after skiing Skoki Mountain Loop.

Crossing meadows near Red Deer Lakes, looking toward Mount Hector.

76 NATURAL BRIDGE
Ski touring 1

Grade Easy
Distance 16 km return
Time 5-6 hours
Height gain 80 m
Max elevation 2200 m
Map Hector Lake 82 N/9
Barrier Mountain 82 O/12

This trail is an extension of the tour around Skoki Mountain. It is a little longer and provides a full day ski. The destination is a natural rock bridge at the end of a small valley behind Oyster Peak.

Facilities The Cyclone Warden Cabin (locked) can be visited on this trip.

Hazards A map and some proficiency in reading it can be very helpful on this tour. In the vicinity of Red Deer Lakes, where several valleys meet, it can be difficult to decide which one to follow.

Access The trail begins and ends at Skoki Lodge.

Follow the Skoki Mountain Loop as far as the Cyclone Warden Cabin. From here continue east down the Red Deer River for several kilometres, then work your way to the right through the woods and over into the drainage behind Oyster Mountain. An alternative is to follow the summer trail from the Cyclone Cabin along the hillside, down the left hand side of the valley, to a trail junction. Turn right on a branch trail which goes to the Natural Bridge. The trail up the small valley to the Natural Bridge can be hard to follow. Towards the end follow the creek bed up to the Natural Bridge. Return to Cyclone Cabin then follow either wing of the Skoki Mountain Loop back to Skoki Lodge.

77 OYSTER LAKE

Ski touring 3

Grade Easy/intermediate
Distance 12 km return
Time 4-5 hours
Height gain 150 m
Max elevation 2290 m
Map Hector Lake 82 N/9

This is a very pleasant tour, through open terrain, to a scenic destination. There is even a thrilling bit of skiing coming back down the creek bed from the lake to Cottongrass Pass.

Hazards When you round the corner of Fossil Mountain do not try to cut high but take the low trail through the trees, it is much safer.

Options This tour can be combined with the Fossil Mountain Loop.

Access The trail begins and ends at Skoki Lodge.

From Skoki Lodge head south up the valley. Within a hundred metres the trail curves to the left and heads up, through the trees, to Jones Pass. Descend at a very gentle angle down the other side, staying to the left. Do not linger on these large avalanche paths. Ski down the draw keeping your eye out for flagging and a sign marking a trail to the right. This trail works its way up and right through the trees and out into the open again. Ski across the open meadows to Cottongrass Pass below the drainage coming down from Oyster Lake. You can either ski up the drainage or ascend the sparsely treed shoulder on the right. Near the top climb the drainage itself, up an open slope to the right, then cut sharply to the left and over a little notch to the lake.

Of Historical Interest

Cliff White, a great ski pioneer of the Canadian Rockies, was one of the first to see the ski potential of the region. With his brothers Peter and Jack he founded the Banff Ski Club in 1917, and in 1928 formed the Mount Norquay Ski Club, building a cabin on the mountain that same year. With Cyril Paris in 1930 he established legendary Skoki Lodge and, eight years later, Temple Chalet. Here he spent many years guiding and introducing skiers to our Canadian mountains. His son is quoted as saying "He was ahead of his time, a primary force in bringing skiing as a successful business to the Canadian Rockies." Banff historian Ted Hart said of Cliff, "There were lots of people in the 1930s who enjoyed skiing, but he actually made it his life's work...." All of us today benefit from Cliff White's pioneering vision.

Cliff White, ski pioneer. Courtesy Whyte Museum.

78 FOSSIL MOUNTAIN LOOP

Grade Intermediate
Distance 11 km loop
Time 5-6 hours
Height gain 300 m
Max elevation 2470 m
Maps Lake Louise 82 N/8
Hector lake 82 N/9

This is perhaps the most challenging tour from Skoki Lodge and will take a good part of the day to complete. Some experience with routefinding and map reading is an asset. There will probably be some trail breaking across open areas because they drift over easily in the wind. This tour can be skied in either direction.

Hazards There is some avalanche potential on this tour and you should be knowledgeable and prepared for emergencies.

Options This tour can be combined with a trip to Oyster Lake. It can also be used as an optional return route from Skoki to Temple Lodge.

Access The trail begins and ends at Skoki Lodge.

Follow the Oyster Lake tour (see opposite page) as far as Cottongrass Pass. From here work your way around to the right through open trees to reach Baker Lake at its northeast corner. Ski across the lake then climb the headwall at the west end to the flats above, being sure to stay away from the steep slopes on the right. Climb up the lower angled slopes towards Deception Pass high on the right. From the pass ski north across the slopes of Fossil Mountain following stakes driven into the snow, then descend down and to the left into the valley. Follow the snowmobile track along the valley down to Skoki Lodge.

Of Historical Interest

Skoki Lodge has been the home of many colourful characters over the years. One of the first was Sir Norman Watson, a British Baronet. He was an early shareholder in the Ski Club of the Canadian Rockies which owned Skoki Lodge and by the late 1930s had become the major shareholder. He had dreams of turning the Lake Louise, Temple and Skoki areas into a little Switzerland, complete with cows in the meadows.

One of the most wonderful individuals to have been associated with Skoki Lodge was Lizzie Rummel who ran the lodge from 1943 to 1949. Her personality, her generosity and her love of the mountains was eventually rewarded with The Order of Canada in April of 1980.

Ken Jones first came to Skoki Lodge in 1936 to work on the second story addition. It was Ken who brought the 60 foot ridge pole over from Red Deer Lakes. For many years during the 30s, 40s and 50s he worked as a guide at Skoki Lodge. Ken loved to tell stories and for decades he entertained guests at Skoki Lodge with his tales of pioneer days in the Canadian Rockies.

79 MERLIN VALLEY

Grade Advanced
Distance 6 km return
Time 3-4 hours
Height gain 210 m
Max elevation 2230 m
Map Hector Lake 82 N/9

A challenging trail which takes you into a beautiful high valley. There is excellent terrain for making turns in the upper Merlin Valley. The climb from the meadows to Lake Merlin is steep and difficult and requires some route finding.

Hazards This trail is very demanding and only experienced skiers will be able to handle the descent back down from Lake Merlin.

If you plan on skiing the slopes above Lake Merlin be aware that you are in potential avalanche terrain and should be prepared accordingly.

Access The trail begins and ends at Skoki Lodge.

Ski down the trail north of Skoki Lodge to the meadows. Turn left and cross the meadows in a southwest direction for several hundred metres then climb up on the right bank at a very large and tall tree. Continue across an open avalanche path, then work your way into the trees. After several hundred metres the trail begins to climb to the right up an open area with sparse trees. The angle is very steep but eventually eases off and the trail cuts left into the trees where it continues to climb but at a more moderate rate. There are numerous blazes along here which makes it relatively easy to follow the trail. It climbs up to the base of some cliffs then traverses left across very steep terrain (in the trees) just below them. After a few hundred metres the terrain flattens out. If you are only going to the lake you can reach it easily now by a short descent down to the left. If your destination is Merlin Ridge then continue climbing and angling up to the right.

Alternative Ascent Route: Cross the meadows to the furthest southwest end then climb an open slope on the right (this is a rock slide in the summer). From the top traverse left to Castilleja Lake. Climb the treed slope above the lake, working your way up by traversing back and forth through the trees. Traverse left (west) to Lake Merlin when you are high enough.

The real problem with both these ascents is the steep descent back down afterwards. Neither are easy.

Opposite: Throughout the 1930s, 40s and 50s all the supplies for Skoki were packed in on the backs of men. The loads were often very heavy, up to 35 kg, and the wages were poor—a dollar a day at the start. But it was a good life out in the open air, skiing and enjoying all that beauty around you. Two of the early packers and guides were Sam Evans (left) and Ken Jones. The legend says that they carried loads into Skoki from Lake Louise for 65 days straight one year. Packers Pass is a more direct route to and from Skoki and it may be that these fellows used it to save a little time.
Photo Karen McDairmid.

80 PACKERS PASS

Grade Intermediate
Distance 11 km from Skoki to Temple Lodge
Time 3-4 hours
Height gain 300 m
Max elevation 2470 m
Map Lake Louise 82 N/8
Hector Lake 82 N/9

An interesting variation offering a slightly more direct way from Skoki back to Temple Lodge. It takes the pass between Packers Peak and Ptarmigan Peak just west of Deception Pass. It is more difficult than Deception Pass and is subject to some avalanche risk.

Facilities There are facilities at either end of the trip (Temple Lodge or Skoki Lodge) and there is the rustic Halfway Hut in the middle.

Hazards This tour is subject to significant avalanche hazard and should be undertaken only by experienced backcountry skiers.

Access This tour begins at Skoki Lodge.

From Skoki Lodge start up the trail towards Deception Pass. In less than a kilometre turn right up the creek that drains Skoki Lakes. Direct access to the lakes is blocked by cliffs so one must climb the small drainage to the left, below Packers Peak, then cut back to the right above the cliffs. Rather than descending along the bench back down to Skoki Lakes, angle up and over the shoulder of Packers Peak, then make a rising traverse high on the northwest slope of Packers Peak up to Packers Pass. Descend the other side easily, down a ramp to the southwest, to Ptarmigan Lake. Here you rejoin the regular trail from Skoki back to Temple Lodge.

81 SKOKI TO LAKE LOUISE VIA PIPESTONE RIVER   Ski touring 1

Grade Intermediate
Distance 24 km one way
Time This tour normally takes all day
Height loss 600 m
Max elevation 2160 m at Skoki Lodge
Maps Lake Louise 82 N/8
Hector Lake 82 N/9

This tour offers an alternative way to ski from Skoki Lodge back to Lake Louise. It is a long tour and trail breaking will be

required. It is a full day trip for most of us and in deep snow might be even more than that. The Pipestone Valley is wide and beautiful and the solitude is wonderful—it is unlikely that you will run into any other parties.

Hazards If the snow is deep and you anticipate that you will be breaking trail give yourself plenty of time.

Access The tour begins at Skoki Lodge and ends at the parking lot for the Pipestone Trails (see page 117).

From Skoki Lodge follow the trail heading north down Skoki Creek. After about 1 km, at the meadows, ski through the campground and carry on straight ahead (do not take the trail which climbs up to the right over to Red Deer lakes). Carry on down Skoki Creek on a good trail which is well flagged at first. Stay on the right bank a short distance above the creek. The trail descends steeply for another kilometre then flattens out. Continue along the gentle valley bottom through the trees on the right side of the creek. After about one more kilometre the valley begins to open up as you reach Little Pipestone Creek and it is best to simply follow the creek bed.

Cross some large open meadows with huge avalanche paths above on the right and then climb up onto the right bank of the creek where you will find a very clear and well defined trail through the trees. Follow this trail easily for about

2 km until it starts to descend. The trail drops steeply for a short distance then levels out and you leave the trees and enter an open meadow.

From here the trail is tricky to follow although there are a large number of blazes on the trees. Head west, doing your best to follow the blazes, through the trees, to the junction with the Pipestone River. You could also head for Little Pipestone Creek and follow it down to the junction with the Pipestone River. Along this section of the tour it might be advisable to pull your compass out and follow it if necessary. From the junction of Little Pipestone Creek and the Pipestone River head down the Pipestone River across beautiful open meadows for about 5 km. Eventually the trees close in and the meadow narrows but it is still best to follow the river itself for another 7 km. About 6 km before reaching the highway look for the Pipestone Trails up on the right bank of the Pipestone River—they are easy to miss. Ski down the Pipestone Trails back to your waiting car at the parking lot.

Rest stop in the remote Pipestone Valley.

GETTING IN SOME TURNS AT SKOKI

Ski touring 2

All of these areas present avalanche risk. Exercise caution at all times.

Packers Pass
The Northwest flank of Packers Peak, above Zigadenus Lake, offers excellent skiing on a slope of about 300 vertical metres. See the tour to Packers Pass (page 133).

Merlin Ridge
The slopes above Lake Merlin offer excellent opportunities for making turns on moderate terrain. The descent is about 360 vertical metres from top to bottom. This area is tricky to reach due to the steep climb from the valley up to the lake. See the tour to Merlin Valley (page 132).

Wolverine Slopes
These slopes are found low down on the west flank of Fossil Mountain. They are just above the trail from Skoki Lodge to Deception Pass. They are short but offer some entertaining skiing.

Skoki Valley
Good terrain to make turns can be found in several locations near the lodge:
- Just above the lodge on the slopes of Skoki Mountain there are opportunities for tree skiing. In fact years ago runs were actually cleared and groomed up here.
- There is some open glade skiing across from Skoki Lodge, in the trees at the base of the Wall of Jericho.

YOHO NATIONAL PARK

82 Sherbrooke Lake	intermediate/advanced	p. 140
83 Ross Lake Circuit	intermediate	p. 140
84 Lake O'Hara Fire Road	easy	p. 141
85 Lake O'Hara Circuit	easy	p. 143
86 McArthur Pass	intermediate	p. 143
87 Morning Glory Lakes	intermediate	p. 144
88 Opabin/Wenkchemna Circuit	advanced	p. 145
89 Yoho Valley Road	easy	p. 147
90 Little Yoho Valley	intermediate/advanced	p. 148
91 Kiwetinok Pass	easy	p. 150
92 Field to Emerald lake	intermediate	p. 151
93 Emerald Lake Trails	easy	p. 153
94 Kickinghorse Trail	easy	p. 154
95 Amiskwi Fire Road to Amiskwi Pass	easy	p. 154
96 Ottertail Valley Fire Road	easy	p. 155
97 Chancellor Peak Campground	easy	p. 155
98 Ice River Fire Road	easy	p. 156
99 Wapta Falls	intermediate	p. 157

Yoho Park offers some of the finest ski touring in the Rocky Mountains and sees a lot of activity. There are two ACC huts and a commercial lodge in the park which provide a wonderful backcountry ski experience. The park gets lots of snow, has spectacular scenery and has a long tradition of ski activity. In fact The Alpine Club of Canada ran its first ski camp at Lake O'Hara in 1936 and almost every year through the 1940s ran a ski camp in the Little Yoho Valley. These two areas are now amongst the most popular in the Rockies. In addition the Wapta Icefields straddle the continental divide between Banff and Yoho Parks.

Access The Trans Canada Highway traverses Yoho Park as it makes its way from Lake Louise to Golden. This road is the main highway across Canada and is kept in top condition in all weather. The only town in the park is Field located along the Trans Canada Highway 26 km west of Lake Louise.

Facilities The town of Field offers limited facilities. There is a service station along the highway and a small hotel in town. There are several bed and breakfasts, a liquor store, post office and a small grocery store. Emerald Lake Lodge (250- 343-6321) offers luxurious accommodation with ski trails starting right from the door. It is reached via a spur road which turns off the highway 2.5 km west of town. Ten km east of Field is West Louise Lodge (sometimes known as Wapta Lodge) with a gas station, hotel, restaurant and lounge.

Information There is a Parks Canada Information Centre along the Trans Canada Highway at the entrance to Field. The Warden Office is located at the Boulder Creek maintenance compound, 5.5 km west of Field.

Lake O'Hara is world famous for its summer hiking trails. It is also a beautiful destination for ski touring in the winter although some of the trails are not suitable for skiing. The region is so beautiful that many people come here simply to look and enjoy the grandeur of the mountains. There are, however, several trails which can be skied safely and Lake O'Hara Lodge and the Elizabeth Parker hut are very popular in winter.

The Little Yoho Valley also offers great ski touring potential. In fact this valley has been the scene of ACC ski camps for six decades. Much of the skiing is up high in alpine terrain but there are also some Nordic tours lower down. The presence of the Stanley Mitchell Hut makes this the perfect location for a ski holiday. It is always a treat at the end of a hard tour to return to a hut and warm yourself around the fire.

Lake O'Hara Lodge

This luxurious lodge was built in the 1920s and today offers a truly comfortable winter experience.
Location On the west shore of Lake O'Hara (GR 463895)
Map Lake Louise 82 N/8
Facilities In the winter only the central lodge is open offering guest rooms, lounge area, dining room, indoor plumbing and central heating.
Capacity 16 in winter
Hosts Bruce and Alison Miller
Cost About $200 per person. All meals and guiding service provided.
Reservations Lake O'Hara Lodge, Box 55, Lake Louise, Alberta, T0L 1E0 Website: www.lakeohara.com Phone: 250-343-6418 (mid-June to September 30, mid-January to mid-April) or 403-678-4110 (off season).

Elizabeth Parker Hut

A beautiful log building surrounded by some of the most spectacular peaks in the world.
Location In a meadow about 500 m west of Lake O'Hara (GR 457893).
Map Lake Louise 82 N/8
Facilities Fully equipped with foamies, cooking and eating utensils, propane cook stoves and lanterns, and a wood heating stove.
Capacity 20 in winter
Water In winter water can often be found flowing in the creek about 100 m east of the hut.
Reservations The Alpine Club of Canada 403-678-3200
Note! This hut is locked when no custodian is present and a combination number is required.

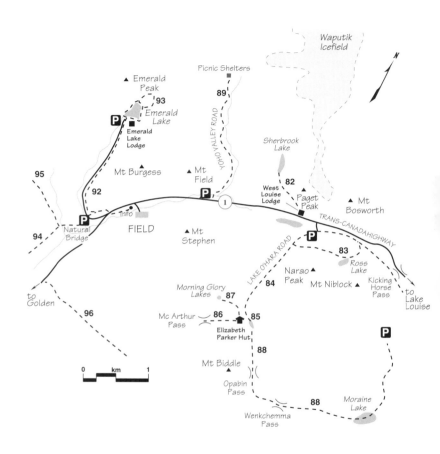

Stanley Mitchell Hut

This delightful log hut sits on the edge of a meadow in a high alpine valley. Out the front window is a spectacular view of the President Range.

Location At the edge of the trees, about 100 m back from the right bank of the creek, near the head of the Little Yoho Valley (GR 303082).

Map Blaeberry River 82 N/10

Facilities Fully equipped with foamies, cooking and eating utensils, propane cook stoves and lanterns, and a wood heating stove.

Capacity 22 in winter

Water From the creek directly south of the hut (you must dig down in the snow).

Reservations The Alpine Club of Canada 403-678-3200

Note! This hut is locked when no custodian is present and a combination number is required.

Ski pioneer Hans Gmoser at the Stanley Mitchell hut in the 1950s. Photo Leo Grillmair collection.

Stanley Mitchell hut under a heavy snow load.

82 SHERBROOKE LAKE

Ski touring 1

Grade Intermediate/advanced
Distance 6 km return
Time 3 hours return
Height gain 180 m
Max elevation 1800 m
Map Lake Louise 82 N/8

A steep and challenging trail. If it is icy or rutted it is even more difficult. However, Sherbrooke Lake is a beautiful destination and the trail is popular.

Facilities West Louise Lodge is at the trailhead with toilets, telephones and a restaurant.

Hazards The trail is marked incorrectly on the topographical map.

Options Sherbrooke Lake is the usual exit from the Wapta Icefields. The descent from the Scott Duncan Hut (see page 183) can be skied in reverse to reach the icefields.

Access Park at West Louise Lodge which is located on the north side of the Trans Canada Highway near the summit of Kickinghorse Pass, 10 km east of Field.

The trail begins behind the lodge and immediately climbs up and left through the trees. Most of the tour climbs at a moderately steep angle across the slopes of Paget Peak and the trail can be hard to follow in some places. After 2 km the trail rounds the shoulder of the peak, breaks out of the trees, and continues easily through the open area along the creek to the lake.

83 ROSS LAKE CIRCUIT

Ski touring 1

Grade Intermediate
Distance 9 km loop
Time 3 hours
Height gain 200 m
Max elevation 1830 m
Map Lake Louise 82 N/8

This is an interesting tour that takes you to an impressive mountain cirque.

Facilities There are toilets at the Lake O'Hara Fire Road parking lot.

Access Turn south off the Trans Canada Highway, 2.5 km west of the Alberta/ B.C. border. Drive a short distance, cross the railway tracks then turn right down the hill for several hundred metres to the parking lot for the Lake O'Hara Fire Road.

Walk back up the entrance road for a short distance, turn right, put on your skis then ski along the old Highway 1A.

After about 2 km you will see a trail sign on the right for Ross Lake. Turn right and climb gradually up a trail through the forest for about 1.5 km to reach Ross Lake, surrounded by great mountain walls. Turn right (west) at the lake along another trail and continue for about 3 km to reach the Lake O'Hara Fire Road. Turn right along the road and ski about 2 km back to your car at the parking lot.

84 LAKE O'HARA FIRE ROAD

Ski touring 1

Grade Easy
Distance 24 km return
Time 3-4 hours to Lake O'Hara, the run back out takes about 2 hours
Height gain 430 m
Max elevation 2030 m
Map Lake Louise 82 N/8

This is a very popular tour and many folks stay overnight at Lake O'Hara Lodge or the Elizabeth Parker Hut. The trail requires little snow as it follows a road and the snow comes early. Often this tour can be skied by mid November. The route is very easy to follow and usually the trail is well packed.

Facilities Toilets at the parking lot.

Options At Lake O'Hara there are several pleasant tours to do. You can also continue over Opabin and Wenkchemna Passes to Lake Louise. On rare occasion folks continue to Marble Canyon on the Kootenay Highway or over McArthur Pass and out the Ottertail Fire Road.

Access Turn south off the Trans Canada Highway 2.5 km west of the Alberta/B.C. border onto a side road (the old 1A Highway). Cross the railway tracks then immediately turn right and drive a short distance down a hill to the parking lot.

The route to Lake O'Hara follows the snow covered summer road which leaves the parking lot at the near (east) end. To begin, the road climbs at a steady angle for about 2 km. For the next 5 km the road is level and all around you is impressive mountain scenery. Just before crossing the creek the road begins to climb again and gains elevation until just before the lake. The return trip can be quick and lots of fun particularly if the trail is packed and there are good tracks.

The first buildings you see as you reach the lake are the Warden Cabin on the left and the summer kiosk, called Le Relais, on the right. The lodge is just a few hundred metres beyond on the shore of the lake.

To reach the Elizabeth Parker Hut you must follow a trail which turns off right at Le Relais. At first the trail climbs steeply through the trees, then it crosses a crest, descends a short distance to the left and breaks out of the trees at the creek. Turn sharply to the right and follow along the edge of the creek to the

The road to Lake O'Hara

Lake O'Hara Lodge. Courtesy Lake O'Hara Lodge.

Crossing meadows near Schäffer Lake on the way to McArthur Pass.

85 LAKE O'HARA CIRCUIT

Ski touring 1

Grade Easy
Distance 2 km loop
Time 1 or 2 hours
Height gain Nil
Max elevation 2030 m
Map Lake Louise 82 N/8

A pleasant tour for skiers of all ability. There are no hills, the scenery is superb and you can spend a few hours revelling in the beauty of Lake O'Hara.

Hazards Be sure the lake is well frozen and covered with a deep layer of snow.

Access This trail begins and ends at Lake O'Hara Lodge.

From Lake O'Hara Lodge ski along the south side of the lake on the shoreline trail. As the trail rounds the east end of the lake beneath the cliffs it heads out onto the lake then returns to the lodge across the lake. Do not attempt to follow the shoreline trail on the north side of the lake as it is up on a small cliff above the lake and steer clear of the shoreline as there are avalanche slopes above.

86 MCARTHUR PASS

Ski touring 2

Grade Intermediate
Distance 4 km return from the Elizabeth Parker Hut
Time 3-4 hours return
Height gain 150 m
Max elevation 2210 m
Map Lake Louise 82 N/8

A delightful tour. It gets you up high with superb views of Mount Victoria across the valley. There is a pleasant little run back down the draw to the hut.

Options There is opportunity to make some turns on the slopes of Mount Odaray above the pass.

Hazards People often ski on the open slope above Schäffer Lake. While this slope does offer good skiing potential it is also very dangerous and has been the scene of several avalanche fatalities in the past.

Access This trail begins and ends at the Elizabeth Parker Hut.

From the back door of the Elizabeth Parker Hut ski straight ahead, just to the right of the trees. After about 150 metres you will find an open draw which leads up the hill. Ski up this draw, gaining about 150 metres in elevation, to reach the meadow beside Schäffer Lake. If it is early in the season it may be best to follow the trail through the trees to the left of the draw.

To reach McArthur Pass cross the meadow, aiming for the lowest point in the pass. Follow the drainage towards the pass for several hundred metres until the way is barred by a cliff band. Make several short switchbacks through the trees on the left of the drainage to get above the cliff then follow open terrain to the pass.

Some good ski terrain can be found to the north on the lower slopes of Mount Odaray. This is a great spot to sit in the sun and eat your lunch.

87 MORNING GLORY LAKES

Ski touring 1

Grade Intermediate
Distance 7 km return
Time This is an easy day tour
Height loss 40 m
Max elevation 2050 m
Map Lake Louise 82 N/8

An enjoyable tour that takes you into a deep cirque beneath the impressive northeast face of Mount Odaray. There is a long climb back up at the end of the day.

Hazards Do not attempt this trail when conditions are icy or crusty.

Access This tour begins and ends at the Elizabeth Parker Hut.

Ski north from the Elizabeth Parker Hut across the meadows then continue up a sparsely treed draw for a short distance to reach a crest. Just before the ground begins to drop away to the north turn left and locate a trail through the woods. This trail runs level for about 0.5 km then descends moderately steeply for about 1 km to Morning Glory Lakes. Note that you will need good grip wax or skins to get back up the hill again.

Setting out for Morning Glory Lakes from the Elizabeth Parker Hut. Photo Leon Kubbernus.

Returning at days end to the Elizabeth Parker Hut. Photo Markus Kellerhalls.

88 OPABIN/WENKCHEMNA CIRCUIT   Ski touring/ski mountaineering 3

Grade Advanced
Distance 24 km one way (Lake O'Hara to Lake Louise)
Time Some parties do this trip in a long, hard day. You can also overnight at the Elizabeth Parker Hut but that means carrying a sleeping bag.
Height gain 430 m from the highway to Lake O'Hara, 570 m from Lake O'Hara to Opabin Pass, 340 m from Eagles Eyrie to Wenkchemna Pass
Height loss 330 m from Opabin Pass, 730 m from Wenkchemna Pass
Max elevation 2600 m at both Opabin and Wenkchemna Passes
Map Lake Louise 82 N/8

One of the best high mountain tours on the Rockies. It is long and challenging and takes you through superb high mountain terrain. It is a serious trip and there is some very real avalanche risk. Use caution!

Options It is possible to cross Wastach Pass to Paradise Valley, then exit down the Paradise Valley Trail. This makes for a longer and harder day.

Hazards The slopes below all three passes: Opabin, Wenkchemna and Wastach have significant avalanche risk. Take all safety precautions. This trip is not recommended unless the avalanche hazard is low. There are small glaciers on both sides of Opabin Pass and there are some crevasses. It is advisable to carry a rope just in case.

Skiing toward Opabin Pass. Mount Biddle is on the right.
Photo Art Longair

Access Begin this tour by skiing up the Lake O'Hara Fire Road (see page141).

From the lodge ski around the south side of Lake O'Hara to the drainage coming down from Opabin Plateau, where you will find a trail junction. Ski up the steep trail (skins advised!) to gain the hanging valley, then head south along the valley towards Opabin Pass. The terrain is open and in good visibility the way is not hard to find. The route ascends a small glacier with some large crevasses. The final climb to the pass is steep and may require step-kicking.

The descent from Opabin Pass is steep for a short distance then becomes a very pleasant ski run for about 300 vertical metres down to Eagles Eyrie. The climb from here up to Wenkchemna Pass is a risky slope. It is moderately steep and underneath the snow pack the ground surface is smooth scree. Use caution! The last part of the climb to the pass is often wind blown and bare and you may be climbing the last few metres over loose rocks.

The descent from Wenkchemna Pass to Moraine Lake is pleasant and follows an easy line over moraine and open meadow. Stay well south of Eiffel Lake and marvel at the walls of the Ten Peaks high above you. Ski along the margin of the forest and the moraine until you reach the drainage which flows down to Moraine Lake. Descend this drainage then ski across the lake to reach the lodge on the opposite side. Continue to Lake Louise along the Moraine Lake road (see page 105).

89 YOHO VALLEY ROAD

Ski touring 2

Grade Easy
Distance 26 km return
Time This is normally a full day trip to Takakkaw Falls and back.
Height gain 150 m
Max elevation 1480 m
Map Lake Louise 82 N/8

A straightforward and easy ski up a snow covered road. You can ski as far as you like—a few kilometres or all the way to Takakkaw Falls. At the end of the road you get a good view of Takakkaw Falls frozen in its winter splendour. You might even see some ice climbers on it.

Facilities There are toilets at the parking lot. There is a campground at Takakkaw Falls which has an enclosed camp shelter and toilets.

Hazards The avalanche slopes off Wapta Mountain should be crossed quickly. This trail should be avoided in periods of high avalanche hazard.

Options This trail ties in with the tour up the Little Yoho Valley to the Stanley Mitchell Hut.

Access There is a large parking lot at the trailhead which is reached by taking the turn off for the Yoho Valley Road, 4 km east of Field. If you are coming from Lake Louise the turn is on your right, just after you descend the big hill from Kicking Horse Pass.

This tour follows a road throughout, to a campground located not far from Takakkaw Falls. The road begins from the east end of the parking lot and is simple to follow. After about 5 km the road climbs several switchbacks. Just after the switchbacks the road is threatened by giant avalanche slopes high on Wapta Mountain. In fact the road is often piled high with avalanche debris. You should proceed as quickly as possible through this area without stopping. At the end of the road you can ski over to the right to get a better view

of the falls or carry on straight ahead to find the campground.

Although the return journey should in fact be downhill and should give a fun glide back to the cars, it is sometimes noted that the road appears to be unique—it is uphill in both directions!

Skiing back down the Yoho Valley Road from Takakkaw Falls.

90 LITTLE YOHO VALLEY

Grade Intermediate/advanced
Distance 10 km one way from Takakkaw Falls to the Stanley Mitchell Hut (Note: the trip from the parking lot to the ACC Hut in the Little Yoho Valley and back to your car is about 46 km!)
Time From the highway the hut can be reached in one very long day (depending on conditions) by strong skiers. Many, however, will find that two days are necessary for the trip. The return journey, from the hut back to the highway, is normally done in one day.
Height gain 150 m from the highway to Takakkaw Falls, 575 m from Takakkaw Falls to the Stanley Mitchell Hut
Max elevation 2060 m
Maps Lake Louise 82 N/8
Hector Lake 82 N/9
Blaeberry River 82 N/10
Touring the Wapta Icefields (Murray Toft)

The tour to the Little Yoho Valley and a stay at the beautiful Stanley Mitchell Hut is one of the great experiences in the Canadian Rockies. The area abounds in superb skiing and the cabin is the postcard image of what a mountain hut should look like.

Facilities There are toilets at the parking lot. There is a camp shelter at Takakkaw Falls which is completely enclosed. It is often used by parties who cannot make it to the Stanley Mitchell Hut in one day. There are toilets nearby and a pile of firewood under the snow. Usually there is an axe in the camp shelter.

Hazards On the way back down watch out for the steep descents down the Laughing Falls Hill and the Hollingsworth Hill, particularly if conditions are icy.

Cross the Wapta Mountain slide paths quickly with no stopping.

Allow plenty of time to reach the hut when you leave the Takakkaw Falls Shelter. If you are breaking trail you will find the going very slow. It is best to spend a comfortable night at the shelter rather than push on, late in the day, and find yourself in the dark frantically trying to find the hut. It has happened many times!

Access This tour begins by skiing up the Yoho Valley Road (see page 147) to the campground.

The trail leaves from the north end of the campground, crossing a large open area which in summer is a stream outwash, then enters the woods on the opposite side. The trail is easy to follow to begin with, along a wide straight cut through the forest. After several kilometres the trail climbs a long and uniform hill (the Hollingsworth Hill), then continues through the woods beyond (the trail can be hard to follow here).

After 4.5 km (from the campground) the trail crosses a bridge over a creek near Laughing Falls then turns left and begins its climb out of the Yoho Valley into the Little Yoho Valley. The turn off point is sometimes hard to find, particularly if the trail signs are buried deep under the snow. Nowadays there are enough people skiing this trail to make it easier to follow than in the past. The trail now switchbacks up through mature, open forest on the west wall of the valley. If it has just snowed the trail can at times be hard to follow.

A moment of quiet contemplation along the Little Yoho River.

After about 240 vertical metres of climb, when the angle begins to ease off, the trail angles left over towards the Little Yoho River. It continues above the river into the valley along the hillside on the north bank. After a while the steep hillside that the trail is traversing levels off and the trail meanders through forest and open glades to the hut. Stay on the north bank of the river throughout. The trail can be hard to follow at times because it crosses glades then re-enters the forest on the opposite side at points that are hard to locate. The hut is located in the trees on the edge of a meadow, on the north side of the Little Yoho River, about 5 km from the Laughing Falls turn-off.

The return journey to the highway can be an exciting challenge for inexperienced skiers. This is particularly true in the spring time when the trail can be icy. The descent of the steep hillside above Laughing Falls is not a laughing matter if you are unsure on your skis. Be careful here and take your time. The same holds true for the Hollingsworth Hill which is steep and long. For your return journey, be sure to get away early in the morning to allow plenty of time to return to the highway in one day.

Telemark Areas

If the weather is overcast there is good tree and glade skiing below the Vice President, on the far side of the valley, opposite the hut. The runs are generally 100-150 vertical metres through glades and on open slopes. There is lots of good, skiable terrain here, but take care, there is avalanche potential!

91 KIWETINOK PASS

Ski touring 2

Grade Easy
Distance 7 km return
Time 3-4 hours
Height gain 400 m
Max elevation 2450 m
Map Blaeberry River 82 N/10

This is a very enjoyable tour in beautiful surroundings. Highly recommended!

Access The tour begins at the Stanley Mitchell Hut.

From the hut ski across the creek and follow it upstream for about 150 m. Turn left and follow a shallow draw in the trees for about 100 m up into a bowl. Climb up and right out of the bowl and over the crest of a moraine to reach a large open stretch which is the drainage from the President Glacier. Cross this in a southwest direction to reach a draw along the left margin of the trees. Continue ascending, staying on the left edge of

the trees in open terrain. Near the edge of treeline there is a moderately steep slope to climb. Remain on the left side of the creekbed and ascend the slope at its lowest and least steep point. High on the left are prominent cliffs. Above the steep hill traverse out right into the creek bed, then continue climbing over alpine terrain to reach Kiwetinok Lake and, a short distance beyond, Kiwetinok Pass. You can ski through the pass to the brow of a hill overlooking the Amiskwi Valley and sit here in the sun while you eat your lunch.

Ken Jones guiding a group back to the Stanley Mitchell Hut hut after a tour to Kiwetinok Pass.

92 FIELD TO EMERALD LAKE

Grade Intermediate
Distance 10 km one way
Time 3-4 hours one way
Height gain 200 m
Max elevation 1300 m
Map Golden 82 N/7

This is an excellent trail with stunning views of Mount Stephen at the start. At time of writing (2001) the trail is trackset.

Facilities There are toilets and telephones at both ends of the trail, at the Park Information Centre in Field and at Emerald Lake.

Options This trail can be skied one way if you leave a car at the other end or can be skied return if you only have a single car.

Access Park at the Park Information Centre, on the south side of the Trans Canada Highway, at the entrance to Field. If you are only skiing the trail one way leave a second car at Emerald Lake.

From the Park Information Centre ski west along the river flats between the highway and the river. After 1 km cross the highway to the right (take your skis off and use caution!). On the other side a wide trail climbs at a moderate angle through the trees for about 1.0 km. The trail then levels off and turns the shoulder of the mountain to the right. Descend gradually for about 0.5 km to a trail junction.

If you take the left hand branch you descend steadily for about 1 km to the Emerald Lake access road at the parking lot for the Natural Bridge. If you take the right hand branch it is about 8 km to Emerald Lake. To start the trail is the wide Tally Ho Carriage Road, but after about 2 km the trail narrows and now meanders up and down through the woods. There are several steep, narrow hills to deal with. Eventually the trail comes out at the parking lot at Emerald Lake.

Of Historical Interest Mount Stephen, which towers high above the town of Field, was named for George Stephen one of the central figures in the construction of the Canadian Pacific Railway. The mountain was first climbed in 1887 by surveyor J.J. McArthur and his assistant T. Riley. This ascent is considered by many to be the start of mountaineering in Canada.

Mount Stephen looms high above the trail from Emerald Lake to Field.

Skiing along the river flats near Field with Mount Stephen towering above.

Skiing across Emerald Lake. Emerald Lake Lodge in the background.

93 EMERALD LAKE TRAILS

Grade Easy
Distance The loop around the lake is 5 km and can be extended by 2-3 km
Time 2 hours to complete the loop
Height gain Nil
Max elevation 1300 m
Map Golden 82 N/7

A lovely tour in a beautiful setting. The skiing is easy and the trail will almost always be packed or trackset. The valley is oriented southwest and gets sunshine most of the day. Highly recommended.

Facilities There are toilets at the parking lot and the Emerald Lake Lodge is nearby with all amenities. There is a sports shop which rents cross country ski equipment beside the bridge, near the start of the trail (250-343-6377).

Hazards You should not linger on the large avalanche path on the southwest side of the lake.

Access Turn north off the Trans Canada Highway 3 km west of Field and follow the road for 6 km to the end where there is a large parking lot.

The summer trail starts just above the sports shop near the bridge and heads into the trees. It then crosses the large avalanche path at the southwest corner of the lake. The trackset trail avoids the avalanche path, starting just below the lodge and crosses the lake to the northwest shore. You can start either way, then continue along the trail on the northwest shore of the lake. At the end of the lake the trail turns east, heading across an open area to enter the trees on the opposite side. At this point you can make a loop back into Emerald Basin and ski several additional kilometres. This extra loop trail eventually swings back and rejoins the main trail which continues along the east and south shores of the lake back to the lodge. Along here the trail rolls through the

woods beside the lake, making several short climbs and descents. Eventually it reaches the furthest east corner of the lodge where it is necessary to remove your skis and walk through the lodge area back to the parking lot.

Skiing at Emerald Lake.
Photo Tony Daffern.

94 KICKING HORSE TRAIL

Grade Easy
Distance 13 km return
Time 4-5 hours return
Height gain 60 m
Max elevation 1220 m
Map Golden 82 N/7

This is a very nice half day tour. Most of the trail runs through forest but there are a few open views along the way. At the moment (2001) the trail is trackset.

Access Turn north off the Trans Canada Highway onto the Emerald Lake access road, 4 km west of Field. Continue 1.5 km and park at the Natural Bridge parking lot.

The trail starts from the right (north) side of the parking lot. Ski gently downhill on a wide road (which is double track set) for about 2.5 km, then cross a small bridge over the Emerald River. In another 100 m cross a larger bridge over the Amiskwi River. Continue another 100 m through a picnic area to a trail junction. Turn left and for about 50 m the trail narrows to one track then it opens up

into two tracks again. Ski about 2 km along a road through the forest to a large open area where there is a terrific view of the surrounding peaks. On the left is the Kicking Horse River.

Ski another kilometre on a wide double track set road then the trail narrows to single track. Continue another kilometre to a trail junction. The branch to the right heads up the Otterhead River (ski touring/trail breaking). If you turn left you can ski about 0.5 km on a single track trail to a bridge over the Otterhead River. This is the end of the trackset trail.

95 AMISKWI FIRE ROAD TO AMISKWI PASS

Grade Easy
Distance 76 km return
Time You can ski along this road for several hours or for several days
Height gain 800 m
Max elevation 1960 m
Maps Golden 82 N/7
Blaeberry River 82 N/10

This trail offers a long tour in a wilderness setting. You will likely be all by yourself to enjoy the exercise and fresh air.

Facilities Amiskwi Lodge (GR 228187) is located near Amiskwi Pass.

Access Turn north off the Trans Canada Highway onto the Emerald Lake access road, 4 km west of Field. Continue 1.5 km and park at the Natural Bridge parking lot.

The trail starts from the right (north) side of the parking lot. Ski gently

downhill, on a wide road, for about 2.5 km then cross a small bridge over the Emerald River. In 100 m cross a larger bridge over the Amiskwi River. Continue another 100 m through a picnic area to a trail junction. Turn right, take a deep breath and start skiing. It is about 35 km to Amiskwi Pass.

96 OTTERTAIL VALLEY FIRE ROAD

Ski touring 2

Grade Easy
Distance 28 km return to McArthur Creek
Time It is a full day tour to ski to McArthur Creek and back, but you can ski as far along the road as you like
Height gain 300 m
Max elevation 1500 m
Maps Golden 82 N/7
Lake Louise 82 N/8

An easy and enjoyable tour which is not often skied. A pleasant way to get some fresh air and solitude.

Options Occasionally skiers will cross McArthur Pass from Lake O'Hara then descend McArthur Creek to the Ottertail Fire Road, then continue out to the highway. This is a good adventure for those looking for something a little different.

Access There is a plowed parking area on the southeast side of the Trans Canada Highway 8 km west of Field.

This tour follows a fire road so it is wide and the grade is gentle. The road does much of its climbing over the first 3 km then levels off. Ski as far as you like then turn back when you've had enough. If you have the time and energy to make it all the way to the McArthur Creek Warden Cabin you will be treated to a spectacular view of the towers of Mount Goodsir to the south.

97 CHANCELLOR PEAK CAMPGROUND

Ski touring 1

Grade Easy
Distance 4 km return
Time 1-2 hours return
Height gain Nil
Max elevation 1120 m
Map McMurdo 82 N/2

A short, easy tour to a campground. Ideal for those who would like to try winter camping in a safe and accessible location.

Facilities There are toilets and picnic shelters at the campground.

Options There is a fire road which leaves from the back of the campground.

Access There is usually a small cleared parking area at the trailhead. This is located on the north side of the Trans Canada Highway, 23 km west of Field, at the west end of the Leanchoil Bridge over the Kicking Horse River.

From the parking area simply ski along the road for 2 km to the campground. There are very impressive views of Mounts Chancellor and Vaux along the way.

98 ICE RIVER FIRE ROAD

Grade Easy
Distance It is 32 km return if you ski all the way to the park boundary at Ice River
Time As long as you wish
Height gain 150 m
Max elevation 1300
Maps Mount Goodsir 82 N/1
McMurdo 82 N/2

A long and easy ski along a fire road. It offers an opportunity to get out on a quiet trail and wander.

Access Park your car at the Hoodoo Creek Campground, on the southeast side of the Trans Canada Highway, 22 km west of Field.

From the parking lot ski along the road for about 0.5 km. Just before the entrance to the campground turn right and ski down a side road for 0.5 km. The fire road starts here. Ski around the gate and head up the road. Put your mind in neutral, breathe deeply and listen to your skis as they swish through the snow.

Of Historical Interest Yoho is a Cree Indian word meaning astonishment or wonder. Yoho Park, created in 1886, was Canada's second national park. It is indeed a place of wonder. One of the finest treasures in the park is the Burgess Shale. This fossil bed was discovered by American Charles Walcott in 1907. It is unique for the soft bodied fossils from the Cambrian era which are preserved in the rocks and has completely changed our view of evolution. The Walcott Quarry in the Burgess Shale was designated a World Heritage Site in 1980 by UNESCO.

99 WAPTA FALLS

Grade Intermediate
Distance 9 km return
Time 3-4 hours return
Height gain 80 m
Max elevation 1120 m
Map McMurdo 82 N/2

This is a pleasant half day tour. Although it is only graded intermediate, the trail is narrow towards the end and requires caution and skill. There is a limited view of the falls from the top of the hill. To see them properly one should really descend the hill which can be tricky—walking down is a good idea.

Hazards Take care at the viewpoint above the falls. It is slippery and a long way down. Walk down the hill if you are unstable on your skis.

Access There is a small parking lot on the south side of the Trans Canada Highway, 25 km west of Field. The parking lot is about 2 km west of the Leanchoil Bridge over the Kicking Horse River—keep a sharp eye out as it appears very quickly.

From the parking lot ski around the closure barrier and head down the road. The first 1.5 km is along a road and is wide and easy. At the end of this section the trail continues along a cutline for another 1.5 km, following the left side of the slash. Eventually the slash peters out and the trail enters the woods.

For the next kilometre the trail is narrow and climbs at a moderate angle. This takes you to a viewpoint above the Kicking Horse River, overlooking Wapta Falls. Unfortunately it is not easy to see the falls from here and you must continue along the trail for another 0.5 km to get a good look. The trail is steep, particularly at the start, and you should walk down if you are unsteady on your skis. The trail initially angles out to the right then lower down traverses back to the left.

At the bottom of the hill you can ski a few metres back along the river to the base of the falls. They are large and impressive from this vantage point.

ICEFIELDS PARKWAY SOUTH

The Icefields Parkway, which stretches from Lake Louise to Jasper, is one of the most scenic drives in the world. In winter, however, it is a remote stretch of highway and there are no service stations for a distance of 230 km.

The southern portion of the highway, from Lake Louise to Saskatchewan Crossing (where the David Thompson Highway (Highway 11) comes in from Rocky Mountain House) is rarely closed in winter. It is well maintained although sanding is minimal, so expect some snow and ice on the road. On the rare occasion when the highway is closed north of Saskatchewan Crossing it may be possible to complete your journey by driving east on the David Thompson Highway to Red Deer and heading north from there.

Num-ti-jah Lodge.

Be certain that you are prepared to deal with cold weather and snow. This includes a strong battery, good snow tires, jumper cables, a shovel and survival gear.

In Emergency There is a Warden Station near Saskatchewan River Crossing, about 2 km south of the junction of the Icefields Parkway and the David Thompson Highway (Highway 11) which may or may not be manned. There are pay telephones at the Saskatchewan River Crossing restaurant and motel complex. Num-ti-jah Lodge is open year round and has pay telephones.

Num-ti-jah Lodge

This beautiful log lodge provides a delightful mix of old fashioned ambiance and modern convenience. Although you can drive to the door of this 1940s structure it has the feel of a backcountry lodge. It has all the modern conveniences and offers access to some of the best ski touring in the Rockies.
Location On the shore of Bow Lake, about 40 km north of Lake Louise along the Icefields Parkway (GR 369253).
Map Hector Lake 82 N/9
Facilities A large log lodge with private rooms, lounge area, dining room, full bar, central heating, hot showers and indoor plumbing.
Capacity 25 rooms for up to 90 guests
Hosts Tim Whyte and Lee O'Donnell
Cost Rates for two range from $65 to $125 per night. Meals are not included.
Reservations Write: Num-ti-jah Lodge, Box 39, Lake Louise, Alberta, T0L 1E0 Email: reserve@num-ti-jah.com Website: www.num-ti-jah.com Phone: 403-522-2167 Fax: 403-522-2425

Accommodation There is a hostel at Mosquito Creek which offers rustic but affordable accommodation. Num-ti-jah Lodge offers deluxe accommodation and first-class meals. The campground at Mosquito Creek is plowed in winter and there is a camp shelter and firewood available.

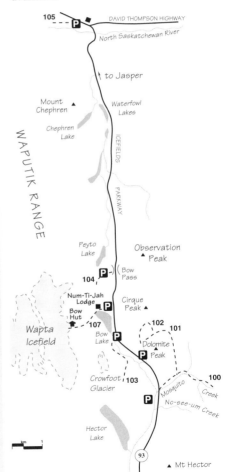

159

100 MOSQUITO CREEK TO MOLAR MEADOWS   Ski touring 2

Grade Intermediate
Distance 18 km return
Time A full day tour for most skiers
Height gain 450 m
Max elevation 2270 m (at the meadows)
Map Hector Lake 82 N/9

This is a very popular tour that gets you up high into alpine meadows. It is an easy trail to begin but towards the end climbs at a steady angle through the trees up to Molar Meadows. On a sunny day this is a beautiful place practice your Telemark turns.

Hazards Ski carefully in Molar Meadows and follow avalanche safety precautions.

Options For the well prepared and adventurous skier it is possible to continue beyond Molar Meadows over North Molar Pass and down to Fish Lakes. You can descend to the Pipestone River and follow it back to Lake Louise. This tour would require several days and involve winter camping.

Access Parking is available in the Mosquito Creek Hostel parking lot on the west side of the Icefields Parkway, 24 km north of the junction with the Trans Canada Highway. The parking lot is just before the highway crosses Mosquito Creek. Additional parking can be found in the Mosquito Creek campground on the other side of the bridge.

Along Mosquito Creek.

From the parking lot walk across the road and cross the bridge. Put your skis on and locate the trail which starts very near to the bridge. To begin with it climbs steeply through the trees up the hillside above then the angle eases off quickly and the trail climbs at a more moderate angle. The trail levels off and rambles through the forest, descending to the creek after about 2.5 km.

The trail now follows along the valley floor for another 1.5 km then begins to curve right. Cross two small creeks then continue through the woods for about a kilometre eventually crossing Mosquito Creek to the right (west) side of the valley. From here the trail climbs steeply so make sure you have a good wax (or skins). Gain about 150 vertical metres then drop down left into the creek bed again. Cross the creek and climb steeply for another 120 vertical m up to Molar Meadows. The trail is hard to follow on this last climb but it is possible to switchback where necessary through the trees.

On the Dolomite Peak circuit. Photo Alf Skrastins.

101 DOLOMITE PEAK CIRCUIT

Ski touring 3

Grade Advanced
Distance 19 km loop
Time This is a full day tour
Height gain 650 m
Max elevation 2500 m
Map Hector Lake 82 N/9

The Dolomite Peak Circuit is one of the finest ski tours in the Canadian Rockies. The beauty of this tour, across alpine snowfields high above treeline, is extraordinary. The first part of the trip, up Helen Creek, is straightforward and the final run down Mosquito Creek is an exhilarating way to end the day. But the middle section of the trip, high above treeline, can present difficult route finding in poor visibility.

Hazards Route finding on this tour can be a problem in poor visibility. It could be very easy to get lost in a whiteout.

There is significant avalanche potential on this tour so caution is advised.

Much of the tour is above treeline, out in the open, so adequate protection against the elements is a must.

Access Because this tour does not return to the same point on the highway as the departure point, two cars are required. It is customary to begin the tour at the Helen Creek trailhead, just north of the Helen Creek bridge, 29 km north on the Icefields Parkway. Leave a second car at the Mosquito Creek Hostel parking lot, about 5 km south along the highway.

The trail climbs steeply above the Helen Creek trailhead for about 100 vertical metres, to the crest of a ridge. The angle eases here and the trail continues northwest along the crest of the ridge for a short distance. Then it descends to the right to the creek bed. Cross the creek on a bridge and continue along the opposite bank. The trail along here crosses large avalanche paths with thick forests in between. After about 1.5 km it starts to climb, then crosses the creek again and works its way up through the trees to an elevation of about 2150 m where the trees begin to thin out.

From here there is no clearly defined trail and you work your way up and right over some steep rolls, then over a rocky shoulder to gain a broad pass at about 2400 m. Be careful of avalanche hazard here. A gentle descent now takes you down to Katherine Lake.

Cross the lake then continue through Dolomite Pass. A huge boulder on the right makes a good wind break for a lunch stop. From the pass descend about 70 vertical metres down the drainage to the northeast, until it is possible to begin turning right (southeast) towards an unnamed pass (GR 442265) which can now be seen about 2 km distant. It is not advised to cut this corner along a high line as some steep and potentially dangerous avalanche slopes will be encountered. The climb from the valley to the unnamed pass is about 150 vertical metres and straightforward.

From the pass descend the slope to the southeast with some caution, then follow the drainage down to a large open area. Carry on descending the drainage until you reach a point where the right bank is threatened by slopes above. During periods of high instability it would be advisable to continue for a short distance, down the sparsely treed slopes on the left bank, away from the danger. At an elevation of about 2150 m cross the creek on a large bench to gain the right hand bank. Continue descending and traversing in a southerly direction (i.e. trending right). Some glades can be found through the trees where you can get in a few turns.

Do not descend directly down the creek bed because the steep banks can pose a serious avalanche threat.

At the bottom, just before reaching Mosquito Creek, you will hit the trail. Turn right and follow it back to the Icefields Parkway (see page 160).

Dolomite Peak circuit. Photo Alf Skrastins.

On the headwall below Helen Lake looking over the Icefields Parkway to Crowfoot Pass. Photo Gillean Daffern.

102 KATHERINE LAKE/HELEN LAKE CIRCUIT

Ski touring 2

Grade Advanced
Distance 8 km return
Time 4-6 hours
Height gain 650 m
Max elevation 2470 m
Map Hector Lake 82 N/9

An excellent tour that takes you high above treeline into alpine terrain. This trip requires good weather and good visibility.

Hazards You are in high alpine terrain far from shelter so you should be well clothed and prepared for emergencies. You are in potential avalanche terrain so take the appropriate precautions.

Access There is a small parking lot on the northeast side of the Icefields Parkway, just across the bridge over Helen Creek, 29 km north of the junction with the Trans Canada Highway.

Follow the Dolomite Peak Circuit tour (see page 162) as far as Katherine Lake. From here ski easily to the west for about 1 km, up open slopes to gain the pass located immediately south of Cirque Peak. Descend the southwest slopes of the pass to Helen Lake. At the top the slopes are steep and you should proceed with caution. Stay to

the right on your descent as there are some small cliffs below on the left. Descend to the lake and cross it. From the south end of the lake contour around to the left at about the same level, through a notch and into a draw. You can descend this draw or traverse a little further to your left to reach your up-track. It is also possible to descend directly down Helen Creek from Helen Lake but the creek can be awkward at the point where it reaches treeline and there is also some avalanche danger.

103 CROWFOOT PASS

Ski touring 2

Grade Intermediate
Distance 10 km return
Time This is a full day tour
Height gain 430 m
Max elevation 2350 m
Map Hector Lake 82 N/9

The tour to Crowfoot Pass is one of the finest in the Rockies. From the pass there are excellent views down the Bow Valley to Mount Temple, Pilot Mountain and farther south to the tower of Mount Assiniboine. Save this one for later in the season when there is lots of snow and the sun lingers in the pass.

Hazards There is avalanche hazard on this tour. The creek route has claimed a life in the past.

Options Folks sometimes cross this pass and descend to Hector Lake then cross the lake back to the highway. Be warned—the descent is very steep!!! Not recommended.

Access Park at the Crowfoot Glacier viewpoint on the west side of the Icefields Parkway about 32 km north from the junction with the Trans Canada Highway. This viewpoint is 3 km south of the turn-off to Num-ti-jah Lodge.

From the parking lot head straight over the snow bank and down a short steep hill to the trees below. This hill is about 20 vertical metres high and may require several kick turns. Once in the trees head out towards the valley bottom for a short distance to reach the flats at the end of Bow Lake. Turn left and ski down the open flats, then round a corner into another open area. From here there are two routes to the pass.

The Ramp Route
After skiing about 1 km from the end of the main body of the lake turn right up a small but clearly defined creek bed. It soon curves left and goes through a large boulder field then across an open area. It now curves right and soon you can branch left through the trees. Within about 100 m you enter a draw and you begin to climb (GR 397218). If there is

lots of snow you can continue ascending the draw. If not, you can traverse out left onto a crest and wind your way upwards. After about 200 vertical

Looking south from Crowfoot pass toward Mount temple.

165

Looking toward Crowfoot Pass from Num-ti-jah Lodge.

metres of ascent the angle lays back and the trees begin to thin out. From here the tour continues along the ramp, gradually gaining elevation. Eventually the angle lays right back and you continue for several kilometres across to the pass. On the last 2 km there are several small steepish hills and rolls that must be treated with caution.

The Creek Route
Continue skiing down the flats until they pinch out and the river begins, then ski up onto the right bank and proceed through the trees. The travelling is excellent along here and after about 1 km through open forest you reach the drainage coming down from Crowfoot Pass (GR 413218). At this point it is a small canyon which is easily entered. Put your skins on and begin heading straight up the creek. The travelling is easy and the angle is reasonable. The creek gains about 100 vertical metres and approaches a cliff looming above through the trees. At this point the creek begins to curve to the left. Continue up the creek for some distance—it is usually quite distinct and easy to follow. At one point the creek levels out for a short distance but soon it begins to climb again through open trees. Eventually you break out of the trees completely and can continue straight ahead up the drainage to the pass where there is a nice outcrop of quartzite to sit on.

104 BOW SUMMIT

Ski touring 2

Grade Easy/intermediate
Distance 1 km to base of ski slope
Time You can spend a few hours or the entire day skiing in this area
Height gain The most popular slope is about 100 m high, from the parking lot to the highest area skied is about 330 m
Max elevation 2250 m on the bench above the most popular slope, 2410 m in the upper bowl
Maps Hector Lake 82 N/9
Blaeberry River 82 N/10

Bow Summit has long been a popular destination for ski touring and for making turns. On a sunny, spring day it is a magical spot. There is lots of snow, the slopes are only a short distance from the car and the views are excellent. Note that the area is closed to skiers early in the season, until there is sufficient snow to prevent damage to the fragile alpine vegetation.

Hazards Bow Summit has been the scene of several avalanche fatalities in the past. Although the slopes are not large they should be treated with caution.

Access Turn west off the Icefields Parkway at Bow Pass, 40 km north of the Trans Canada Highway. Drive a short distance up the road towards the Peyto Lake Viewpoint, then turn right into a large plowed lot.

Approaching the main hill at Bow Summit.

From the parking lot ski up the unplowed road for 3-400 m then angle out left to the base of a prominent hill. This hill is the main attraction at Bow Summit and although not large can give many hours of enjoyable skiing. Highly recommended.

There is also a bowl higher up where turns can be made. To reach this bowl ski along the bench which runs along the top of the hill (there is an old road along here). The trail (road) crosses a creek drainage after about 1 km and just beyond turns up into a wild alpine cirque. Some of the slopes here are skiable but offer avalanche potential.

On rare occasions the skiing is good on the wind swept shoulder above the Peyto Lake Viewpoint. This slope, however, is susceptible to wind slab and is often a very dangerous proposition. If you are thinking of skiing here you should know what you are doing and take all precautions.

There are excellent opportunities for short tours at Bow Summit.

1. Ski from the car park up the road for several hundred metres then angle out left below the prominent hill. Continue along the base of the hill until you reach a creek then work your way back taking a lower line if you chose. This is a nice spot to introduce someone to the joys of ski touring.

2. From the parking lot you can ski up the road to the Peyto Lake Viewpoint then continue farther up the hill on the old road. This road climbs in a southerly direction until it reaches the bench along the top of the prominent hill. Ski south along the bench for about 1 km to the point where the road crosses a creek drainage. You can continue a bit farther along and have an outstanding view down the Bow Valley.

105 GLACIER LAKE

Ski touring 1

Grade Intermediate
Distance 14 km return
Time A moderate day tour
Height gain 50 m following the river, 250 m following the trail
Max elevation 1420 m following river, 1670 m following trail
Map Mistaya Lake 82 N/15

This can be a wonderful ski tour in a wilderness setting. However, the valley is low in elevation and receives little snowfall. Consequently the river flats are often blown bare and when spring comes the snow disappears quickly.

Access There is a parking lot on the southwest side of the Icefields Parkway about 1 km north of the turn off for the David Thompson Highway.

The trail starts from the southwest corner of the parking lot. It heads south for a short distance, turns west and continues for about 1 km to a bridge over the North Saskatchewan River. Cross the bridge and continue west until the trail descends to the flats of the Howse River.

From here follow the river flats for 5 km. At about GR 125519, turn north up the creek which drains Glacier Lake. If the creek is open and it is not possible to ski a short canyon, climb up on the right bank and find the trail which is followed to Glacier Lake.

Instead of following the river flats it is also possible to follow the summer trail which works its way into the forest and climbs 250 vertical metres over a hill before descending steeply to the lake.

WAPTA ICEFIELDS

The Wapta Icefields have become the most popular area for ski mountaineering in Canada. The mountains are spectacular, the glaciers are extensive and relatively safe, access from the highway is easy and there is an excellent system of huts operated by The Alpine Club of Canada.

The Wapta Icefields are really composed of two distinct icefields—the Wapta and the Waputik. The are both usually referred to as 'The Wapta'. It is a large area, perhaps 3-400 km sq., of which about 150 km sq. is actually covered by glaciers and icefields.

On a sunny day it is a joy to explore the icefields. You can make ski ascents of the surrounding peaks and there are enough variations of 'The Wapta Traverse' to keep the ardent ski mountaineer busy for a number of years. There are also many fine slopes to satisfy those who want to make turns.

The area is included in this book to help you make the transition from valley trail skiing to ski mountaineering. The Wapta Icefields are usually the location where ski tourers make this exciting step into high mountain adventure.

Although the Wapta Icefields have come to be regarded as pretty tame adventure, one should not take lightly the dangers that are awaiting the unsuspecting. In winter time, with extremely cold temperatures and violent storms, survival can become an issue for the most experienced ski mountaineer. With reduced visibility, navigation becomes a challenge for all of us, and getting lost up here with limited survival gear can be very serious indeed. Avalanche terrain demands good route finding skills and the numerous crevasses required experience in roped glacier travel. In the event of an emergency you should be prepared to extricate a companion from a crevasse or dig them from an avalanche. It is recommended that for your first few trips you travel in the company of an experienced leader or perhaps even a guide.

Wapta Icefields

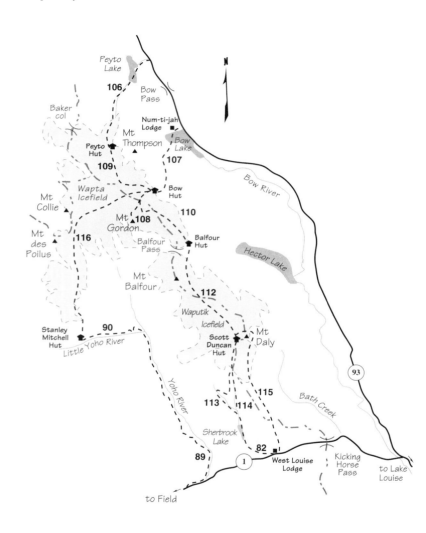

170

Crossing Bow Lake toward the Wapta Icefields.

The Wapta Icefields are normally traversed in one of four ways. These are:

1. The Complete Traverse from Peyto Lake to Sherbrooke Lake (there are three possible exits).

2. The Partial Traverse from Bow Lake to Sherbrooke Lake (three exits).

3. The Mini Traverse from Bow Lake to Peyto Lake.

4. The East-West Traverse from Bow Lake to the Little Yoho Valley.

Maps The Wapta Icefields are covered by 4 topographical maps. However, there is one map that covers the entire region. It is printed on waterproof, tear-proof and eraseable material and on the back has aerial photographs showing the major routes. It is recommended that you purchase this map and use it as a companion to this guidebook.

It is called "Touring the Wapta Icefields" and it was prepared by Murray Toft.

Huts There are four huts on the Wapta Icefields and a fifth nearby in the Yoho Valley (the Stanley Mitchell Hut see page 139). In poor visibility it may be difficult to locate these huts and so you should be equipped to bivouac.

Balfour Hut

A comfortable, modern hut in the heart of spectacular, wild country.
Location On low, rocky hills at the toe of the Vulture Glacier (GR 375157).
Map Hector Lake 82 N/9
Facilities Foamies, cooking and eating utensils, propane cooking stoves and lanterns.
Capacity 18
Water Snowmelt
Reservations The Alpine Club of Canada 403-678-3200
Note! This hut can be difficult to find in whiteout conditions.

The Freshfield Group Mount Ayesha Ayesha Glacier Mount Forbes

A thirteen-photo panorama from the top of Mount Gordon. Photos Gillean Daffern.

Peter and Catharine Whyte Hut (Peyto Hut)

A comfortable, modern hut with a great view out the front door.
Location On the moraine below the NW ridge of Mount Thompson (GR 314237)
Map Blaeberry river 82 N/10
Facilities Foamies, cooking and eating utensils, propane cooking stoves and lanterns.
Capacity 18
Water Snowmelt
Reservations The Alpine Club of Canada 403-678-3200

Scott Duncan Hut

A comfortable, modern hut which services the south end of the Wapta Icefields.
Location On a bench at the bottom of the NE ridge of Mount Daly (GR 417084).
Map Hector Lake 82 N/9
Facilities Foamies, cooking and eating utensils, Coleman cooking stoves and lanterns.
Capacity 12
Water Snowmelt
Reservations The Alpine Club of Canada 403-678-3200
Note! This hut can be difficult to find in whiteout conditions.

Mount Forbes Rhondda North Rhondda South Peyto Peak Peyto Glacier

Bow Hut

A thoroughly modern hut, the flagship of the Wapta Fleet, set amongst spectacular surroundings.
Location NE of St. Nicholas Peak, on a rocky ridge overlooking the main drainage leading down to Bow Lake (GR 355203).
Map Hector Lake 82 N/9
Facilities Two buildings (a cooking room and sleeping quarters) separated by a vestibule. Foamies, cooking and eating utensils, propane cooking stoves and lanterns, and a wood heating stove.
Capacity 30
Water Snowmelt in winter, in spring from a small creek to the west of the hut.
Reservations The Alpine Club of Canada 403-678-3200
Note! The cooking room is locked when a custodian is not present and a combination number is required.

Bow Hut.

Peyto Glacier   Mount Thompson   Portal Peak   Mount Jimmy Simpson

106 PEYTO GLACIER APPROACH

Grade Intermediate
Distance 10 km one way to the Peyto Hut
Time This tour usually takes all day
Height gain 550 m
Max elevation 2480 m
Map Blaeberry River 82 N/10
Touring the Wapta Icefields

This is a very pleasant way to access the Wapta Icefields. Depending on conditions, the weight of your pack and your fitness and skill level, it can be an easy day trip or a marathon march. The route is generally easy to follow.

Facilities The route passes by a glaciological research camp with a small wooden building which has been known to provide shelter in an emergency.

Hazards There are slopes on this tour which could slide in certain conditions. In addition, caution should be exercised when circling around the crevasses at the upper end of the Peyto Glacier. The rope should be worn when near these crevasses.

Access There is a small parking lot on the west side of the Icefields Parkway about 2.5 km down the hill, north of Bow Pass.

From the parking lot find an old road which is just a short distance away. It is easiest to walk north along the highway for about 100 m, then descend west down the bank for a few metres to hit the road.

Descend the road for several hundred metres keeping your eyes open for a trail which takes off through the woods to the left—usually there is a piece of flagging to mark the spot. Follow the trail as it rolls up and down through the woods for about 1 km to Peyto Lake. This section can be very tricky and sometimes it is best to do it with skins on!

St. Nicholas Peak

Cross the lake heading for the Peyto Creek drainage on the other side. Be certain that the lake is adequately frozen and snow covered.

Once you reach the gravel flats on the far side of the lake, head toward the narrowing. At the first narrows, only a short distance from the lake, it is usually necessary to cross the creek then climb onto the left bank for a short distance. Cross the creek again, then continue along the gravel flats for about 0.5 km. When the stream begins to curve to the left towards a narrowing canyon, climb up slopes on the right towards a large and prominent moraine that can be seen higher up.

Climb up into a protected little basin behind the moraine, then continue to the point where the crest of the moraine butts up against the hillside. Take off your skis and climb the hillside (careful—avalanche potential), then continue climbing on foot another 75 vertical metres until the angle lays back. Here you can usually put your skis on again and traverse across to the

Peyto Glacier (passing the glaciological research station).

Ascend the glacier in a southwest direction, aiming for the groove in the slope at the end. Ski up the groove staying well to the right of the crevasses. Above the crevasses circle back to the left (east). The Peyto Hut is directly to the east on a knoll, below the slopes of Mount Thompson. The precise grid reference is 314237.

ACC ski course ascending Peyto Glacier.

Mount Olive East Peak

107 BOW LAKE APPROACH

Grade Intermediate
Distance 8 km one way to the Bow Hut
Time 4-6 hours
Height gain 390 m
Max elevation 2330 m
Maps Hector Lake 82 N/9
Blaeberry River 82 N/10
Touring the Wapta Icefields

This is the most popular and easiest access onto the Wapta Icefields. It takes you to the Bow Hut which is the largest and most luxurious of the Wapta Huts. The trail is usually broken and easy to follow, however, if there has been a heavy snowfall and you are unfamiliar with the route it can be much more challenging.

Facilities Num-ti-jah Lodge is located near the parking lot on the shore of Bow Lake. Telephones are available and there is a restaurant.

Hazards There is avalanche hazard on this route in several places: along the narrow canyon, climbing the hillside above the canyon and then on the final steep hill before Bow Hut. Use caution!

Access There is a large parking lot on the west side of the Icefields Parkway, about 6 km south of Bow Pass, at the turn off to Num-ti-jah Lodge. Do not park in the lot for the lodge as this is reserved for guests.

From the parking lot ski beside the road down to the lake. Cross the lake (be certain that it is well frozen and snow covered) to the gravel flats on the far side. Continue up the stream for about 0.5 km until you can see that the way ahead is blocked by a narrow canyon. At this point angle left and follow a trail through the trees, climbing gradually up a small side drainage. Soon it bumps up against a steep mountainside beneath a large avalanche path. Do not linger here

Mount Olive West Peak

but climb quickly a short hill to the right, traverse around the corner, then descend into the main drainage again. You have now circumvented the first canyon.

Follow the creek, heading almost due south, up the second canyon. The walls above you are steep and hung with snow—you should not linger here. In the late spring the creek may be open in places and present difficulty. After about 1 km the way ahead becomes difficult and the route ascends to the left, up onto the east bank. Continue through broken forest, climbing gradually, until the trees end and the route breaks out into a large mountain cirque.

Cross the cirque in a southerly direction, climbing gradually, and contour around to the base of the steep hillside on the right. It is critical that you pick the safest point to climb this hillside as there is avalanche potential here. The route normally ascends a shallow groove at the left end of the hillside, making a series of traverses and kick turns, until it can break over the right edge of the groove onto the slopes above. Continue

up these slopes for about 100 vertical metres to reach the hut. The precise grid reference for the Bow Hut is 355203. This is a relatively new hut, built in 1989, and any information of an earlier date will give an incorrect hut location.

Skiing up the gorge on the way to Bow Hut.

177

Mount Hector
Mount Douglas
Mount St. Bride
Hector Lake

108 ASCENT OF MOUNT GORDON

Ski mountaineering 2

Grade Easy/intermediate
Distance 12 km return
Time An easy day trip
Height gain 850 m
Max elevation 3200 m
Maps Hector Lake 82 N/9
Blaeberry River 82 N/10
Touring the Wapta Icefields

One of the most scenic ascents on the Wapta Icefields. It is possible to see the entire icefield stretched out before you. The 13 page panorama above was taken from the summit of Mount Gordon. The ascent is straightforward in good weather but can be tricky in a whiteout.

Access The tour begins a Bow Hut.

From Bow Hut head up the hill in a northwest direction. Climb the toe of the glacier with long switchbacks, ascending west beneath the impressive north face of St. Nicholas Peak. Continue angling southwest towards Mount

Gordon. The route ascends easily to the right hand shoulder of the mountain, passing a deep wind scoop below some outcropping rocks, then works its way up and left to the ridge. Once on the ridge the angle eases and the summit is only a short distance away. The run back down to the hut is excellent.

Balfour High Col
Mount Balfour
Mount Lefroy
Mount Victoria
Mount Hu...

109 PEYTO HUT TO BOW HUT

Ski mountaineering 2

Grade Easy
Distance 6 km one way
Time 3-4 hours
Height gain 150 m to Rhondda/Thompson Col
Height loss 300 m to Bow Hut
Max elevation 2670 m
Maps Hector Lake 82 N/9
Blaeberry River 82 N/10
Touring the Wapta Icefields

This connection is straightforward in good visibility but can be a challenging route-finding problem in a whiteout.

From the Peyto Hut ski southeast to the broad pass between Mount Thompson and Rhondda South. Continue southeast, traversing so as to maintain your height. The most common mistake here is to lose elevation too quickly and be drawn down into the Bow Glacier drainage. Stay high above the Bow Glacier and traverse through a little notch (GR 343209) beside a small rounded summit (referred to locally as The Onion). From here descend southeast to the Bow Hut. Watch out for crevasses.

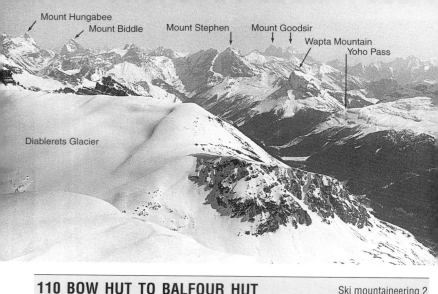

Mount Hungabee
Mount Biddle
Mount Stephen
Mount Goodsir
Wapta Mountain
Yoho Pass
Diablerets Glacier

110 BOW HUT TO BALFOUR HUT

Ski mountaineering 2

Grade Easy
Distance 7 km one way
Time 4-6 hours
Height gain 580 m to Olive/St. Nicholas Col
Height loss 430 m to Balfour Hut
Max elevation 2930 m

Maps Hector Lake 82 N/9
Blaeberry River 82 N/10
Touring the Wapta Icefields

This connection is also straightforward in good visibility but can be challenging in a whiteout.

From Bow Hut climb up the hill in a northwest direction. Once you reach the glacier the direction of travel becomes westerly. Climb up beneath the impressive north face of St. Nicholas Peak and work your way around the west side of the peak until you can ski up into the pass between St. Nicholas Peak and Mount Olive.

From the pass head east out onto the Vulture Glacier, then curve around to the right. Continue descending in a southeast direction to the hut. There are numerous crevasses at the toe of the glacier, directly in your path, so it is best to pick a line that takes you along the east

side of the glacier, then curves around to the south at the very end.

In poor visibility the best tactic is to ski east (with the aid of a compass) from the Olive/St. Nicholas Col until the escarpment which runs along the east side of the Vulture Glacier can be seen. Then descend the glacier using this escarpment as a handrail (it shows up through the mist as assorted cliffs and scree slopes). As you near the end of the glacier, the escarpment can be followed to the right (south) to the hut (GR 375157). The location of the Balfour Hut changed in 1990 so any information prior to this date will be incorrect.

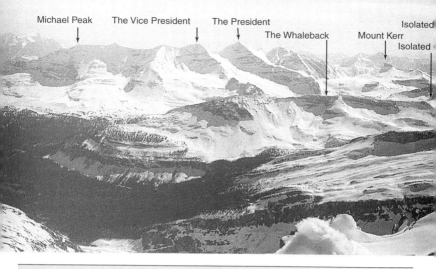

Michael Peak   The Vice President   The President
                                        The Whaleback   Mount Kerr   Isolated
                                                                        Isolated

111 PEYTO HUT TO BALFOUR HUT

Ski mountaineering 2

Grade Easy
Distance 7 km one way
Time 5-7 hours
Height gain 430 m to Olive/St. Nicholas Col
Height loss 430 m to Balfour Hut
Max elevation 2930 m
Maps Hector Lake 82 N/9
Blaeberry River 82 N/10
Touring the Wapta Icefields

This tour offers the essence of icefields touring. It stays high and traverses across 'endless' expanses of snow. In some conditions the descent to the Balfour Hut can be fast and fun.

Many people ski directly from the Peyto Hut to the Balfour Hut. The trip is straightforward when there is good visibility. Refer to pages 179 and 180 for the route. These two tours can be connected easily—instead of descending to Bow Hut when traversing from the Peyto Hut, simply continue high across the icefield to the Olive/St. Nicholas Col and follow the usual route down to the Balfour Hut.

ated Col   Isolated Peak   Mount McArthur

Glacier Des Poilus

112 BALFOUR HUT TO SCOTT DUNCAN HUT   Ski mountaineering 3

Grade Intermediate
Distance 10 km
Time 6-8 hours
Height gain 520 m to Balfour High Col
Height loss 320 m to Scott Duncan Hut
Max elevation 3020 m
Map Hector Lake 82 N/9
Touring the Wapta Icefields

This is one of the most challenging sections of ski mountaineering on the Wapta Icefields. It should only be undertaken in good visibility as it is hard to navigate by map and compass in the complicated terrain below Mount Balfour.

From the Balfour Hut, descend a short distance then ski across the flats in a southerly direction to reach the lower slopes of Mount Balfour. Ascend the slope and ski out onto the glacier, heading towards a rock cliff that sticks out prominently in the middle of the glacier. High above you on the right is another bench which is sometimes used as a route up the glacier. As you approach the rock cliff the route turns up to the right and climbs steeply up a narrow ramp. The angle then eases, the route turns left and continues another kilometre to Balfour High Col. This route

is subject to icefall from the northeast face of Mount Balfour and you should travel as quickly as possible without rest stops.

From the col the route descends in a southeast direction across the Waputik Icefield, heading almost directly for Mount Daly. There are a few crevasses across here and you should ski with caution. The hut is located at the base of the spur that descends in a northwest direction from Mount Daly (GR 417084).

Mount Des Poilus

113 SCHIESSER/LOMAS ROUTE

Ski mountaineering 3

Grade Intermediate in the upper section. Below Sherbrooke Lake, where the trail descends through the trees to West Louise Lodge, the skiing is more difficult
Distance 12 km from the Scott Duncan Hut to West Louise Lodge
Time This descent takes most of the day
Height loss 1060 m
Max elevation 2710 m
Maps Hector Lake 82 N/9
Lake Louise 82 N/8
Touring the Wapta Icefields

This is the safest and the most pleasant way to descend from the Scott Duncan Hut to the Trans Canada Highway. In reasonable visibility it is easy to follow. However, if you are unfamiliar with the terrain it can be difficult in a whiteout, requiring advanced navigational skills in the upper section.

From the Scott Duncan Hut descend to the glacier below. Traverse south toward the pass between Mount Niles and Mount Daly. Ski around the right side of the small peak in the centre of the pass and descend a slope that takes you out onto a broad bench high above Niles Creek.

Descend along the bench for about 2 km. Very near the end of the bench the route swings to the right and begins to curve back around the shoulder, towards the west. Be sure to swing right around to the west so that you are clearly above upper Sherbrooke Creek. Descend open slopes, then ski through the trees into upper Sherbrooke Creek. Continue directly down the creek bed to the flat, open meadow where it joins Niles Creek. There are a few short steep sections in this creek bed which can be difficult in crusty or icy conditions.

Mount Collie

After you reach the junction of Niles Creek with Sherbrooke Creek, continue to just short of the brow of a steep hill, not far above Sherbrooke Lake. From here it is best to traverse out to the right, through the trees, to the brow of the hill. Descend steeply for a short distance until you reach an open slope which descends to more gentle terrain. Ski down to the lake and cross it (be sure the lake is well frozen).

Once across the lake continue above the left bank of Sherbrooke Creek for a short distance, then search up to the left to find the summer trail. From here the trail turns east and heads down and around the shoulder of Paget Peak to West Louise Lodge. This section of the trail is steep and challenging—it can be the most difficult part of the descent, particularly if you have a large pack and the trail is icy or rutted.

114 TRADITIONAL SHERBROOKE LAKE EXIT   Ski mountaineering 3

The Scott Duncan Hut was built to enable parties exiting the Wapta to get an early start and descend this route while conditions were well frozen. Previously, parties had been forced to descend dangerous slopes late in the day. The traditional exit down Niles Creek can still be dangerous and is not recommended unless the snowpack is very stable. The route goes through the pass between Mount Niles and Mount Daly, staying on the left side of the little peak in the pass, then descends the Niles Creek drainage.

115 BATH GLACIER EXIT   Ski mountaineering 3

Grade Intermediate
Distance 11 km from the Scott Duncan Hut to West Louise Lodge
Time This descent takes most of the day
Height loss 1060 m
Max elevation 2800 m
Maps Hector Lake 82 N/9
Lake Louise 82 N/8
Touring the Wapta Icefields

The exit via the Bath Glacier offers an interesting variation and in good conditions can be a viable alternative to the Schiesser/Lomas route. There is one very steep slope, about 300 m high, that you should feel very certain about before descending.

From the Scott Duncan Hut head north and curve around to the right (east). Ski through a gentle pass on the northeast side of Mount Daly and out onto the Bath Glacier. From here the route continues south across the Bath Glacier, high above the valley. The route is generally safe along here, but there are a few sections where the slope is steep enough to be dangerous in certain conditions.

After about 8 km the route climbs to a pass between Paget Peak and Mount Bosworth. The descent down the south side of this pass is extremely steep and should be undertaken only if you are absolutely certain of the safety of the slope (often it is windblown and bare). From the bottom of this slope continue south down the valley. After about 1 km swing right above the upper edge of the trees and work your way over to a large avalanche path which descends from Paget Peak. Ski down this path, then continue through the trees to West Louise Lodge almost directly below.

Opposite: Chic Scott, Don Gardner and Charlie Locke at Balfour High Col in 1967 on the last day of the Great Divide ski traverse. Photo Neil Liske.

116 THE YOHO TRAVERSE

Ski mountaineering 3

Grade Advanced
Distance 20 km one way
Time The tour from Bow Lake to Little Yoho usually takes two days. From Bow Hut it can be done in one very long day
Height gain 820 m
Height loss 1100 m
Max elevation 2900 m
Maps Hector Lake 82 N/9
Blaeberry River 82 N/10
Touring the Wapta Icefields

From the Bow Hut you can traverse to the Stanley Mitchell Hut in the Little Yoho Valley. Most parties will find this a very long day—so be prepared to camp along the way. There are several slopes which provide serious avalanche potential in certain conditions, so it is best to wait for a period of high stability before attempting this trip. Routefinding in whiteout conditions would be extremely difficult on this tour.

From Bow Hut climb northwest up the hill and head west out onto the icefield. Ski west to the broad, open pass between Rhondda South and Mount Gordon. From the pass descend gently

for several kilometres and ski across to the broken section of glacier descending southeast from Mount Collie. This is the first challenge of the trip—to find a way through these crevasses.

Once above them head southwest to the top of a very steep slope above the Des Poilus Glacier. This is the second challenge of the tour—to descend this slope safely. In certain conditions it may not be possible.

Cross the Des Poilus Glacier heading south. People often camp in this area rather than stay at the Bow Hut. The third challenge is to ascend the steep ramp which works its way from right to left under Isolated Peak, up to Isolated Col (GR 298101). Caution is required here as the slope is steeper than it appears.

The descent of the south facing slope of Isolated Col is also steep and requires caution. Continue down the valley, then descend steeply through the trees to the Stanley Mitchell Hut which is located on the edge of a meadow, along the banks of the Little Yoho River (GR 303081). To ski out to the highway refer to the Little Yoho Valley (see page 148) and Yoho Valley Road (see page 147).

The south side of Isolated Peak and Isolated Col on the right. This slope has serious avalanche potential.

ICEFIELDS PARKWAY NORTH

117 Nigel Pass	intermediate	p. 189
118 Wilcox Pass	intermediate/advanced	p. 190
119 Parker Ridge	intermediate	p. 191
120 Hilda Ridge	intermediate	p. 192
121 Sunwapta Falls/Athabasca River	intermediate	p. 194
122 Poboktan Creek	easy	p. 195
123 Maligne Pass	advanced	p. 197
124 Fryatt Creek	advanced	p. 198

The northern section of the Icefields Parkway stretches from the junction with the David Thompson Highway (Highway 11) at Saskatchewan River Crossing to Jasper. It is a remote highway and the section from the bottom of the 'Big Bend' over Sunwapta Pass and past the Athabasca Glacier is subject to avalanche and poor visibility. There are no service stations and little sign of civilization. Apart from several hostels and a campground there is nowhere to stay. It is a bit of a backcountry experience just to drive this road in the winter. Be certain that you have enough gas to reach your destination and return before you start.

The highway itself is an excellent road. It is well maintained and in good weather virtually any driver in any type of vehicle can handle it. However, during the big storms, when the snow comes, driving conditions can be very difficult. The highway is occasionally closed while avalanche slopes are bombed and snowplows do their work.

Be certain that you are prepared to deal with cold weather and snow. This includes a strong battery, good snow tires, jumper cables, survival gear and a shovel. Starting your car after a day or two of skiing in extremely cold weather can be a major problem.

Accommodation There are hostels located at Rampart Creek, Hilda Creek, Beauty Creek and Athabasca Falls. Some of these have saunas which can be a real treat on a starlit winter night after a hard tour. There are enclosed picnic shelters at the Columbia Icefields Campground, located just south of the information centre.

There are two warden stations, one at Saskatchewan River Crossing (which may or may not be manned) and one at Poboktan Creek. There are pay telephones along the road at the tourist complex at Saskatchewan River Crossing, the Information Centre at the Columbia Icefield, Poboktan Creek and the Valley of the Five Lakes trailhead.

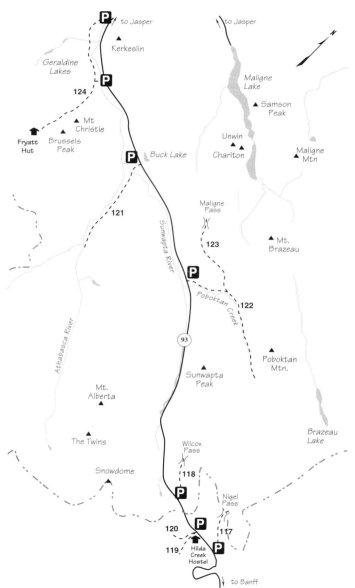

117 NIGEL PASS

Ski touring 2

Grade Intermediate
Distance 16 km return
Time 4-6 hours return
Height gain 280 m
Max elevation 2120 m
Map Columbia Icefield 83 C/3

This is a very pleasant tour through spectacular mountain terrain. It is varied and interesting but not too difficult. The valley gets a lot of sun. This trip offers and easy day tour with lots of time for lunch breaks and exploring around.

Hazards Approach the pass with caution as cornices can overhang the cliffs above the Brazeau River.

Options To continue over the pass and down the Brazeau River it is necessary to climb up to your right (east) about 1 km before the pass. Gain about 100 vertical metres and cross into the Brazeau drainage which is followed down to your left (west).

Access There is a parking lot on the east side of the Icefields Parkway about 7 km south of Sunwapta Pass.

From the parking lot ski straight ahead up the old road. Do not follow the trail which is off to the right, across the stream. After about 1.5 km, where a large avalanche path descends from the left, turn right into the trees for a short distance, to the old Camp Parker Warden Cabin. Ski past the cabin on the left side and angle down through open timber to Nigel Creek (a steep but short descent). Follow the creek bed for another kilometre until the sides begin to pinch in. It is possible to continue up the creek if there is lots of snow, but it is better to climb up onto the right bank and gain a bench about 50 m higher. Here there is a trail in the woods. Follow the trail along this bench for 1 km until the terrain starts to open up and the canyon disappears. Continue easily, just above the creek, for another kilometre until it is necessary to climb up on the right bank again to pass a rocky canyon below. Soon the trail descends to the creek and the way ahead is clear. Follow the drainage straight ahead, climbing gradually through meadows

and clumps of trees, up to Nigel Pass. If you stay to the left and ski to the lowest point in the pass, you will end up looking down a very steep cliff into the headwaters of the Brazeau River.

Of Historical Interest Joe Weiss was a Swiss adventurer and photographer who lived in Jasper. Between 1929 and 1933 he undertook five major ski expeditions in the Rockies. In 1930 he and four companions (Frank Burstrom, A.L. Withers, Vern and Doug Jefferys) skied the valley route from Jasper to Banff. They crossed Nigel Pass en route and spent a night at the Camp Parker Warden Cabin. The trip took them 15 days and they arrived in Banff just in time for the winter carnival. Joe skied the traverse a second time in 1931 with Cliff White (of Skoki fame) and Russell Bennett. Along the way they made the first winter ascent of Snow Dome. Joe's last great tour was in 1933 when he and his companions very nearly made the first winter ascent of Mount Columbia. There is a very fine book about Joe entitled *One Man's Mountains* by Helen Colinson. If you can locate a copy it makes a very interesting read.

118 WILCOX PASS

Ski touring 2

Grade Intermediate/advanced
Distance 8 km return
Time 4-6 hours return
Height gain 360 m
Max elevation 2360 m
Map Columbia Icefield 83 C/3

An exciting tour that gets you up high very quickly. There is an outstanding view, out west, of the Columbia Icefield.

Hazards The steep initial section of this tour may be tricky to descend.

Access Park at the plowed turn-off into the Wilcox Creek Campground, on the north side of the Icefields Parkway, 2.5 km south of the Columbia Icefield Chalet.

The trail climbs up the hillside almost immediately above the parking area. It is advisable to put skins on your skis for the initial part of this tour. The trail can be found in the trees straight ahead of the parking area. At first the trail climbs at a reasonable, though steep, angle. After a short distance, the trail enters a gully and it becomes necessary to make several switchbacks. After gaining about 50 m elevation, ski out left to the brow of the hill. The angle eases off here and the way ahead follows a gentle bench which climbs gradually through the trees. After a short distance you can climb up to your right through some trees, for about 75 vertical metres, onto a higher bench. Follow this higher bench easily to the northwest, for about 3 km, to the pass.

119 PARKER RIDGE

Ski touring 2

Grade Intermediate
Distance 2 km to reach the ridge
Time 2 hours to the ridge
Height gain 410 m
Max elevation 2440 m
Map Columbia Icefield 83 C/3

Parker Ridge is the classic location in the Rockies to make a few turns. The slope is excellent, the views are outstanding and the snow is deep. The hillside starts within a stone's throw of the car and, if you chose to stay overnight, there is a hostel right at the bottom of the run. Because the snow comes early and stays late, this is a favourite autumn and springtime ski hill. Note that the area may be closed to skiers until there is sufficient snow to prevent damage to fragile alpine vegetation.

Facilities Hilda Creek Hostel is located just off the road, at the bottom of Parker Ridge.

Hazards Parker Ridge is avalanche country and there have been several fatalities here over the years. Ski with caution and use all safety procedures.

Access Parking is available in a large lot on the north side of the Icefields Parkway overlooking Hilda Creek, about 3 km south of Sunwapta Pass (directly across the road from the Hostel).

From your car, walk across the highway and continue a short distance east along the highway until it is possible to put your skis on and ski up to the hostel which is located just south of the highway. From the hostel make your way up through the trees for several hundred metres, then angle off to the right about the point where you break out of the trees. Above you on your left is a steep slope that has killed several people in the past. Ski a short distance along to the right, to a point where the angle of the hillside lays back and there is a poorly defined drainage.

Turn up to the left and climb the hill at the lowest and safest point to reach the bench above. Now begin to work your way out to the southeast, climbing gradually up to Parker Ridge. Once you reach the ridge you can continue along the crest, gaining another 150 vertical metres. Most people stop at about this point, where the ridge becomes narrow, to admire the incredible view.

The safest descent is to return along the route you just climbed. There are, however, many alternatives lines of descent, if conditions are safe.

Of Historical Interest Parker Ridge was the scene for many years of the Sunwapta Giant Slalom. This ski race, organized by the Calgary Mountain Club, was held on the Victoria Day long weekend during the 1960s. It was a great springtime event, attracting up to 2000 spectators, skiing and partying in the sun and the snow. A young skier by the name of Nancy Greene was the winner one year.

Opposite: Returning from Wilcox Pass. Across the valley lies the Columbia Icefield, Athabasca Glacier and Snow Dome.

The view from Parker Ridge over the Saskatchewan Glacier is superb.

120 HILDA RIDGE

Ski touring/telemarking 2

Grade Intermediate
Distance 2.5 km to reach the ridge
Time 2 hours to the ridge
Height gain 410 m
Max elevation 2440 m
Map Columbia Icefield 83 C/3

An enjoyable alternative to Parker Ridge which will often be in shape when Parker Ridge is skied out or windblown.

Facilities Hilda Creek Hostel offers rustic accommodation.

Hazards Some of these slopes are steep enough to avalanche. Ski with caution and use all avalanche safety procedures.

Access Park your car and make your way to the Hilda Creek Hostel (see Parker Ridge page 191).

Ski west beyond the hostel, through the trees, over to Hilda Creek. Continue up the creek bed for a short distance, until it appears reasonable to begin climbing the hillside on your right (north). Work your way up through the trees for about 180 vertical metres until you break out of the forest onto the crest of a ridge. Continue working your way up the ridge for another 100 vertical metres. You can descend to Hilda Creek a number of different ways: the descent straight down to Hilda Creek is the obvious line. Use caution!

Skiing the trail from Sunwapta Falls to the Athabasca River.

193

121 SUNWAPTA FALLS/ATHABASCA RIVER   Ski touring 1

Grade Intermediate
Distance 12 km return to the junction with the Athabasca River
Time 4-5 hours return
Height loss 100 m
Max elevation 1390 m
Maps Athabasca Falls 83 C/12
Fortress Lake 83 C/5

This is a pleasant and popular trail and there are great views of the surrounding peaks from the Athabasca River. The trail is unique in that it descends on the way out and climbs coming back to your car.

Options You can continue along the Athabasca River flats for another 8 km to the junction of the Athabasca and Chaba Rivers.

Access Turn west off the Icefields Parkway onto the Sunwapta Falls access road, 55 km south of Jasper. Drive about 0.5 km along this road to a parking lot.

From the parking lot drop steeply down a few feet in front of the cars onto the trail. The trail then descends steeply and immediately crosses a bridge over the chasm of Sunwapta Falls. Climb a few feet on the other side of the bridge then continue through the woods. The trail descends gradually for about 2.5 km then flattens out for another 2 km. The final kilometre is a moderately steep descent down to the Athabasca River.

Skiing along the Athabasca River toward Mount Quincy.

122 POBOKTAN CREEK

Grade Easy
Distance 26 km return
Time A full day tour for most skiers
Height gain 400 m
Max elevation 1940 m
Map Sunwapta Peak 83 C/6

The tour up Poboktan Creek is a pleasant valley trip. The trail through the trees is sometimes well packed by wardens with their snow machines.

Facilities Toilets at the parking area.

Hazards Do not attempt to ski along the bed of Poboktan Creek as there is a narrow canyon about 4 km below Waterfall Warden Cabin which is impassable.

Access There is a large parking lot on the east side of the Icefields Parkway, on the south side of Poboktan Creek, about 70 km south of Jasper (just across the creek from the warden station).

From the parking area descend almost directly down to Poboktan Creek. Cross the creek on a bridge, then ski for about 0.5 km along the north side of the creek. At this point the trail begins to climb steeply and soon gains about 100 vertical metres. It now continues high on the north slope, working its way into the valley. After about 3 km the trail drops down to the creek again and follows it along for a short distance. Then, once again, it climbs up onto the north bank and for several kilometres works its way through the trees, until it reaches Poligne Creek. At this point a trail branches north toward Maligne Pass (see page 197).

Cross this creek and follow the trail as it winds its way through the woods for about 1 km, until it reaches another creek. The trail crosses this creek and continues up the valley, climbing steadily. After several kilometres of traversing along the northeast side of the valley, the trail descends to Poboktan Creek. Follow the creekbed for about 1 km to a major fork. The way up the left fork looks clear but is actually a dead end. Follow the right fork for a very short distance then climb the open slope up onto the left bank. In the angle between the two forks you will find the trail again (and the Waterfall Camping Area as well). Follow the trail through the trees for about 1 km until it descends to the open meadows along Poboktan Creek. Ski across the meadow to the far end (1.5 km) where the Waterfall Warden Cabin is located at the edge of the trees, on the northeast side of the meadow.

Looking back down Poboktan Creek from beyond Waterfall Warden Cabin. Photo Mike Potter.

The old Fryatt Hut before extensive renovations. Photo ACC Collection.

123 MALIGNE PASS

Grade Advanced
Distance 28 km return
Time This is a full day tour
Height gain 700 m
Max elevation 2240 m
Map Sunwapta Peak 83 C/6

This tour should be undertaken by experienced skiers who can handle very tricky downhill skiing on narrow trails. The way up the narrow valley of Poligne Creek is difficult and the route does not get any easier until very near Maligne Pass. The descent to Poboktan Creek is an exciting ride to say the least. Maligne Pass, however, is high, alpine, very beautiful and well worth the trip.

Facilities Toilets at the parking lot.

Hazards This tour should be undertaken only when the avalanche hazard is low as the upper part is very exposed.

Access There is a large parking lot on the east side of the Icefields Parkway, on the south side of Poboktan Creek, about 70 km south of Jasper (across the creek from the warden station).

From the parking lot follow the Poboktan Creek trail for 7 km to its junction with Poligne Creek (see page 195). From the junction, ski north, up the hill, for several hundred metres, then cross a bridge to the east bank of Poligne Creek. The trail climbs very steeply now and skins are recommended. It does one very long switchback to the right then swings to the left and begins to head into the valley at a more reasonable angle. The trail continues along horizontally for some way, then descends to the creek.

Cross a bridge, then continue along the trail as it climbs into the trees on the west bank. The trail descends to the creek again after about 1 km. Cross the creek on a bridge located at the edge of a large avalanche path. Follow the trail through the trees, climbing steadily, high above the east bank of the creek. After another kilometre the trail again descends to the creek. Cross a bridge to the west bank. You are now in the V-angle formed by the junction of two creeks, about 2.5 km up the trail, north of Poboktan Creek. Continue following a trail through the trees to reach the most westerly of the two creeks, the one which descends from Maligne Pass. Follow this creek, staying on the east bank, for about 0.5 km, until you cross it on a small bridge. You are now on the west bank of the most westerly creek. Continue angling up the treed hillside above and soon the trail peters out. Traverse right into the creek bed itself, which is followed for a short distance, until you come out into the open at a giant avalanche path. Cross the avalanche path and ski up a draw to your right to regain safer ground in the trees. Now work your way up towards the pass, through the trees, staying well back from the avalanche slopes on your right. After a while the trees thin out, then disappear. Continue climbing at a moderate angle for several kilometres to the pass. The last 4 km, beyond the avalanche path, is very beautiful and the pass itself is outstanding.

124 FRYATT CREEK

Ski touring 2

Grade Advanced
Distance 13 km one way from the Athabasca River Crossing
Time It is a full day tour to reach to hut
Height gain 780 m
Max elevation 1980 m
Map Athabasca Falls 83 C/12

An adventurous ski tour with a cabin as your reward. The headwall at the end, up to the cabin, can be a killer—try to leave plenty of time to deal with this obstacle in daylight.

Facilities The Fryatt Hut is located just above the headwall at the end of the valley. Note that it is incorrectly marked on the map—the correct grid reference is 403174.

Hazards Use care when crossing the Athabasca River—be sure it is well frozen.

Access Park on the west side of the Icefields Parkway at a plowed parking lot about 41 km south of Jasper.

Ski carefully across the river, climb the bank, and head into the woods to find the trail.

If it is not possible to cross the river you can follow the summer trail from Athabasca Falls. Ski along the road for a short distance from the Athabasca Falls parking lot, crossing the bridge over the Athabasca River and round the curve. Turn left up the Geraldine Fire Road and follow this for about 2 km to the junction with the Fryatt trail. Turn left again and follow the trail along the valley bottom for 6 km to reach the river crossing point.

From the river crossing point follow the trail south for 3.5 km to where it crosses Fryatt Creek. From here the trail turns southwest and climbs steeply through the forest along the south side of the valley for about 4 km. The creek is reached again and the way becomes easier. Follow the drainage up the valley, cross the lake, then continue up the drainage to the headwall. The summer trail is hard to follow up the steep headwall and the skiing is very difficult. It is often a good idea to just take off your skis and climb the hill on foot. Ascend the hill on a diagonal from right to left, staying to the right of the waterfall. The Alpine Club of Canada informs me that the route up the headwall is now marked with yellow markers. The cabin is just above the northwest side of the creek, not far beyond the rim of the headwall.

Sydney Vallance (Fryatt) Hut

A very pleasant hut in a beautiful location. It has been completely refurbished in recent years.
Location Above the headwall at the head of Fryatt Creek GR 403174 (note that the cabin site marked on the map is incorrect).
Map Athabasca Falls 83 C/12
Facilities Foamies, Coleman cooking stoves and lanterns, cooking and eating utensils and a wood heating stove.
Capacity 12
Water From the creek a few metres east of the hut.
Reservations The Alpine Club of Canada 403-678-3200
Note The hut is locked when a custodian is not present and a combination number is required.

JASPER AREA

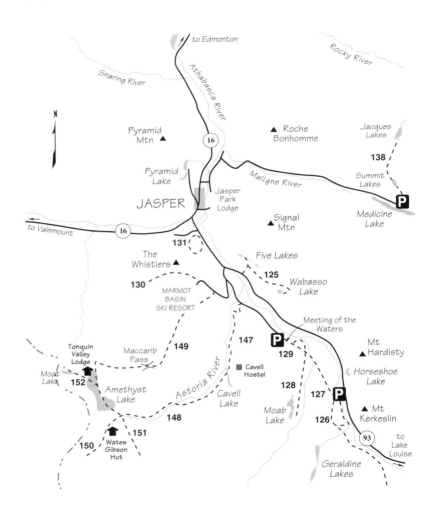

Jasper National Park is the largest of the mountain parks, covering 10,878 square kilometres. It offers extensive opportunities for cross country skiing in a wilderness setting. The town of Jasper is quiet in winter but still has everything that you may require. The Athabasca Valley is very low in elevation, consequently Jasper area trails can often suffer from lack of snow. The trails near Maligne Lake however, have a much deeper snow pack.

Access Jasper is most easily reached by a 360 km drive from Edmonton via Highway 16. One can also reach Jasper after a 230 km drive along the Icefields Parkway (Highway 93) from Lake Louise. Mount Robson Provincial Park is located 88 km west of Jasper along Highway 16. Many of the ski trails in this chapter are found along the Maligne Lake Road which branches off Highway 16, 5 km east of Jasper.

Facilities The town of Jasper has a population of about 2500 and offers all the amenities a ski adventurer could want. There are gas stations, grocery stores, book stores, restaurants, hotels, a liquor store and a post office. The best bargains in accommodation are the Jasper Hostel, located 7 km from town along the road to the Sky Tram or the Maligne Canyon Hostel, located 11 km east of Jasper on the road to Maligne Canyon (phone 780-852-3215 for both these hostels). For your equipment needs try Gravity Gear (888-852-3155) or Totem Ski Shop (780-852-3078).

Information There is a Park Information Centre located across from the VIA Station in the centre of downtown (780-852-6176). The Park Warden Office can be reached at 780-852-6155.

History Jasper has a rich skiing history dating back to the late 1920s. Between 1929 and 1933 Joe Weiss made five ski expeditions into the heart of the Rockies, including two traverses all the way from Jasper to Banff. His companions on many of these trips were Jasper locals such as Vern and Doug Jeffery, Pete Withers and Frank Burstrom. In 1930 a young adventurer by the name of A.L. Parsons made a solo winter ascent of Resplendent Mountain, near Mount Robson.

During the 1940s and 50s The Alpine Club of Canada hut in the Tonquin Valley was the scene of much ski activity. Rex Gibson was a leading force at the time and after he died the hut was named in his honour (and that of Cyril Wates).

Several ski cabins were built in the area near Maligne Lake. The most famous of these is the Shangri-La cabin, built by legendary guide Curly Phillips at the head of Jeffery Creek. The skiing above the cabin in Snow Bowl is some of the best in the Rocky Mountains. Phillips was killed in 1938 in an avalanche at Elysium Pass.

During the war a Scottish Regiment trained in the Jasper Area. The Lovat Scouts, as they were called, learned mountain skills from some of Canada's most prominent ski guides and were led by noted British mountaineer Frank Smythe. The Canadian officer in charge was none other than Major Rex Gibson. Unfortunately, many of these soldiers were to lose their lives in the Italian Campaign.

125 VALLEY OF THE FIVE LAKES/WABASSO LAKE   Nordic skiing 1

Grade Easy/intermediate
Distance 2 km one way to the Valley of the Five Lakes, 6 km one way to Wabasso Lake
Time 1 hour one way to the Valley of the Five Lakes, 2 hours one way to Wabasso Lake
Height gain 75 m
Max elevation 1130 m
Maps Jasper 83 D/16
Medicine Lake 83 C/13

A short and pleasant ski tour that can be lengthened substantially by skiing to Wabasso Lake. The terrain is rolling and on an overcast day it would be easy to get turned around. It is recommended that you carry a map and compass.

Facilities There are telephones, picnic tables and toilets at the trailhead.

Hazards Note that the trails are incorrectly drawn on the topographical map. Also the Fifth Lake is incorrectly labelled Wabasso Lake. Wabasso Lake is about 4 km farther southeast (GR 352482).

Options Although there are trails which lead from the Valley of the Five Lakes back to Jasper, they are very difficult to follow. You should not attempt to ski them unless you are skilled at route finding in complicated terrain.

Access There is a parking lot on the northeast side of the Icefields Parkway, 9 km south of Jasper.

From the parking lot ski straight into the woods. Follow a clear trail in a northeast direction through the lodgepole pine forest. After about 800 m the trail drops down to a creek bed. From here you have two choices—Wabasso Lake is along the creek to the right and the Valley of the Five Lakes is straight ahead.

Wabasso Lake Turn right and ski along the creek bed. The terrain is gentle and makes easy travelling. The summer trail is actually on your left in the forest, but it is best to simply follow the creek. After about 5 km the woods close in around the creek and it is best to find the trail which curls around to the right, turning almost 180 degrees around the edge of a ridge. It then travels west several hundred metres to Wabasso Lake.

Valley of the Five Lakes From the junction at the creek, climb the hill above in a northeast direction (be careful of snow stability). At the top of the hill you have two choices.

1. You can angle off to the left, climbing at a gradual angle for about 200 m to a crest. Then descend the other side for 0.5 km to the First and Second Lakes.

2. To reach the Third, Fourth and Fifth Lakes angle to the right from the top of the hill and climb through the woods for several hundred metres to the top of a crest. Descend the other side, ski along a small open space, then climb to another crest. Descend the other side and continue down for about 200 m to the lakes.

126 ATHABASCA FALLS LOOP
Nordic skiing 1

Grade Easy
Distance 7 km loop
Time 2 hours
Height gain 40 m
Max elevation 1220 m
Map Athabasca Falls 83 C/12

A very pleasant trail over varied terrain.

Facilities There are telephones and toilets at the parking lot.

Options You can continue up the Geraldine Fire Road for another 7 km and gain over 500 m in elevation. The view from the top is excellent but the road is steep and relentless.

Access Drive south from Jasper along the Icefields Parkway for 31 km, then follow Highway 93A a short distance to the Athabasca Falls parking lot.

Ski along snow covered Highway 93A and cross the bridge over the Athabasca River. The impressive frozen waterfall will be seen on your left. Continue along the road for about 0.5 km as it curves north to the turn-off for the Geraldine Fire Road. Turn left and ski up the fire road for about 2 km gradually gaining elevation through the forest, to the Fryatt Creek trailhead. Turn left and follow the trail for about 1 km until it veers left along a marsh. Follow the trail east for 1 km to the Athabasca River, then turn left again and ski along the shore back to the road and the parking lot.

127 ATHABASCA FALLS/MEETING OF THE WATERS
Nordic skiing 1

Grade Easy
Distance 10.5 km one way
Time 3-4 hours one way
Height gain 60 m
Height loss 120 m
Max elevation 1240 m
Map Athabasca Falls 83 C/12

A gentle trail which follows snow covered Highway 93A. There are some good views of the valley and the surrounding peaks.

Options This trail can be skied in either direction. It can be extended by skiing the Moab Lake Trail and/or the Whirlpool Campground Trail.

Access This trail is most often skied from south to north. One car can be left at the Meeting of the Waters picnic site on Highway 93A. The road is only plowed as far south as this point. Then drive around via the Icefields Parkway to the Athabasca Falls parking lot, 31 km south of Jasper, and begin your tour here.

From the parking lot the trail simply follows Highway 93A. It begins by crossing the bridge over the Athabasca River, then continues around a long curve, past the intersection with the Geraldine Fire Road. The road climbs very gradually for about 4 km then, just beyond Leach Lake, begins a gradual descent for about 2 km. The road levels off towards the bridge over the Whirlpool River. The road then continues another 2.5 km to your waiting car at the Meeting of the Waters parking lot.

128 MOAB LAKE
Nordic Skiing 1

Grade Easy
Distance 18 km return
Time 5-6 hours return
Height gain 110 m
Max elevation 1230 m
Map Athabasca Falls 83 C/12

A long, easy ski tour, much of it following a road through the forest. Some portions of the tour run parallel to the Whirlpool river, offering expansive views.

Options Can be extended up the Whirlpool River along the fire road for another 8.5 km to the Tie Camp Warden Cabin.

Access Drive south of Jasper for 7 km along the Icefields Parkway then turn right onto Highway 93A which is followed to the Meeting of the Waters picnic site. This is as far south as the road is plowed.

From the parking lot ski south along the snow covered road. After 2 km turn right onto the Whirlpool River Fire Road and follow it for another 6.5 km to what is the summer parking lot and trail head. Continue about 0.5 km beyond this point and you will see the trail for Moab Lake leaving the road on the right (large sign). The lake itself is just a short distance down the hill.

129 WHIRLPOOL CAMPGROUND LOOP
Nordic Skiing 1

Grade Easy
Distance 4.5 km return
Time 1-2 hours
Height gain Nil
Max elevation 1130 m
Map Athabasca Falls 83 C/12

A short and pleasant trip with some fine views.

Access Drive south of Jasper for 7 km along the Icefields Parkway, then turn right onto Highway 93A which is followed to the Meeting of the Waters picnic site. This is as far south as the road is plowed.

From the parking lot ski 2.2 km south along the snow covered road, as far as the Whirlpool River Bridge. Turn left and circle back through the campsite to return to the parking lot.

Of Historical Interest
The Meeting of the Waters and the trail up the Whirlpool River to Athabasca Pass is very historic. This is the route of the early fur traders and was discovered by David Thompson in the winter of 1810-11. Be sure to read the fascinating historical signpost at the Meeting of the Waters, then think of the early explorers and fur traders as you slide peacefully along the snowy trail.

130 WHISTLERS CREEK

Ski touring 2

Grade Easy as far as the creek then advanced beyond this point
Distance 10 km to upper creek return
Time 4-5 hours
Height gain 300 m
Max elevation 2100 m
Map Jasper 83 D/16

This tour is popular with locals, particularly when there is little snow in the valley near Jasper. It is a pleasant, easy ski for the first 2 km, as far as the intersection with Whistlers Creek, but beyond this it is more difficult.

Facilities The tour starts from the Marmot Basin Ski Resort where restaurants, toilets and telephones are available.

Hazards The steep slopes at the head of the valley offer avalanche potential and only experienced skiers, taking all the appropriate precautions, should venture beyond this point.

Options There is good potential for ski mountaineering and for making turns in the upper basin.

Access Drive south of Jasper along the Icefields Parkway for 7 km, then turn right onto Highway 93A. Follow this road for 2.5 km then turn right onto the Marmot Basin access road and follow it for about 11 km to the ski resort. Drive as far as you can, past the big ski lodge, to the highest parking lot #3.

The trail begins across the road from parking lot #3 and a few metres down the hill. Climb up the bank and head north into the trees. Climb gradually for about 400 m along a good trail until it reaches a small lake. Round the lake on the right on a trail through the trees, then continue north along the brow of a hill. A diversion of a few metres out to the right along here will give you a view across the Athabasca Valley to Jasper. The trail gains elevation very gradually and curves around to the left for about 1 km then, just after crossing the bottom of an avalanche path, it descends to the right to reach the creek bed. To this point the trail is reasonably level and wide.

From here the trail follows the stream bed and climbs more steeply. It is a tricky trail to descend so it is only recommended for more experienced skiers. After several kilometres the trees open up and the views improve. Beyond this point is ski mountaineering terrain for experienced skiers only.

131 WHISTLERS CAMPGROUND LOOP

Nordic skiing 1

Grade Easy
Distance 4.5 km loop
Time You can spend a few hours here or the whole day if you chose
Height gain Nil
Max elevation 1060 m
Map Jasper 83 D/16

The trackset trails of Whistlers Campground provide excellent skiing for skiers of all ages and abilities.

Facilities There are tables and fire pits for picnics.

Access Drive south from Jasper along Highway 93 and turn right after 3 km at Whistlers Mountain Road. Immediately turn left again along the campground road and follow this to the parking lot.

From the parking lot ski a short distance along the access road to join the campground perimeter road. This road forms a loop around the campground and offers enjoyable, easy skiing.

132 MARJORIE AND CALEDONIA LAKE

Ski touring 1

Grade Easy
Distance 4 km to Marjorie Lake return, 8 km to Caledonia Lake return
Time 1.5 hours to Marjorie Lake return, 3 hours to Caledonia Lake return
Height gain 70 m
Max elevation 1170 m
Map Jasper 83 D/16

This tour starts right at the edge of town. It is an easy way to get away from it all and spend a few hours in the woods.

Options Adventurous skiers can carry on around the Saturday Night Lake Circle, an additional 20 km of skiing and, most likely, trail breaking.

Access The trail starts at the southwest edge of town, along Cabin Creek Road, where the access road to the water supply begins.

From your car at the start of the access road, descend a few metres then cross the creek. Ski behind some houses for a short distance, then turn up to the right. Ski up the hill for about 100 m, turn sharply to the left and climb to a crest overlooking the houses of Jasper. The trail continues gaining elevation through the forest for about 0.5 km then descends and breaks out into a clearing. Cross the clearing, descending slightly, and enter the forest on the far side. The trail now climbs gradually for another kilometre along the south facing slope, then levels off and continues 0.5 km to Marjorie Lake.

Follow the trail along the right shore of the lake to an intersection at the far end. Stay to the left at the intersection and carry on into the forest. Follow along the edge of the delta at the end of the lake, then ski up a draw for about 1 km. The trail then traverses along a south facing hillside, through aspen and pine, for another kilometre to another intersection. Climb up a few metres to the right, then break out left and continue for about 1 km to Caledonia Lake.

133 CABIN LAKE FIRE ROAD

Ski touring 1

Grade Easy
Distance 6 km return
Time 2 hours
Height gain 80 m
Max elevation 1200 m
Map Jasper 83 D/16

A pleasant tour along an easy trail.

Options The adventurous can attempt to ski the Saturday Night Lake Circle. This 27 km tour is not often skied and the route finding can be tricky.

Access There is a parking lot on the left, 2 km up the Pyramid Lake Road, next to Cottonwood Slough.

From the parking lot ski southeast along a trail parallel to the road. After about 200 m turn right onto the Cabin Lake Fire Road. Head up the hill and in a few metres the road opens up into a large swath through the trees (this is the town of Jasper fire break). The tour continues along this fire break all the way to the lake. The trail passes under

some power lines in about 0.5 km, jogs left, then climbs to the brow of a hill. It descends a short distance, passing some large Douglas Firs, climbs over another hill then descends to Cabin Lake.

For an outstanding view, ski south along the dike at the east end of the lake, then descend to the left for about 0.5 km to the brow of a hill. This is an excellent viewpoint, overlooking the Athabasca Valley.

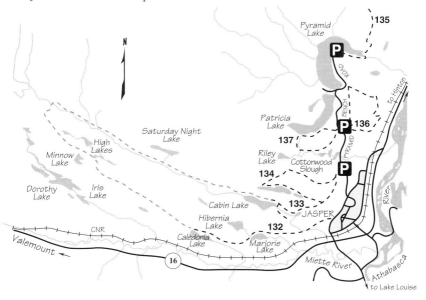

207

134 MINA LAKE LOOP

Nordic skiing 1

Grade Easy/intermediate
Distance 6.7 km loop
Time 2 hours
Height gain 110 m
Max elevation 1230 m
Map Jasper 83 D/16

An excellent trail which is varied but never too difficult.

Options This tour can be combined with a trip to Cabin Lake. A side excursion to Riley Lake is also possible.

Access As for Cabin Lake Fire Road.

From the parking lot head south, parallel to the road, for about 200 m to reach the Cabin Lake Fire Road. Turn right and follow the road up the hill. Within a few metres the road becomes a wide swath through the trees (it is actually the fire break for the town of Jasper). Follow the open path up the hill, under some power lines and continue up the clearing. The trail ascends for about 1 km and crosses over a hill then descends gently down the other side. You will see a trail, marked #8, on the right entering the forest. Turn onto this trail and ski through the forest for about 0.5 km to the first lake. Ski along the right bank of the lake, then ski 100 m to the second lake. Ski

along the right side of this lake through an open forest of mature Douglas Fir trees. From the end of the second lake the trail curves around to the right and descends steeply to a junction with the Riley Lake trail. If you chose to make a side trip to this lake it is off to your left about 0.5 km away. The trail descends steeply at one point and can be hard to follow.

To continue along the Mina Lake Loop turn right at the junction and climbed easily for about 0.5 km until the trail begins to descend. The last part of this tour is a fun downhill run for about 1 km through the woods to rejoin the Cabin Lake Fire Road. Turn left for some more downhill fun back to your car.

135 PALISADE LOOKOUT

Ski touring 1

Grade Intermediate
Distance 22 km return
Time 6-8 hours return
Height gain 890 m
Max elevation 2070 m
Map Jasper 83 D/16

A ski tour up a fire road which gives great views if you reach the top.

Access Park you car at the end of the Pyramid Lake Road, 6 km from Jasper.

This tour follows a road through forest all the way to the lookout. The grade

is moderate along the early part of the tour. After 7.5 km the road forks and you should follow the right-hand branch. The view from the top is worth the effort. Bundle up for the run back down.

136 PYRAMID BENCH LOOP

Nordic skiing 1

Grade Easy
Distance 4.5 km loop
Time 1-2 hours
Height gain Nil
Max elevation 1200 m
Map Jasper 83 D/16

The view across the valley towards the Colin Range is outstanding and there is an excellent chance of seeing wildlife, particularly sheep, along the bench. This trail should be avoided when there is little snow cover.

Access Same as the Patricia Lake Loop.

The trail starts just beyond the end of the parking lot and undulates through aspen forest in a northeast direction to a junction. Turn right here and ski up the trail through Douglas Fir forests. Soon you arrive at the top of the bench overlooking the Athabasca Valley. If it is not too windy this is a lovely place to take a break. Turn right and ski along the bench through the Douglas Firs. Eventually the trail turns back to the right, away from the bench, and the depth of snow immediately increases. Along this section there is a downhill which may be a challenge for novice skiers. The trail winds its way back to the parking lot.

Photo Gillean Daffern

137 PATRICIA LAKE LOOP

Grade Intermediate
Distance 6 km loop
Time 2 hours
Height gain 100 m
Max elevation 1210 m
Map Jasper 83 D/16

One of the most interesting tours in this area. The terrain is varied, the scenery is excellent and the trail holds the snow better than some of its neighbours. It is best skied in a clockwise direction.

Options The trailhead for this loop and the Pyramid Bench Loop are the same. You can ski both trails easily in a day.

Access Follow the Pyramid Lake Road from town for 3 km, then turn right into the Pyramid Riding Stables parking lot.

Ski back to the Pyramid Lake Road along a narrow trail which parallels the access road. Cross the road and the trail proper starts on the other side. In a very short distance the trail divides and you are urged to turn left. Work your way through the trees to the top of a bench overlooking Cottonwood Slough. Descend to the creek, then follow it west to the beaver pond. At this point the trail begins to climb steeply to the outlet creek from Patricia Lake. It crosses and re-crosses the creek before reaching the south shore of Patricia Lake. There is a long flat section along the lake with views of Pyramid Mountain and other peaks in the Victoria Cross Range. Make a sharp turn to the right near a building by the lake, then climb steeply up and over a ridge crossing two powerlines en route. A long pleasant downhill is your payoff and this takes you back to the intersection at the start of the trail.

Photo Gillean Daffern.

138 SUMMIT LAKES/JACQUES LAKE

Ski touring 1

Grade Easy to first Summit Lake, intermediate to Jacques Lake
Distance 10 km return to first Summit Lake, 24 km return to Jacques Lake
Time It is a half day trip to ski to first Summit Lake and back, it is a full day tour to ski to Jacques Lake and back
Height gain 80 m to Summit Lakes
Max elevation 1530 m at Summit Lakes, 1490 m at Jacques Lake
Map Medicine Lake 83 C/13

An excellent novice trail as far as Summit Lakes. The trail follows the valley along Beaver Creek between the Colin Range and the Queen Elizabeth Range and is very scenic. To carry on to Jacques Lake is more challenging and it may be necessary to break trail along this narrow path.

Facilities There are toilets at the trailhead and there is a picnic shelter just before reaching Beaver Lake.

Hazards Do not linger in the obvious avalanche path which crosses the valley just before Summit Lakes.

Access Drive 27 km along the Maligne Lake Road to the Beaver Creek picnic area which is on your left at the southeast end of Medicine Lake.

For the first 2 km, as far as Beaver Lake, the trail is a wide, gentle road. The trail then continues along the west shore of Beaver Lake, offering superb views of the immense slabby wall of the Queen Elizabeth Range. Beyond the lake the trail crosses to the east side of the valley briefly, then returns to the west side. Shortly after crossing an avalanche path the wide trail ends at the first Summit Lake. To carry on to Jacques Lake follow the right-hand (northeast) shore of both lakes before finding the summer trail again. Follow this trail through dense forests to Jacques Lake.

MALIGNE LAKE TRAILS

The well maintained trails at Maligne Lake offer superb Nordic skiing. The snow is usually excellent, the scenery is beautiful and there are a variety of trails to choose from. The touring into alpine terrain, high above the tree line, is also superb and there is great scope for making turns.

The Maligne Lake Trails are located at the end of the Maligne Lake Road, 45 km from Jasper. There are two parking lots. The first one on the northeast side of the lake, serves Lake Loop only. All the other trails in the area are accessed from the parking lot on the west side of Maligne Lake, across the bridge. Many of the trails begin along the Bald Hills Fire Road which starts where the access road turns left into this parking lot.

The Maligne Lake trails are usually trackset and offer a mix from short and easy to long and advanced.

Note The Maligne Lake area is the wintering ground for Cariboo. Please give them plenty of room—stay well back and keep dogs on leash.

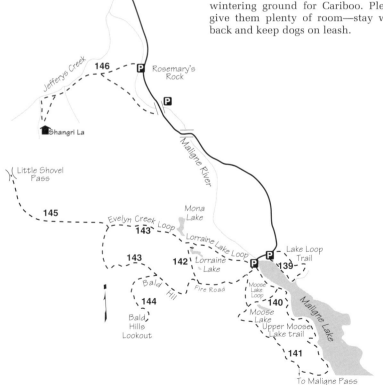

Lake Loop. Photo Gillean Daffern.

139 LAKE LOOP
Nordic skiing 1

Grade Easy/intermediate
Distance 3.5 km loop
Time 1 hour
Height gain 80 m
Max elevation 1720 m
Map Athabasca Falls 83 C/12

This is a wonderful trail but there are several hills that can be tricky for beginners.

Facilities Toilets at the trailhead.

Hazards Be sure the lake is well frozen and snow covered.

Access See introduction to the Maligne Lake trails.

Start at the downhill end of the parking lot, nearest the lake. Ski past the old Curly Phillips boathouse then continue along the edge of the lake for about 1 km. The scenery along here is outstanding. Turn left at a sharp inlet into the shoreline and ski up the inlet to the end. Continue straight ahead up a trail which climbs gradually angling around to the left. After about 1 km you cross a little meadow then the trail begins to climb more steeply for about 0.5 km eventually crossing a ridge crest. Descend gradually until you reach a large meadow on your right. Ski along the left flank of the meadow then turn left and begin descending again. About 0.5 km of gentle downhill takes you back to the parking lot. Along this last section of the trail you will pass several big depressions in the ground. These are called kettles and were left by the melting ice of the last ice age.

140 MOOSE LAKE LOOP
Nordic skiing 1

Grade Easy/intermediate
Distance 4.5 km loop
Time 1 hour
Height gain 60 m
Max elevation 1740 m
Map Athabasca Falls 83 C/12

This would be an easy trail if it were not for the hill down to the lake. Moose Lake is a lovely spot for a break.

Facilities Toilets at the trailhead.

Hazards Be sure the lake is well frozen and snow covered.

Options This trail can be linked with Upper Moose Lake Loop.

Access See the introduction to the Maligne Lake trails.

Start along the Bald Hills Fire Road. In about 100 metres turn left at the Maligne Pass trail sign. There is some very nice rolling skiing along here to the junction with Upper Moose Lake Loop. Turn left again and ski a fast downhill to Moose Lake. From here the trail continues more easily to the shore of Maligne Lake. Turn left once more and ski past the warden cabin to the parking lot.

141 UPPER MOOSE LAKE LOOP

Nordic skiing 1

Grade Intermediate
Distance 7.6 km loop
Time 2 hours
Height gain 90 m
Max elevation 1780 m
Map Athabasca Falls 83 C/12

This is a fun trail. It is always interesting and the views along the lakeshore are beautiful. It should be skied in the anticlockwise direction.

Hazards Be sure the lake is well frozen and snow covered.

Access See the introduction to the Maligne Lake trails.

The first part of this trail is as described for the Moose Lake Loop but at the junction continue ahead up the steep hill. After this it is a winding and narrow trail to the Maligne Pass trail junction.

From here the fun begins. Turn left and descend a draw, curving easily back and forth to the lake. Turn left again and follow the trail along the lakeshore, winding in and out at every indentation, rounding immense boulders to eventually join up with the last part of the Moose Lake Loop.

Skiing past one of the immense boulders along the lake shore. Photo Gillean Daffern.

142 LORRAINE LAKE LOOP

Nordic skiing 1

Grade Intermediate
Distance 7.3 km loop
Time 2 hours
Height gain 120 m
Max elevation 1820 m
Map Athabasca Falls 83 C/12

An entertaining trail which is a little more challenging than the Moose Lake Loops.

Facilities Toilets at the trailhead.

Hazards Watch out for the blind corners.

Options This loop ties in with the Evelyn Creek Loop.

Access See the introduction to the Maligne Lake trails.

Ski up the Bald Hills Fire Road for about 1.5 km then turn right at a sign onto a much narrower trail. The trail rolls along, finishing with a downhill run and a sharp left corner to Lorraine Lake. Ski around the northwest shoreline to join the Evelyn Creek Loop. Turn right at this junction and ski along a narrow twisting trail. It is mostly downhill with blind corners and emerges on the access road just north of the parking lot entrance. Be careful of other skiers ascending this trail.

143 EVELYN CREEK LOOP

Nordic skiing 1

Grade Intermediate/advanced
Distance 12 km loop
Time 3 hours
Height gain 280 m
Max elevation 1960 m
Map Athabasca Falls 83 C/12

A longer trail with a challenging downhill section. It is best skied in a clockwise direction to get the thrill of the long downhill run (about 140 m elevation loss).

Facilities Toilets at the trailhead.

Access See the introduction to the Maligne Lake trails.

Head up the Bald Hills Fire Road for about 3.5 km and at the end of a long straight section leave the fire road and continue straight ahead on the narrow Evelyn Creek trail. Make a long traverse across the hillside then, just past the Evelyn Pass hiking trail turn-off, turn right and descend to Evelyn Creek. At this point you will see, on your left, the bridge over Evelyn Creek. This is a long and exciting downhill run and it keeps the snow well. Turn right again and continue along a very pleasant rolling section to join the Lorraine Lake Loop just past Mona Lake.

Opposite: Looking east over Maligne Lake from the Bald Hills Lookout. Photo Gillean Daffern.

144 BALD HILLS LOOKOUT

Grade Intermediate
Distance 10.5 km return
Time This is a moderate day trip
Height gain 480 m
Max elevation 2170 m
Map Athabasca Falls 83 C/12

This trail takes you high above treeline, where the terrain and the scenery are beautiful. It is worth spending a few hours up here exploring the area.

Facilities Toilets at the trailhead.

Hazards Be prepared up here for the cold and wind. If you wander off into the meadows be careful of avalanche terrain.

Options It is tempting, if you have time, to explore across the meadows to the south.

Access See the introduction to the Maligne Lake trails.

The trail follows the Bald Hills Fire Road to the site of the old fire lookout. The fire road starts directly opposite the entrance to the parking lot. After the Evelyn Creek Loop turn-off (3.5 km) the fire road steepens considerably and climbs to the open ridge at treeline.

The trail continues along the ridge in a southerly direction, over meadows and rises, to reach the lookout site, which is on the left (east) side of the ridge. All along here there are wonderful views to the right of Mount Tekarra and the ridges of the Skyline Trail. However, when you reach the lookout site you are treated to the celebrated view of Maligne Lake and surrounding peaks.

145 LITTLE SHOVEL PASS

Ski touring 2

Grade Intermediate/advanced
Distance 20 km to the pass and return
Time This is a full day trip
Height gain 650 m
Max elevation 2320 m
Map Athabasca Falls 83 C/12

This is one of the finest tours in the Jasper area. It gets you up high into the alpine where there are some outstanding views and some turns can be made.

Facilities Toilets at the trailhead.

Hazards This tour takes you above timberline so be prepared to deal with avalanche terrain, extreme weather and limited visibility.

Options From Little Shovel Pass you can continue out north into Snow Bowl and down to the Shangri La Cabin. This is one of the finest spots for ski touring in the Rockies and is highly recommended (see opposite page).

Access The tour begins at Maligne Lake. Park in the lot at the end of the road, across the bridge from the chalet.

From the entrance to the parking lot walk about 25 m back along the access road. The trail starts on the left. This is the Skyline Trail and also the exit from the Lorraine Lake and Evelyn Creek Loops. The trail is excellent as it climbs and descends at a moderate angle through the trees for about 5 km to the Evelyn Creek Bridge. Keep a sharp eye out for skiers coming down the trail.

From the bridge it is best to follow the drainage to the pass. Head up Evelyn Creek for several hundred metres then angle up the right-hand fork (GR 525427) that comes down from Little Shovel Pass. This branch is not very

distinct to begin and may be hard to find. It might be best to ski up Evelyn Creek for about 200 m then angle up right through a clearing in the trees. The going is easy but the creek is hard to follow. After several hundred metres the creek becomes more distinct and easier to follow. Follow this branch of the creek for about 1.5 km until the creek bed flattens out and one crosses an open meadow near the end of the valley. At this point (GR 503420) angle up right into a very small drainage coming down from the pass. This creek is also not very distinct to begin with and is hard to find. Follow the drainage to the pass (GR 485430).

The summer trail which switchbacks up the hillside above the valley is not recommended as it traverses several open slopes higher up.

146 SHANGRI LA

Grade Intermediate
Distance 8 km one way
Time This tour takes all day and should really be combined with an overnight stay at the cabin.
Height gain 420 m
Max elevation 2000 m
Maps Medicine Lake 83 C/13
Athabasca Falls 83 C/12

Shangri La is a beautiful log cabin located high in the mountains near Jasper.

It is an outstanding destination for skiers of all abilities. Stay a few days and enjoy the peace and quiet of the Canadian Rockies.

The bowl above the hut, 7 km across and rimmed with many small peaks, offers excellent skiing. Days can be filled touring the meadows, admiring the scenery or carving turns and scrambling to the summits. The descents are not long, generally 2-300 vertical metres, but are more than adequate for a good days skiing.

Access From Jasper drive east of town along Highway 16 for about 3 km to the Maligne Lake turn-off. Drive up this road for almost 40 km.

There are two ways to begin the tour.
1. If the river is well frozen you can cross it at Rosemary's Rocks and ascend directly towards the valley of Jefferys Creek. Park your car in a plowed lot on the right at the point where the road leaves the Maligne River (GR 534477) and cuts inland (the large rocks are obvious in the river). Cross the river (Caution!), ascend the far bank and head off northwest, through the trees, following a trail with many blazes. The route initially seems to be going in the wrong direction but after several kilometres turns west and heads up the hillside, climbing steadily.

2. If the river is open, drive another 1 km along the road and park in a plowed lot on the left, just before the bridge. Cross the bridge on foot, then ski along the left bank of the river. Soon the trail begins to climb and works its way up the hillside (many blazes on the trees).

Eventually the two approaches join, then ascend steeply, cross a wooded shoulder, then descend to Jefferys Creek (GR 509476).

Follow the creek bed for about 2 km until it opens into a large meadow. Keep following the creek for several more kilometres, then turn left up a subsidiary stream which enters from the left (GR 478457) and follow it for 1 km to the cabin. The cabin itself is tucked away above the left bank of the stream and can be easy to miss. Usually you spot the water hole dug in the stream and the steep footsteps leading up the bank.

Many people take a short cut for the last kilometre to reach the cabin. Rather than following the small stream up to the cabin they turn up to the left (at about GR 483459) and ascend directly over a wooded shoulder.

Approaching Snow Bowl along Jefferys Creek.

The author at Shangri-la. Photo Tony Daffern.

TOURS AT SHANGRI LA

There are a variety of tours that can be done in Snow Bowl above Shangri La. All of them begin by skiing up the draw to the southwest which you see looking out the front door of the cabin. Very quickly this draw breaks out of the trees into the open meadows. Do not attempt to follow the stream bed itself which continues past the cabin in a southerly direction. The walls of this stream bed are very steep and narrow and pose a real avalanche threat.

Once out in the meadow you can tour for may hours and find many excellent slopes for turns. Here are some suggestions:

1. There is an excellent hill for making turns on the east flank of what is called Aberharts Nose. This is the hill directly in front of you as you enter the meadow beyond the draw. Good ski descents can be had from this ridge (GR 470437).

2. If you feel adventurous, ski and scramble along the ridge above Aberharts Nose to reach the summit of Mount Aberhart (GR 464427) which gives a panoramic view of the area.

3. If you want a pleasant Nordic tour you can ski in a northwest direction to Shovel Pass (GR 440478).

4. At the end of the day, pleasant skiing can be had in the last rays of the sun on the west slopes of Sunset Peak (GR 485435).

Curly Phillips, the man who built Shangri-la, was a Jasper ski pioneer. He perished in 1938 in an avalanche at Elysium Pass. Photo courtesy Whyte Museum of the Canadian Rockies.

Shangri La Cabin

This delightful log cabin was built in 1936 by the legendary outfitter and guide Curly Phillips. It is steeped in the history and magic of a bygone era.
Location Near the head of Jefferys Creek, just below treeline at an elevation of 2000 m (GR 479448).
Map Medicine Lake 83 C/13
Facilities This is a very comfortable cabin with wood and propane heating, propane cook stove, cooking and eating utensils and bunks with foam pads.
Capacity 6
Water From the creek, down the hill in front of the cabin.
Reservations Phone Bette Weir in Jasper at 780-852-3665

The Wates-Gibson Hut. Photo Nancy Hansen.

147 MOUNT EDITH CAVELL ROAD Ski touring 1

Grade Easy
Distance 11 km one way to the hostel
Time 4-5 hours one way to the hostel,
2-3 hours one way back to your vehicle
Height gain 500 m
Max elevation 1730 m
Maps Jasper 83 D/16
Amethyst Lakes 83 D/9

This tour follows a road which is not plowed in the winter. It is a steady uphill plod all the way but it takes you to the Mount Edith Cavell Hostel where you can spend a pleasant night. Nearby the views of the north face of Mount Edith Cavell are very impressive.

Facilities The Mount Edith Cavell Hostel is the destination for this tour. There is a telephone at the parking lot.

Options This tour is the start for the trip into the Tonquin Valley and Amethyst Lakes. It is advisable to ski to the hostel the first day, spend the night, then continue the next day up the Astoria River to the Tonquin Valley.

Access From Jasper drive south on the Icefields Parkway. After 7 km turn right onto Highway 93A which is followed for another 5 km, past the turn-off to Marmot Basin Ski Resort, to a large parking lot at the Mount Edith Cavell Road, located on the left, just across the bridge over the Astoria River.

The tour up the snow covered road begins directly across the highway from the parking lot. It climbs for several kilometres in long switchbacks, then rounds a shoulder into the drainage of the Astoria River. The rest of the way the road climbs at a more gentle angle and is very easy to follow. The hostel is on your left.

After getting settled in and enjoying a hot drink, it is nice to round the day off with a short ski up the remainder of the road to Cavell Lake and admire the impressive north face of Mount Edith Cavell.

TONQUIN VALLEY/ROBSON

The Tonquin Valley offers some excellent touring and has long been the scene of Alpine Club of Canada ski camps. The scenery is outstanding, the snow is deep and there is a variety of terrain to explore. It is a good idea to visit this valley for a week or so and get to know the region. The Wates-Gibson Hut and the Tonquin Valley Lodge offer comfortable accommodation for winter visitors. Although there are only three tours described in this book there is potential for more.

Location of and route to Wates Gibson Hut. Photo Vance Hanna.

Wates-Gibson Hut

A beautiful log building set in the middle of a ski paradise.
Location At the NW corner of Outpost Lake (GR 152353—see photograph below).
Map Amethyst Lakes 83 D/9
Facilities Foamies, cooking and eating utensils, Coleman cooking stoves and lanterns, and a wood heating stove.
Capacity 24 in winter
Water Outpost Lake
Reservations The Alpine Club of Canada 403-678-3200
Note! The hut is locked when a custodian is not present and a combination number is required.

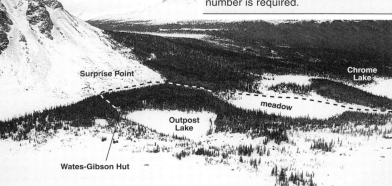

Surprise Point / Chrome Lake / meadow / Outpost Lake / Wates-Gibson Hut

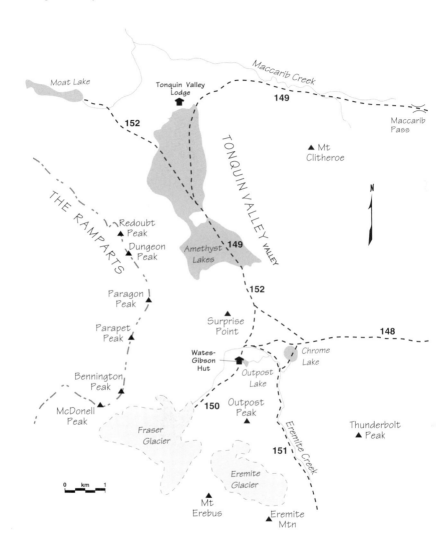

148 TONQUIN VALLEY VIA THE ASTORIA RIVER   Ski touring 2

Grade Intermediate
Distance 14 km from the Mount Edith
Cavell Hostel to the Wates-Gibson Hut,
16 km to Amethyst Lakes
Time 6-8 hours one way
Height gain 150 m to Wates-Gibson
Hut, 240 m to Amethyst Lakes
Max elevation 1970 m
Map Amethyst Lakes 83 D/9

A classic tour which takes you into the heart
of one of the most beautiful regions in the
world. It is really worthwhile to spend a few
days here, exploring the area.

Hazards Many parties arrive late in the
day and have trouble locating the Wates-
Gibson Hut. Plan your schedule so that
you arrive in the daylight and have some
time to hunt around if need be. Refer to
the photograph on page 223 for the hut
location.

Options It is common for parties to ski into
the Tonquin Valley via the Astoria River
then to return to the road via Maccarib
Pass and Portal Creek.

Access This trail begins at the Mount
Edith Cavell Hostel (see page 222).

From the hostel ski up the road for about
75 m then turn down a trail to your right.
This trail crosses a bridge over Cavell
Creek and after a few metres passes
some outfitters shacks and corrals. The
trail proper starts here. For the first 5 km
it stays high on the northwest flank of
Mount Edith Cavell, above the Astoria
River. The trail traverses horizontally at
first, then actually climbs for a short distance. Eventually it works its way down
the hillside, reaching the Astoria River
shortly after crossing Verdant Creek.

The trail crosses to the right (north)
bank of the Astoria River and for most of
the next 9 km, as far as Chrome Lake, it
continues along the north bank. Sometimes the trail follows the river bed itself
but usually it is up on the north side of
the river. Travel along this trail is almost
always easy due to the snowmobile traffic into the Tonquin Valley.

Just before reaching Chrome Lake, a
branch of the trail begins to climb up to
the right, following the drainage which

descends from Amethyst Lakes. This
trail is packed because of the snowmobile traffic. On the map the drainage
divides into two streams—follow the
left (west) branch up to the lake. Here
you will be treated to one of the most
beautiful views in the world, the Ramparts above Amethyst Lakes.

The Tonquin Valley Lodge is located
at the northwest corner of Amethyst
lakes (GR 132413).

To reach the Wates-Gibson Hut on
Outpost Lake you should continue
along the Astoria River to Chrome
Lake. The trail will normally become
more difficult to follow because the
snowmobiles have turned off. As well,
the Astoria River is not as clearly defined along here. From Chrome Lake to
Outpost Lake the route finding is tricky.
Starting from the outlet of Chrome Lake
there are two ways you can go:

1. You can ski across the lake, angling
left (south) to the inflow stream. Climb
up a few metres to your right (west),
through a notch and into the meadows
above. Now turn right (northwest) and

ski up the meadows for several hundred metres, to the north end. This route has simply followed the drainage.

2. Alternatively you can take a short cut from Chrome Lake to the meadows just beyond. From the outlet of Chrome Lake angle up to the right (west) and follow clearings through the trees for about 0.5 km, to the meadow previously mentioned.

From this meadow, the trail climbs up Penstock Creek gaining about 50 vertical metres before it flattens out into another meadow below Surprise Point. On your right (north) you will see a huge pile of jumbled rocks. Ski along the left (south) side of the meadow for about 300 m. The trail then curves around a corner to your left and you will see on the hillside, about 50 m in front of you, a V shaped open slope. Ascend this hillside for about 75 vertical metres, climbing back and forth through the trees, then pop over the crest onto the shore of Outpost Lake. The cabin is nestled in the trees a few metres above the north-west corner of the lake (see photograph on page 223).

The Ramparts from Maccarib Pass. Photo Alf Skrastins.

149 TONQUIN VALLEY VIA MACCARIB PASS   Ski touring 2

Grade Intermediate
Distance 12 km to Maccarib Pass, 28 km to Wates-Gibson Hut
Time It is a full day ski to reach Tonquin Valley Lodge. To ski to the Wates-Gibson Hut on Outpost Lake, in one push, is a long, hard day indeed.
Height gain 300 m to the junction of Portal and Circus Creeks, 740 m to Maccarib Pass
Max elevation 2200 m at Maccarib Pass

Maps Jasper 83 D/16
Amethyst Lakes 83 D/9

The ski to the junction of Portal and Circus Creeks is pleasant but the really nice terrain starts at this point and the next 8 km to Maccarib Pass is beautiful touring country. The tour to the pass is highly recommended. For those contemplating the trip to the Tonquin Valley it is easier to ski in via the Astoria River then ski out over Maccarib Pass.

Access There is a parking lot on the left (west) side of the Marmot Basin Ski Resort access road, at the point where the road crosses Portal Creek. Drive south from Jasper along the Icefields Parkway (Highway 93) for 7 km, then turn right onto Highway 93A. Follow this highway for another 2.5 km, then turn right again onto the road to Marmot Basin. Drive up this road for about 6 km to Portal Creek.

From the parking lot walk along the road, across the bridge, to the north side of Portal Creek. Put your skis on, ski past some corrals and log buildings and head up the trail. The trail is straightforward to follow and provides easy going. It runs through the trees just above the right bank of the creek. In heavy snow years or later in the season it is easy to follow the creek bed itself. After about 4 km the trail drops down into the creek bed of Portal Creek just beyond its junction with Circus Creek. The point where you break out of the trees is a nice spot to stop for a drink and a bite to eat.

Beyond here the travel becomes much more pleasant and the skiing is lovely. For 5 km follow the creek up the valley through open, rolling terrain until you begin to approach the end of the valley. Just before the end start climbing up to the right towards Maccarib Pass. It is an easy and simple climb. The route follows open, alpine terrain and the slopes are mostly of a lower angle. Be sure not to turn up to the right too soon. The pass you are looking for is tucked up close to the north side of Mount Maccarib (if you turn up too early there is another pass which looks inviting). The last part of the climb to the pass and then through the pass is easy, however, in whiteout conditions route finding could be tricky.

From the pass descend gradually down the other side for 5 km, losing 180 vertical metres. At the point where the valley is about to close in and the creek bed begins to narrow and drop steeply, angle to the left through the

trees (you can see evidence of a campground across the creek at this point). A gentle, descending traverse, around the corner, through open woods, for about 1 km, brings you down to the valley bottom at the north end of Amethyst Lakes. The Tonquin Valley Lodge is located at the northwest corner of the lake (GR 132413).

To continue to the Wates Gibson Hut on Outpost Lake ski south along the north arm of Amethyst Lakes. Cut across a narrow spit of land which sticks out into the lake, then continue south to the far shore. From this point the going gets tricky. You want to traverse high around the head of the Astoria River, just below Surprise Point, to gain the upper valley of Penstock Creek. This 2 km stretch can prove difficult or it can be not too bad if done correctly.

From the end of the lake follow the right-hand drainage which exits the lake on the west flank, near Surprise Point. Ski for about 1 km until this drainage begins to drop more steeply towards the valley. At this point begin angling around through the forest to the right. It is not necessary to climb up at all and a traverse through the trees should bring you into the upper reaches of Penstock Creek. There is no well defined trail through here in the winter and you will be forced to do a bit of bushwhacking.

You should aim to reach upper Penstock Creek in the open meadow below Surprise Point. Above you to the north, on Surprise Point, you will see a slope strewn with large boulders. Cross the meadow to the south side where there is an obvious open slope on the treed hillside above. Climb back and forth, through the trees, up the hillside to the left of this slope for about 75 vertical metres. Pop over the ridge to reach the Wates-Gibson Hut on the shores

150 FRASER GLACIER

Ski touring 2

Grade Intermediate
Distance 2 km one way
Time 2 hours one way
Height gain 400 m
Max elevation 2250 m
Map Amethyst Lakes 83 D/9

An exciting tour which takes you into high alpine terrain, to the toe of the Fraser Glacier. Some turns can be made up here as well. To ski up onto the glacier and beyond is ski mountaineering and you should be familiar with glacier travel techniques.

Access This tour begins at the Wates-Gibson Hut on the edge of Outpost Lake.

From the hut work your way up the hillside, through the trees, in a westerly direction. After about 50 vertical metres the terrain lays back and you can continue west through sparse trees over rolling hills. Make your way out into the open drainage of Penstock Creek. Be certain not to cut the corner on your left too tight as there is a steep open slope here that could be dangerous! The trail up to the edge of the glacier follows the drainage and is open and straightforward. Stay well back from any steep slopes or hanging glaciers. At about 2200 m the angle lays back just before the glacier begins.

Tonquin Valley Lodge

A delightful lodge located in one of the most beautiful places on earth.
Location At the NW end of Amethyst Lakes in the Tonquin Valley (GR 132413)
Map Amethyst Lakes 83 D/9
Facilities A central dining lodge surrounded by several cabins. Wood heating and outdoor plumbing are part of the experience.
Capacity 14
Host Kable Kongsrud
Cost About $100 per person
Reservations Write: Tonquin Valley Pack and Ski Trips, Box 550, Jasper, Alberta, T0E 1E0. Email: packtrp@telus.net Website: www.tonquinvalley.com Phone: 780-852-3909 Fax: 780-852-3763.

151 EREMITE VALLEY

Grade Easy/intermediate
Distance 5 km one way to the toe of the glacier
Time 2-3 hours one way
Height gain 400 m
Max elevation 2200 m at toe of glacier
Map Amethyst Lakes 83 D/9

This is a beautiful day trip from the Wates-Gibson Hut. You can explore around and make a few turns high in the valley.

Hazards Do not linger beneath the avalanche slopes off Outpost Peak.

Options If you are equipped and prepared for glacier travel you can continue up to the pass between Alcove Mountain and Angle Peak. The descent from this pass is excellent.

Access This tour begins at the Wates-Gibson Hut on the shores of Outpost Lake.

From the hut ski north down the hill, through the trees, to the open meadow below Surprise Point. Continue down Penstock Creek, losing about 75 vertical metres, to reach the meadow just above Chrome Lake. Continue south along the meadows bordering Eremite Creek. Generally the route follows the creek bed up the valley, eventually breaking out into open, alpine terrain after about 2.5 km, at Arrowhead Lake. The slopes on your right on Outpost Peak contain some giant avalanche paths, so you should travel quickly across any area that is threatened.

You can continue beyond Arrowhead Lake up into the basin. You can ski up to an unnamed pass on the east side of the valley, which overlooks the head of the Whirlpool River. If you are prepared for glacier travel, you can ski, without difficulty, up to the pass between Alcove Mountain and Angle Peak. The descent back down the glacier offers excellent skiing.

Rex Gibson, ski and climbing pioneer in the Jasper area, outside the original cabin on Penstock Creek. Photo Joan Dunkley Collection.

Of Historical Interest
The Tonquin Valley was pioneered as a ski touring area by the Edmonton Section of The Alpine Club of Canada. Cyril Wates and Rex Gibson, who were both prominent members of the club, spent a great deal of time in the area. The cabin at Outpost Lake which bears their names is the third generation hut in the valley and is in excellent condition thanks to major renovations performed by the Edmonton Section of The ACC.

The Ramparts across Amethyst Lake. Photo Alf Skrastins.

152 AMETHYST LAKES/MOAT LAKE

Ski touring 2

Grade Easy/intermediate
Distance 20 km return to Moat Lake
Time This is a full day tour
Height gain 120 m
Max elevation 1940 m
Map Amethyst Lakes 83 D/9

This tour is a little tricky to start. It can be difficult to work your way around from Penstock Creek to Amethyst Lakes. Once you are there, however, the tour across the lake, underneath the wall of the Ramparts, is outstanding.

Access This tour begins at the Wates-Gibson Hut on the edge of Outpost Lake.

From the hut ski north, down the hill to the meadows along upper Penstock Creek. From here you must work your way northeast, around Surprise Point towards Amethyst Lakes. There is no well defined trail in the winter and you may have to do a little bushwhacking and route finding. You should gradually climb as you work your way around the hillside, gaining about 100 vertical metres over 1 km.

If you are unsure of this route, you can descend Penstock Creek to Chrome Lake, then descend the Astoria River for a short distance to reach the drainage coming down from Amethyst Lakes. It is then a simple matter of climbing back up this drainage, perhaps along a well packed snowmobile trail, to reach the lakes. This route will add about an extra hour to the tour (each way).

Once you reach Amethyst Lakes the imposing wall of the Ramparts appears. The rest of the tour across the lakes and around the corner to Moat Lake is straightforward and one of the most spectacular tours in the world. Be sure to take your camera.

153 BERG LAKE VIA KINNEY LAKE   Ski touring 2

Grade Advanced
Distance 17 km one way
Time Depending on the depth of the snow, the strength of the party and the weight of their packs this may be a one or two day trip to get to the lake.
Height gain 780 m
Max elevation 1640 m
Map Mount Robson 83 E/3

A real adventure tour that takes you well into the backcountry. You feel like you have truly gotten away from it all at Berg Lake. The scenery is outstanding.

Access Mount Robson Provincial Park is located 88 km west of Jasper along Highway 16. Turn right, pass the information centre, and drive up a short access road to the trailhead.

The trail is initially wide and easy. It follows alongside the Robson River gaining elevation gradually. Just before Kinney Lake cross a bridge to the east shore. Continue around the lake along the right shore, past the camp shelter, then head across the gravel flats at the end of the lake.

The valley narrows and you must climb up on the left flank to gain the higher Valley of a Thousand Falls. This can be a tricky routefinding problem. After the trail levels off, cross the Robson River to the east bank (suspension bridge). Near here you will see the Whitehorn Shelter.

Carry on up the east bank of the river for a little more than a kilometre then cross to the northwest side (suspension bridge). The trail then climbs steeply, switchbacking up the hillside. Caution is advised.

Facilities There is a camp shelter along the northeast shore of Kinney Lake and another at the Whitehorn Campground, located on the east side of the Robson River, just after the suspension bridge, near the start of the Valley of a Thousand Falls. There is a shelter at Berg Lake itself, along the northwest shore, towards the end of the Lake. This shelter is completely enclosed and has a wood heating stove.

Hazards The climb at the north end of the Valley of a Thousand Falls, alongside White Falls and Emperor Falls, is steep and potentially dangerous.

Beyond Emperor Falls the angle lays back and the skiing becomes more reasonable. Follow the trail until it breaks out onto the open gravel flats and ski across to the lake. Either ski down the lake or along the north shore, almost to the other end, where you will find the Berg Lake Shelter up on your left.

Berg Lake (Hargreaves) Shelter

A rustic log building in a spectacular setting which can provide shelter on those cold winter nights.
Location Along the north shore of Berg Lake not far from the NE end of the lake.
Map Mount Robson 83 E/3
Facilities Heating stove, benches and tables. Wood pile nearby. No bunks, foamies, cook stoves, cooking or eating utensils.
Capacity N/A
Water Snowmelt
Reservations Phone Mount Robson Provincial Park for information 250-566-4325.

MULTI-DAY ADVENTURES

One of the nice things about ski touring is that you can pursue it at any level that suits you. You can ski for an hour or two along an easy trail, tour for 10 or 15 km into the backcountry or, if you are really adventurous, try one of these multi-day expeditions which require a very high level of experience and skill. When you head off on one of these trips no one is expecting you back for days or even weeks, so if something goes wrong you may have a long wait for assistance. You must be prepared to deal with all eventualities yourself.

The four multi-day adventures included here are just a sample of what you can do if you are so inclined. In the Rocky Mountains in winter, you can point your skis up almost any valley and just go where your spirit takes you. In this world of overcrowded ski resorts and contrived adventure it is nice just to roam freely in the snow covered hills. I hope that the information provided in this book will inspire others to leave the tyranny of the rat race behind for a while and discover something that is still whispered in the wind, out there on the wilderness trail.

The North and South Boundary Trails are infrequently done. Unless you have some "in" with Jasper National Park and can get a key to the warden cabins, be prepared to camp.

The Jasper to Banff Traverse was first done in 1930 by Joe Weiss and four companions from Jasper; Vern and Doug Jeffery, A.L. 'Pete' Withers and Frank Burstrom. It took them 15 days and much of the distance they followed what is now the Icefields Parkway. The very next year Weiss repeated his monumental tour, this time with Cliff White and Russell Bennett. The tour from Jasper to Banff as described in this book, along the east side of the highway, was first done in 1976 by Don Gardner and Larry Mason. Three years later, in 1979, it was repeated by Bob Saunders and Mel Hines. Both these trips took 14 days and these guys are strong skiers—it is a long way.

The Southern Rockies Hut to Hut Traverse was first skied in 1994 by Chic Scott, Art Longair, Doug Bell and John and Louise Davidson. It is an outstanding tour and can be done in a variety of ways using a mixture of huts and camping if you like—whatever suits your taste and budget.

Before heading out on one of these trips it is a good idea to have a chat with the wardens and let them know your plans. They will have some good advice to offer and always like to know of folks undertaking major ski expeditions in their parks.

154 SOUTH BOUNDARY TRAIL
Ski touring 2

Grade advanced
Distance About 200 km
Time 7-10 days
Height gain 1500 m
Max elevation 2200 m
Maps Medicine Lake 83 C/13
Mountain Park 83 C/14
Southesk Lake 83 C/11
George Creek 83 C/10

Job Creek 83 C/7
Sunwapta Peak 83 C/6
Columbia Icefield 83 C/3
Jasper National Park MCR 221

This is a wilderness adventure. You will be camping and breaking trail the whole way. The trail follows the valley bottom so route finding is reasonably simple.

Access Park as for Summit/Jacques Lakes along the Maligne Lake Road (see page 211). Leave a second car at the Nigel Pass trail head (see page 189).

This tour roughly follows the east and south boundaries of Jasper National Park. It normally begins by skiing to Summit and Jacques Lakes then continues northeast to the Rocky River. Turn southeast and ski for several days along the Rocky River and the Medicine-Tent River to Southesk Pass. Descend the Cairn River to the Southesk River, then turn east and follow the Southesk River to its confluence with the Brazeau River. Turn sharply to the southwest and follow the Brazeau River for about 60 km to Nigel Pass. Descend Nigel Creek to the Icefields Parkway.

155 NORTH BOUNDARY TRAIL
Ski touring 2

Grade Advanced
Distance About 200 km
Time 7-10 days
Height gain 1200 m
Max elevation 2000 m
Map Mount Robson 83 E/3
Twin Creek Lake 83 E/6
Blue Creek 83 E/7
Jasper National Park MCR 221

Another wilderness adventure involving trail breaking and camping. The trail follows the valley bottom so route finding is relatively simple.

Options There are several variations to this trip. Blue Creek offers an alternative to the upper Snake Indian River. Moose Pass and the Moose River offer an alternative finish to the trip.

Access The trip begins from Highway 16 at the east end of Jasper Lake. Leave a second car at the Berg Lake trailhead (see page 232).

This tour roughly follows the north and west boundaries of Jasper National Park. It begins by ascending north up the Snake Indian River for almost 100 km to Snake Indian Pass. It then descends Twintree Creek to the Smoky River. The route then turns south and follows the Smoky River to Robson Pass. It finishes along the Berg Lake trail via Kinney Lake to Highway 16.

156 JASPER TO BANFF TRAVERSE

Grade Advanced
Distance About 350 km
Time 14-21 days
Height gain About 7500 m
Max elevation 2500 m
Maps Medicine Lake 83 C/13
Athabasca Falls 83 C/12
Southesk Lake 83 C/11
Sunwapta Peak 83 C/6
Job Creek 83 C/7
Cline River 83 C/2
Pentland Lake 82 N/16
Hector Lake 82 N/9
Lake Louise 82 N/8
Castle Mountain 82 O/5
Banff 82 O/4
Jasper National Park MCR 221
Banff, Kootenay and Yoho National Parks MCR 220

This is about as challenging a ski adventure as you can imagine. It is rarely done and then only by very strong skiers. Plan this expedition well, train all winter, then give it everything. March is the best time of year when the days are longer, the temperature more moderate and the snow is deep. It is possible to bail out from this tour at a number of points along the way (Poboktan Creek, Nigel Creek, Pipestone Creek and several more). Additional food can be picked up when you cross the David Thompson Highway (Highway 11), about halfway along the tour, and food caches can be placed in advance from the Icefields Parkway.

Hazards This is big time adventure and you must be well prepared.

Access If you do this trip in its entirety you can start almost from the town of Jasper and ski all the way to the town of Banff.

The trip begins by skiing up the Signal Mountain Fire Road just outside Jasper. It then continues across the Skyline Trail (see *Summits and Icefields*, Chic Scott, Rocky Mountain Books, 1994) to Little Shovel Pass and down to Maligne Lake. From here climb back up to the Bald Hills Fire Lookout (see page 217) and continue south across the rolling terrain of the Six Pass Route (see *Summits and Icefields*, Chic Scott, Rocky Mountain Books, 1994) to Maligne Pass. Descend Poligne Creek to Poboktan Creek (see page 197) and then continue up to Jonas Shoulder and Jonas pass. Descend to the Brazeau River then ascend to Cline Pass. Descend the Cline River all the way to the David Thompson Highway (Highway 11). You can pick up a food cache here and maybe a change of clothes.

It is necessary to walk along the highway for about 5 km to reach the Siffleur River, which is then followed all the way to Pipestone Pass. Descend the Pipestone River then ascend Little Pipestone Creek and Skoki Creek (see page 134) to Skoki Lodge. Cross Deception Pass (see page 126) then continue down Baker Creek. Follow Wildflower Creek up to Pulsatilla Pass then descend Johnston Creek. Cross Mystic Pass (see page 63) and follow Forty Mile Creek (see page 61) back to the Mount Norquay Ski Resort.

157 SOUTHERN ROCKIES HUT TO HUT TRAVERSE   Ski touring 2

Grade Advanced
Distance 125 km
Time 7-10 days
Height gain 2440 m
Max elevation 2510 m
Maps Spray Lakes Reservoir 82 J/14
Mount Assiniboine 82 J/13
Banff 82 O/4
Castle Mountain 82 O/5
Lake Louise 82 N/8

This tour takes you through some of the most beautiful and dramatic mountain terrain in the world. There are huts along the way so, if you like, you can travel with a light pack.

Facilities The huts along the way are: Bryant Creek Shelter, Assiniboine Lodge, Naiset Huts, Police Meadows Cabin, Sunshine Village Ski Resort, Egypt Lake Shelter, Shadow Lake Lodge and Skoki Lodge. Most of these are described elsewhere in the book. They vary from first class backcountry lodges with four star meals to rustic wilderness cabins. Reservations are required at most of these huts so be sure to take care of this before you start.

Options You could also start by skiing up Brewster Creek to Sundance Lodge, then crossing Allenby Pass to Assiniboine Meadows. The tour could end by skiing from Lake Louise over Wenkchemna and Opabin Passes to Lake O'Hara.

Access This tour begins at the Mount Shark trailhead (see page 29) and ends at Lake Louise.

Most of the individual sections of this trip are described in detail in the text. It is simply a matter of stringing them all together.

The first section of the tour follows Bryant Creek, crossing Assiniboine Pass to Assiniboine Meadows. This can be done in two days by overnighting at the Bryant Creek Shelter. At Assiniboine you can stay at the Naiset Huts or at Assiniboine Lodge.

The next section continues via Citadel Pass to Sunshine Village Ski Resort. There are old cabins at Police Meadows which can be used overnight if necessary. It may be difficult to get accommodation for one night at the Sunshine Village Ski Resort.

From Sunshine Village continue via Simpson and Healy Passes to Egypt Lake then down Pharaoh Creek to Shadow Lake. You can either descend Redearth Creek to the Trans Canada Highway or cross Gibbon Pass then descend from Twin Lakes to the highway. The trip can end here or after a pleasant night at Lake Louise continue farther.

Perhaps the finest way to end this tour is to ski via Deception Pass to Skoki Lodge. After several pleasant nights here you can return to your car at the Fish Creek parking lot or take the adventurous route out via the Pipestone River to Lake Louise.

This tour allows you to sample many of the wonderful historic lodges of the Rockies in a single trip. It should become a classic one day.

INDEX

Index

PHONE NUMBERS AND WEB SITES

Rocky Mountain Books   www.rmbooks.com

Park Administrative Offices

Kananaskis Country Office (Canmore)	(403) 678-5508
Parks Canada Regional Office (Calgary)	(403) 292-4401

Visitor Information Centres

Waterton	(403) 859-5133
Barrier Lake (Kananaskis)	(403) 673-3985
Peter Lougheed Provincial Park	(403) 591-6322
Banff	(403) 762-1550
Lake Louise	(403) 522-3833
Yoho	(250) 343-6783
Jasper	(780) 852-6176

Travel Alberta	1-800-252-3782

Tourism British Columbia	1-800-663-6000

Weather Reports

Banff	(403) 762-2088
Jasper	(780) 852-3185

Reservations

Alpine Club of Canada Huts	(403) 678-3200
Banff National Park Shelters	(403) 762-1550
Canadian Alpine Centre and Hostel	(403) 522-2200
Banff Area Hostels	(403) 762-4122
Icefields Parkway Hostels	(403) 762-4122
Jasper Hostels	1-877-852-0781
Naiset Huts, Assiniboine	(403) 678-2883

Helicopter Companies

Alpine Helicopters	(403) 678-4802

Internet Web Pages
Kananaskis: www.gov.ab.ca/env/parks/prov_parks/kananaskis
Banff: www.parkscanada.pch.gc.ca/banff
Jasper: www.parkscanada.pch.gc.ca/jasper
Kootenay: www.parkscanada.pch.gc.ca/kootenay
Yoho: www.parkscanada.pch.gc.ca/yoho
BC Parks: www.bcparks.ca
Chic Scott: www.chicscott.com

IN AN EMERGENCY

In an emergency dial 911

You can also contact the RCMP or the nearest Ranger or Warden Office

RCMP Offices

Waterton (Nov-April)	(403) 653-4932
Kananaskis	(403) 591-7707
Canmore	(403) 678-5516
Banff	(403) 762-2226
Lake Louise	(403) 522-3811
Jasper	(780) 852-4421

Park Ranger or Warden Offices

Waterton Park	(403) 859-5140
Kananaskis Country (emergency only)	(403) 591-7767
Banff Park (emergency only)	(403) 762-4506
Banff Park (regular calls)	(403) 762-1470
Kootenay Park (regular calls)	(250) 347-9361
Kootenay Park (emergency only)	(403) 762-4506
Yoho Park	(250) 343-6142
Jasper Park (Sunwapta)	(780) 852-5383
Jasper Park (Jasper)	(780) 852-6155

Avalanche Hazard and Snow Stability

Public Avalanche Information Bulletin (Canadian Avalanche Association)
1-800-667-1105 or www.avalanche.ca

Other books by Chic Scott include Summits and Icefields guide books to alpine skiing in two volumes (the Rockies and the Columbia Mountains), "Pushing the Limits, the Story of Canadian Mountaineering" and 'The Yam, 50 Years of Climbing on Yamnuska" (with Dave Dornian and Ben Gadd).

The author can be contacted regarding any changes, additions or corrections to this book at chic@chicscott.com.